Spirits of the Great Hill

More Haunted Sites and Ancient Mysteries of Upstate New York
(The Sequel to SHADOWS OF THE WESTERN DOOR)

By Mason Winfield

For Frances Ward Winfield,
Daughter of a Revolution

©2001 Western New York Wares Inc.
All rights reserved.
Printed by Petit Printing

Address all inquires to:
Brian Meyer, Publisher
Western New York Wares Inc.
P.O. Box 733
Ellicott Station
Buffalo, NY 14205
e-mail: *wnywares@gateway.net*

This book was published and printed in Buffalo, NY
ISBN: 1-879201-35-6

**Visit our Internet Site at:
www.buffalobooks.com**

CONTENTS

PUBLISHER'S PONDERINGS — 5   INTRODUCTION — 6

1. OTHER COUNCIL FIRES

Kingdoms of the Cattaraugus — 9	King Solomon's Mines — 14
Giants in the Ground — 10	Fort Hill — 15
The Sodus Bay Spearhead — 12	The Great Circle-Henge — 17
The Buried Causeway — 13	The Mastodon Rider — 18

2. THE POWER POINTS

The Peace Queen — 21	Garden of the Gods — 26
Ontario Atlantis — 23	The Devil's Hole — 27
The Angel's Mountain — 24	Valley of Madness — 28
The Spiritual Springs — 25	The Great Hill — 29

3. ON THE SPIRIT WAY

Byzantium by the Lake — 31	"Whosoever Will May Come" — 39
City of Light — 33	Calvin of Oak Knoll — 40
"That Place is Burnt!" — 35	Father X of the Western Door — 41
The Millennial Millerites — 37	

4. SPOOKS, SPECTERS, SPIRITS

The Niagara Frontier:

Psychic Symphony	44
Niagara Square	46
The McKinley Curse	47
Mark Twain's Buffalo Ghost	48
The Lockwood Mansion	49
Lady in Lavender	50
Team Spirit	51
The Imaginary Friend	52
The Lemon Angel	53
Clet Hall	54
Tale of the Tailor	55
The Cold Springs *Whatever*	56
Spirit Sisters	57

Lake and Lakeside Wights:

"Flying Dutchmen"	70
The Black Dog of the Erie	71
The Phoebe Catherine	72
The Point Charles Marker	72
"Wherever you can place your eyes..."	73
The Fyfe and Drum	74
The Box of Red Jacket's Bones	75
Flittin' on the Dock of the Bay	76

Left Side of the River:

The Dollhouse	58
The Lighthouse	59
The Niagara Poltergeist	60
Houdini's Halloween	61
The Buttery	62
The Angel Inn	63
The Kiely	64

Rochester & Region:

Poor Tessie Keating	65
Hill of 1,000 Ghosts	66
Of Widows and Windows	67
Mother of Sorrows	68
Bump & Run	69

Chautauqua-Allegany Spirits:

Boos & Brews	77
Fatal Bellman	78
"New Ireland"	79
The Ashford Hollow Witch	80
The White Inn	81
Little Lucy's Theater	82

Spirits of the Great Hill

The Western Finger Lakes:		Genesee Country Ghosts:	
Portrait of the Grey Lady	83	The Legend of	
Seth Roberts	84	Buttermilk Falls	87
Message from Mehitabel	85	The Abell House	88
Eliza of the Trackways	86	Flower of Avon	89

5. IROQUOIS SPIRITS

A. The Charmholder's Bundle

		B. Miracles of Mad Bear	
		Medicine Men	97
Seneca Witch Belief	91	The Cattail Healing	98
The Wailing Spirit		Powerline	98
of the Genesee Flats	92	The Lazarus Effect	99
Catching a Blood-Bone	92	The Witching Wall	100
The Hair-bone Token	93	The Djogao Skull	101
The Stealer of Childrens' Hearts	94	Weapons of Friendship	101
Maker of the False Face	95	Mad Bear's Magic Hat	102
A Witch's Bag	96	The Medicine Case	103
The Charmholder's Bundle	96	The Ghost-Talker	104
		Only a Change of Worlds	105

6. WHITE MAGIC

A. The Path of Peace

		B. Children of the Left-Hand	
The Bradford Miracle	107	Bird of Perdition	111
The Witch of the Helpers	108	The Hinsdale Horror	112
Father Baker's Healing	109	Diabolic Frolic	113
Heart of the Mountain	110	The King of the Wood	114

7. THE SACRED ROYCROFT

The Shroud of Roycroft	116	Nightmare on Walnut St.	121
Michael's Mount	117	The Hallway Stalker	121
"Dangerous Negations"	118	The Christmas Spirit	122
Electricks	119	Hub in France	123
John Barleycorn's Curse	119	"Some Particulars..."	124
The Prophecy	120		

8. THE INVISIBLE COLLEGE

Orenda	127	The Cohocton Head-readers	132
Iroquois Masons	128	Cthulhu Country	134
Sacred City	129	Nicola Tesla's Falls Experiment	135
White Shaman of the Landscape	131	Human Dimensions	136

9. THE WNYX-FILES

The Top Ten UFOs	139	The Medina Croppies	146
War in Heaven	142	Anchor of Doom	147
The Randolph Frankenstein	143	The Black Creek Whodat	148
The Lake Erie Serpent	144	The Man Who Lived Twice	149
Creepy Critters	145	The Quest for the	
		Holy Shale	150

Publisher's Ponderings

The Ghosts and Mr. Winfield.

If we were running a television network instead of a regional publishing company, this supernatural saga would be one of our most popular series.

"When are you guys going to do another ghost book?"

It's a question that has been asked repeatedly in recent years.

But unlike the fictional boob tube exploits of Mrs. Muir, Mason Winfield's literary works are rooted in research and realism.

Four years have passed since an East Aurora author contacted us about his plan to write a book about supernatural sites in Western New York. We were captivated by the notion of exploring the darks lanes of upstate legacy.

It turned out to be one our best publishing decisions. *Shadows of the Western Door* will soon move into its fifth printing and has become one of Western New York Wares' five best-selling books. *Shadows* has even inspired a compact disc audio version. In 1999, Mason penned *A Ghosthunter's Journal*, a book that has also performed beyond our expectations.

One can understand why we have high hopes for *Spirits of the Great Hill*, a tome that is sure to delight thousands of Winfield fans.

Mason's exceptional writing talent and attention to detail are key ingredients in any publishing success story. But they aren't the only ingredients.

Michele Ratzel has served capably as our business manager for many years. Even the most creative publishing company can be doomed by a lopsided balance sheet. Shelly has helped to keep a close eye on the dollars-and-cents of our literary adventure. Her involvement in our company also shatters the tired adage that good friends should never be involved in business together.

Tom Connolly has supervised our marketing, distribution and e-commerce activities with the skill a talented circus juggler. His creativity and drive have propelled Western New York Wares to a new level.

Our company also continues to reap spin-off benefits from the former involvement of marketing associates Matt Pitts and Kevin Wilson. While they left the company to pursue exciting careers, I consider them two of my most treasured friends.

Finally, I want to thank my mom, Jean Meyer, and my late father, Bill Meyer. They taught me one of life's most valuable lessons: if you believe in your cause and work hard, even the most lofty goals can be accomplished.

Brian Meyer
July 2001

Introduction

For all its shorthand rep as "the book on Buffalo ghosts," *Shadows of the Western Door* (1997) was regional in scope, and surveyed Western New York's paranormal past across a range of subjects: ancient mysteries, mystical sites, Iroquois magic, hauntings, creepy critters, occult societies, and other prodigies under the paranormal umbrella. This is *Shadows*' sequel.

We knew there'd be another book like *Shadows* someday, because there was so much more to tell. *Spirits of the Great Hill* contains new material in most of *Shadows*' subjects. Like *Shadows*, its target area is the traditional Seneca territory, "that part of New York State west of a line dropped south from Sodus Bay," according to Arthur Parker, with a bit of Canada on the other side of the Niagara. Like *Shadows*, this book is titled after another of the Seneca names, "People of the Great Hill," based on their national creation myth. It's only fitting. The Native Americans are the spiritual bedrock of our region. The noble Seneca are its historic inhabitants.

The subject of "ancient mysteries" is a major component of the paranormal industry, and it's nowhere more lively than in the Americas. *Spirits* begins with "Other Council Fires" and a few more out-of-place (or time) artifacts, strange ruins, and crazy skeletons to report.

Modern mysticism puts heavy focus onto the forces of the earth and their interaction with current and traditional supernatural lore. "The Power Points" (a more specialized revisiting of *Shadows*' second chapter) is a tour guide to regional energy-sites and natural "mystery" places.

There's a lot to say about Western New York in most paranormal categories, but the region really stands out for mystical-religious activity. In the 1800s this energy was so proverbial that our region had nicknames like "The Burned-over District" and "The Spirit Way." One might think that *Shadows* had exhausted the noteworthy subjects, but "On the Spirit Way" carries easily on. This may be a very neglected feature of the Erie-Ontario region, which some claim the new spiritual mecca of the world.

About a third of this book is another tour, of hauntings, region-by-Western New York-region. Most of the articles in "Spooks, Specters, Spirits" represent actual reports. Others recycle folklore. A third group recounts single tales picked up through interviews. This list is in no way meant to be comprehensive. The area seems steeped in hauntings, another neglected story. Do a few interviews yourself if you doubt it.

To some people ghosts are nonsense; to others they're the spirits of the dead. Reality may be more flexible. This chapter isn't meant to validate ghosts or spontaneous psychic phenomena of other types. We believe some of it exists, but saw no need to weaken every piece with skeptical disclaimers. Readers should understand how controversial the subject is and simply enjoy the stories.

So much of our history, our speculations about life and afterlife, and our thoughts for our departed loved ones are held in the tales of our ghosts. Even if some of us don't value them, they're worth preserving for others who might. Readers should also understand that, unless intrigue itself is an object of dread, there is no supernatural danger whatsoever in visiting these sites. To whatever extent these "spirits" truly are as the folklore has them, they seem tutelary souls, guardians and well-wishers, for those who can see them that way.

We follow with a chapter of Iroquois supernatural tales, including a profile of "Mad Bear" Anderson, a 20th-century medicine man. Six Nations folklore is rich, and some of the best modern evidence of psychic phenomena is found on "the Res," where they don't make a big deal about it, either.

Few think of religion when the word *paranormal* is mentioned, but established faiths have long dealt with the reports of psychic events. "White Magic" surveys local cases of suspected possession, miracles, and other super-normal events in which mainstream religion or its presumed opposite - alleged "Satanic" activity - was involved. We offer several from both the light and the dark side.

East Aurora's marvelous Arts & Crafts Movement Campus Roycroft has yet to give up all its secrets, material or mystical. Roycroft was a community of artists harnessed into an enterprise of book and magazine publishing and the mass-marketing of crafts. Its founder Elbert Hubbard (1856-1915) was a complex figure who suggested his mystical interests and hallowed his Campus with sacred architecture.

Shadows' chapter "The Supernatural Roycroft" and its bit of ghostlore may have left an impression of the Inn as a haunted castle. Nothing could be further from the truth. *Shadows'* look at Roycroft was mostly technical, dealing with signs of mysticism in Roycroft art, architecture and literature, and showing Roycroft to be a modern sacred site. *Spirits'* treatment is more folkloric, and it's inversely fitting that we call its follow-up "The Sacred Roycroft." Roycroft truly is a shrine, for artists, thinkers, craftsmen, and all who love the beauty of mystery. That's what we meant to show about Roycroft the first time, our area's single most intricate site, and possibly the most intricate in the east when all perspectives are considered.

"In the ancient world," writes Manly Hall, "nearly all the secret societies were philosophic and religious. During the medieval centuries, they were chiefly religious and political, although a few philosophic schools remained. In modern times, secret societies, in the Occidental countries, are largely political or fraternal, although in a few of them, as in Masonry, the ancient religious and philosophic principles still survive." *Shadows'* chapter "Track of the Illuminoids" is revisited here as "The Invisible College," traditional code-lingo for a famous group of British occult scholars and for the pipeline of European religious-mystical knowledge in general. Called "the Hermetic-Cabalist tradition," this system underlies most Western esoteric groups. Readers may be surprised to see its influence.

Its potpourri of paranormal topics may make "The WNYX-Files" the most sensational of our chapters. There is a vivid modern folklore out there, and an active subculture that seldom gets much of a voice.

Most reviewers who actually read *Shadows* were positive. Few saw it as a contribution to the area's history, which was imagined when it was written. There was a good surprise, though. Some readers said that they read only one book a year and couldn't put *Shadows* down. That became more meaningful than the Pulitzer.

"If you can't explain something, don't," is a saying attributed to a great philosopher of the early 1970s, Winfield, we believe. (He's still with us, but he left the environment of American graduate school in the late 1970s and no longer thinks himself a great philosopher.) This book is made of things we can't explain.

July 2001
East Aurora, NY

Other Council Fires

Ancient Mysteries

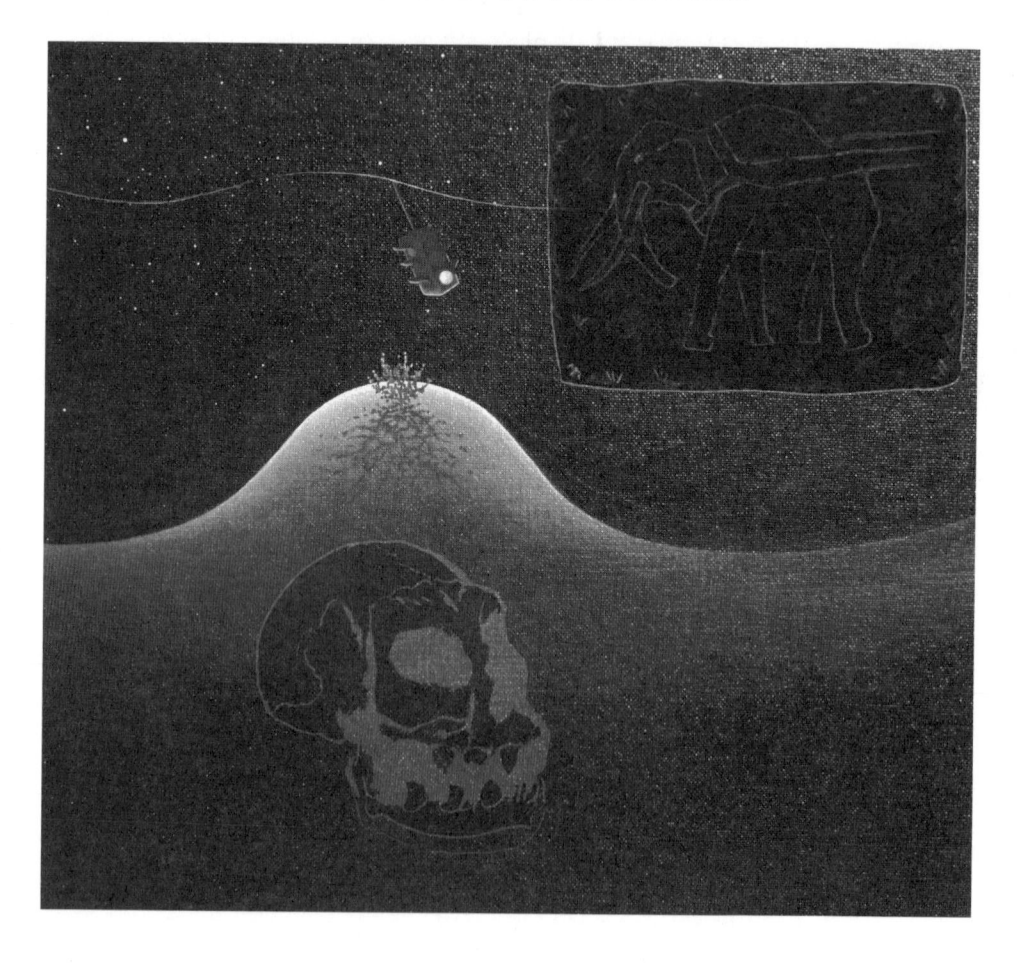

Further examination should precede opinion.

                William Martin Beauchamp

Other Council Fires

KINGDOMS OF THE CATTARAUGUS

In *Shadows of the Western Door* we set forth the established picture of American prehistory: no inhabitants but fully modern Homo sapiens; no ancient human populations but Native Americans; no Old World contact before Columbus. "Other council fires were here before us," the Iroquois have always maintained, and the established picture may be catching up to them. Still, real evidence around Western New York to disprove any of the above tenets would be not only dramatic; it would be amazing. It may be here.

The first Europeans in Western New York encountered the leftovers of prehistoric civilizations - "giant earthworks, massive burial mounds, and stone forts sitting above streams and rivers," in the words of Salvatore Trento. Western New York and parts of Ohio teemed with them. Most were simple ovals or circles, but other shapes and even animal effigies existed, of which Newark, Ohio's Serpent Mound complex is probably the most famous. These monuments have inspired wonder since.

Despite impressively sage conjecture by some colonial observers, among them Thomas Jefferson, many historians and much of the general public were unable to shake the sense that the ancestors of the migratory hunters and farmers of the Northeast Woodlands had not set up these large, numerous, and lasting monuments, to say nothing of the elaborate stoneworks found throughout the region. Many conjectured some influence no longer evident - either vanished Native American civilizations or European, even Atlantean, influences. The term *moundbuilder* to the 19th century became as charged as *druid* or *shaman* to the 20th.

The debate had spinoffs from the start, including a 19th-century industry in literature and excavation for fun and profit. First Mormon Joseph Smith, of course, burrowed into a Palmyra hill and came up with a new religion based on Lost Israelite Tribes and ancient American civilizations. Wags like John Ranking (in a long-titled 1828 book) posed lost Mongol armies of Kublai Khan, conquering the Americas, North and South, with elephant-cavalry. Another early, successful, and silly book was Cornelius Matthews' *Behemoth: A Legend of the Mound-Builders* (1839). (Great. Behemoth the Mammoth - a raging prodigy at last tricked and killed by a clever Mound-Builder hero. We're pitching a manuscript titled *Morris the Tyrannosaurus*. Any takers?) Another winner was *Traditions of the De-Coo-Dah*, by William Pidgeon (1858), replete with legends of warring Mound Builder empires. Ignatius Donnelly (1831-1901) takes the cake. His *Atlantis: The Antediluvian World* set off lost-continent speculation, including elephant-armies in the new world. More recent observers turn to ancient UFOs.

French and Spanish explorers observed earthworks under construction, and today it's generally accepted that native cultures - almost surely the ancestors of ones extant at the first European contact - built most of the earth-and-stone works. That doesn't mean nobody else was here. Somebody was busy, that's for sure.

Spirits of the Great Hill

Giants in the Ground

[Of *Shadows'* eighty articles, only "The Grave of Jack the Ripper" caused near the interest of "Monsters from the Mounds." Weird, human-like, giant skeletons have been reported all over North America, though nowhere so frequently as in Western New York and parts of Ohio. *Shadows* listed a few of the whoppers: human giants seven to nine feet tall; bestial humanoid skulls from Tonawanda Island; human skeletons from Fort Porter (Buffalo), but flat-shinned as if from lives of climbing trees. We have a few more weirdos to mention.]

With weapons, a head pillowed in a turtle-shell, and other signs of a celebrated burial, the bones of a giant Native American were found near Long Point on the east side of Conesus Lake in the early 1800s. In 1806 more large bones - a prodigious shin and a thigh two inches longer than that of the tallest settler - were found in an earthwork at the construction of Olmsted's mill, about 30 rods northeast of Bosley's Mills near the outlet of Conesus Lake.

While digging a cellar in Dansville (which apparently overlies an old Native American town), homebuilders found two skeletons of "giant-sized Indians" in 1869. They were side-by-side and seemed to have been older than others found near them. About 1820 many skeletons were taken from a huge Mt. Morris mound (nearly a hundred feet in diameter, and eight to ten high). One was enormous, its jaw so large that the biggest man in the settlement could fit it over his own chin.

Size was not the only strangeness reported of many Pennsylvania, New York, and Ohio giants. Huge molars, double rows of teeth, and "bilateral protrusions" at the jaw-hinge (cheek-flaps) were often described among the official finds. The strangest "extra" was the brow-knobs, virtual horns, on the titans unearthed from two Pennsylvania locations just below the Western New York state line. These are odd things to make up. Are they merely the symptoms of "acromegaly," a complaint often afflicting people of great height, in which parts of the skull and jaw grow disproportionately? At the least, something curious was going on in prehistory.

Closer to the present, Captains Magellan and Cooke reported living giants in South America's bleak Patagonia. (Cooke reported lashing one nine-footer to the mast, hoping to ferry him back to Europe, but he broke loose and dove into the chill Pacific.) Maybe the giants were elsewhere. Many world cultures have legends about them in the dim past; antennae go up when they tally with actual findings. Many nations of the Eastern woodlands, among them the Iroquois, Delaware, and Algonquin, talk of ancient wars with giant races. Their ancestors would likely have contacted the old Adena, the moundbuilding culture; attempts have been made to stitch their tales into the archaeological record. So far too many bare spots are filled by conjecture.

A good study has been made of giant skeleton reports in Ohio, which, like Western New York, features a high concentration of ancient earthworks. *Adena*, *Hopewell*, and *Mississippian* are names for succeeding stages of these mound-building cultures, none likely predating Christ by more than a few centuries. It would seem that the earliest, the Adena, stretched influence into Western New York and other

Other Council Fires

parts of the northeastern woodlands. The Adena culture was, seemingly, a multi-ethnic coalition of Native American groups. We judge them only from earthworks and grave-goods, so the term *Adena* is one of desperation.

Behind the scenes in anthropological circles it seems accepted that giant human bones were found at at least three sites, none in WNY, though some authorities (like Webb and Snow, *The Adena People*) don't make the dramatic mention we'd expect of them. Other sources find that some Adena were taller on average than any group of people now living. Not only do their bones reveal women well over six feet tall and men nearing seven, but they were wide-bodies, powerfully built, something you wouldn't expect of a freak or two among a short-statured group. They were, apparently, Native Americans, though DNA testing has reportedly established no link between the Adena and any contemporary Native American group.

Even the first observers suggested that huge Adena remains ceremonially treated need not imply a race of giants. Generations of selective breeding might have produced a physically-distinct caste of guardian-servants, warriors, or aristocrats, maybe the ruling class of a normal-sized group of people. We hear that Japan's elite World War Two commandos were all over six feet, and that the Chinese sent to the 2000 Olympics a basketball team with three seven-footers, one of whom is now in the NBA. Heroically buried and unearthed in centuries, they might convince future anomalists that both Asian peoples were super-sized. The matter is still weird. In 2000, most American males are nearly a foot taller than most Native Americans at the time of Christ. The Adena giants would have been more conspicuous about the northeastern woodlands than an NBA team in an airport.

East Aurora antiquarian Rodger Sweetland has a theory: If every mammal species exposed to cold - bears, lions, hoofed animals - grows 50-100% in size (we had 400-pound beavers in the Pleistocene) why couldn't there have been giant Homo sapiens? Why wouldn't they have faded out in warmer climes, as did most other mega-mammals?

A lot is written about giant American skeletons, like other paranormal curiosities. Skeptics conjecture that the reported specimens were simply measured wrong, and that disarticulated bones would look larger held up beside living bodies. Maybe.

One big problem with giant American skeletons is the absence of the bones. The great Iroquois scholar Arthur Parker (1881-1955) weighed the question himself, conceding that it was hard to find a single bone of any sort that had been collected before 1850. North American soil can be treacherous at preserving human bones which, even of normal size, are fragile after centuries in the ground. Few survive amateur handling. The settlers who found such oddities, uninspired by things scientific or Native American, would have been unlikely to house their own collections.

Believers, though, note that many giant skeletons were sent to universities and museums and simply "disappeared." In some cases doctors and scientists were on hand at excavations, testifying to what was found, sent off, and then lost. It is interesting to observe how many theory-crashers of any sort seem to just... vanish. What do you make of it?

Spirits of the Great Hill
The Sodus Bay Spearhead

In the summer of 1929 a storm blew out the breakwater on the west side of Charles Point near Sodus Bay, about a thousand feet from Lake Ontario. The summer residents set to work digging the foundations of a new boathouse. A foot below water level and twenty from shore, a shovel hit something hard. Up came a rusty object about a foot long and an inch across at its broadest. It looked to be a spearhead of European style, and somebody in the party recognized its potential impact. Philanthropist and clock-lover Augustus Hoffman had made a strong and surprise contribution to American history's "X-Files."

At the least, the artifact was curious. The Native Americans didn't have hard metals like iron until the Europeans brought them. Though the recognized European groups of explorers and conquistadors surely used many medieval weapons - and the sword was in actual military use in the twentieth century - this object seemed to fall between the cracks. When, a year after its finding, the Sodus Bay spearhead made its way to the Royal Ontario Museum, conjecture turned in a different direction. Curator Dr. C. T. Currelly judged it to be 600 to 1100 years old. He presumed it was Norse, and Scandinavian experts agreed.

It's been accepted that medieval Scandinavians had settled Greenland and visited parts of the Atlantic coast, but this spearhead came as news, seeming to be evidence that Norse explorers had gone much farther inland and south than previously thought. According to the Seneca we know, Iroquois historians never doubted that Vikings were all over the Atlantic coast and the Great Lakes, and that other Old World visitors were here as well. From his days working with state archaeologist Arthur Parker, Rochester historian J. Sheldon Fisher recalled turning up ancient skulls that were clearly North European in type at several sites about the Western Door. (Now, of course, under the Native American Graves Repatriation Act, they are all being returned to representatives of extant Native American nations for reburial, and thus any chance of solving a mystery will be gone.)

Most "funny" American artifacts are just plain funny. Forget the fact that they look like they don't belong here; they look like they don't belong anywhere, pointing to a high probability that they were forged. Truly ancient artifacts from known cultures have clear "pedigrees" - subtleties of style and manufacture - that cannot be casually faked. Exactly like others in Scandinavian museums, the Sodus Bay spearhead seems to be the real deal, a weapon of an old type very likely from the Viking age. One source regards it as the tenth incontestably Norse relic found around the Great Lakes, and historians in Wayne County see no reason to believe that the artifact is not authentic. The Norse could easily have reached this part of the states, and *America BC* author Barry Fell's theories about ancient Vikings on the Great Lakes are looking better all the time. Take a look at it yourself. The Sodus Bay spearhead is on display at the Wayne County Museum in Lyons, NY.

Other Council Fires

THE BURIED CAUSEWAY

[So far as we know, there was no wheeled traffic, no beast of burden, and no need of mass transportation before the Europeans hit North America. Still, ancient roads were among the curiosities reported by the first of them, most near water.]

"In excavating for the pipes of the Oxygen and Hydrogen Gas Company on Niagara Square," reports the *Buffalo Morning News* on July 10, 1872, "workmen have struck, ten feet below the surface, a number of logs... One of these logs is about two feet in diameter, the others, smaller." They were arranged to imply a road to the modern mind. The article goes on to observe that "the old inhabitants say (these logs) were part of a causeway that existed in that locality in days past."

The next day someone calling himself "Old Settler" writes in the "Notes from the People" column that, from 1816 to 1822, the road - now Niagara Street - west of Niagara Square was causewayed with logs up to the crossing of Mohawk Street. Seeming to sense a disconnect, though, the paper's editor asks, "Will some of our worthy historians brush up their memories and tell us all about the state of affairs in that section of the town before ten feet of earth was added to the surface?" Good point.

A road beneath a two-centuries-young city hardly implies Atlantis, but the depth is suggestive, possibly representing several thousand years. Surely earth moved about Niagara Square as Buffalo formed, but ten feet is a long way down. If the log road was not a recent feature buried by the growth of the city - about six decades old at the time of the article - we have a problem.

Later in his letter "Old Settler" notes a Buffalo house in which a murdered soldier's ghost rushed a shoemaker's bench and blew his candle out. It's a dubious skeptic who finds ghostly marvels to his taste but defies earthly ones. "Old Settler" should get used to both on the Western Door.

Obed Edson notes "the most extensive remains of the county" by Cassadaga Lake, with "an elevated strip of land, the width of an ordinary turnpike bearing the appearance of having been once a graded way." Near a mound from which many human skeletons were taken, it was sixty rods or more in length. A. W. Young notes two old mounds and traces of a roadway at Griffith's Point near the eastern shore of Chautauqua Lake. In his *History of Portland*, Horace Taylor notes several ancient roadways by that Lake Erie landing. This was an ancient portage, and water levels were far higher in earlier times. The Allegany River might have been the goal, part of a water route running through to the Gulf of Mexico.

Frederick Larkin reports several roads about our region "underlayed with stone and covered with sand and gravel to the depth of several feet." The point of such graded ways has always been a mystery, "especially to those who suppose the builders were allied to the Indian tribe." Doc Larkin regarded our region - particularly the then-navigable Cattaraugus Creek - one of the likeliest ancient trade routes from the Erie to the Ohio River. Because of their proximity to water, these old roads would seem to be ramps for portaging - carrying boats - between navigable bodies, perhaps even loading or unloading heavy cargo. What?

Spirits of the Great Hill

King Solomon's Mines

[We all know it's gone; nobody knows who took it or where it went. It's one of the world's most spectacular "ancient mysteries," half a billion pounds of missing Great Lakes copper. Some think Solomon's mines were really in the Americas.]

The first Euroamericans were surprised by the number of mines - about 5,000 - around the northern shore of Lake Superior. Those who knew mining were shocked by the amounts of copper taken - some estimate 500+ million pounds - from bleak Isle Royale, with no accounting for its whereabouts. Charcoal at the bases of the ancient pits gave radiocarbon dates of 2000 (some perhaps 6000!) to 1000 BC, roughly those of the Bronze Age in northern Europe. Copper plus tin makes the harder metal bronze, but there was no American Bronze Age, so we think. But somebody was digging, and there are problems with all the guesses as to who it was:

- *Nobody should have been mining copper there and then.* Native North Americans used copper for ornaments; South Americans used it also for implements. Neither needed to dig. Enough copper for either is found on the surface.
- *So much was taken.* Way more than both continents should have used.
- *So little has been found.* Copper is one metal with a pedigree, and there are several motherlodes in the world. Copper thought to come from Superior has been found all over the Americas, but not in anything approaching these staggering amounts. We'd expect scholars to doubt rumors of ancient Romans and Phoenicians taking vast masses of Great Lakes copper home, even if it had turned up in Europe... but it's not there, either. We could even muse about someone taking it off the planet - UFO's, perhaps? - but the mining technology was typical for the age. But not the place.

Who did it? is the heavy question. Mediterranean empires of the day would have used plenty of copper and tin to make bronze. The Mediterranean has no ready sources of either metal. Many Old world seafarers may have left footprints in the ancient Americas. After extensive examination of the famous Peterborough, Ontario, rock carvings, Harvard prof Barry Fell thought he'd narrowed the Great Lakes action down to 1700 BC and a Scandinavian king named *Woden-Lithi*, whose trade network headquarters was in this neck of the lakes.

Fell has good evidence for something going on here, if not exactly Woden-Lithi. But the subject is important. It might explain other ancient regional mysteries. Water would have been the way to transport almost anything heavy throughout the eastern part of the continent, and routes would go through either the Mississippi system or the Great Lakes. The process would have involved surprisingly little portaging, though ramps and roads would be needed for unloading ships. This could account for Western New York's anomalous ruins and ancient roads.

The Chippewa "Curse of the Copper" is a legendary blight on those who take the soft metal from the region. A memory of an ancient disaster? The miners didn't leave much behind to tell us what happened.

Other Council Fires

FORT HILL

[In 1880 and 1938 several close (for the day) studies were made of a small region of Yates County near Keuka Lake, where four problematic earth-and-stone constructions were found. The Native Americans of the area had been quizzed about them since their discovery, and the matter was a mystery to the oldest Iroquois. In *Shadows* we discussed the oddest of them, "Bluff Point." This could be the best-studied.]

At the behest of the Smithsonian Institute the father-son team of Dr. Samuel Hart and Professor Berlin Hart Wright surveyed and mapped the ruin at the summit of the promontory called "Bluff Point." The stone ramps and alignments of that fourteen-acre site may have been all that was left after other structures were stripped away, but what was observable to the Wrights that July day in 1880 and until its 1930s dismantling was incomprehensible. No firm conclusions have ever been reached about this bizarre stonework on a natural promontory above Keuka Lake.

Ten miles north of Bluff Point and clearly visible to the Wrights from one of its pillars was an elliptical earthen fortification known as "Fort Hill." It's located in Sherman's Hollow in the northwestern part of the town of Jerusalem, about a mile from the community of Jemima Wilkinson, the "Publick Universal Friend," in a town even called "Friend." As it's also known, "The Old Fort" was 545 feet long north to south and 485 feet across, enclosing ten acres. Its dirt embankments (four feet high and ten across a century ago) must have settled over the years.

Fort Hill may have been aptly named. There were twelve breaks in the walls where gates (presumably of wood) could have been, and it held the spring vital for withstanding any siege. A deep, wide trench ran around the inside of the earthwork, and near it is a tall hill with very steep sides, nicknamed "the pinnacle." Smoke signals or fires from this spot would have been visible at Bluff Point, implying line-of-sight communication with a sister settlement. We can almost envision Frederick Larkin's doomed outposts of a "higher" culture, slowly enveloped by the unenlightened hordes. (See "The Mastodon Rider.")

In advance of the Wrights' visit the Smithsonian had sent queries to people living in the area of the ruins, and the family team got a look at whatever relics had been found. They included unspecified iron implements that could have come from historic occupants. One likely ancient artifact that Berlin Wright calls "a Mexican kneading board" we would call a *metate*. This stone butcher's block with an indented curve (on which corn would have been ground) is one of the most distinctive features of Central American housekeeping, as much a fixture of the Mexican kitchen as is a sink to the modern American. Versions of it are found among many Native American societies, including the Iroquois. This one, however, was of a fine, compact type of sandstone "radically different from any geological formation found in that region."

About twenty rods southeast of the enclosure was an ancient graveyard. Skeletons had been found seated, facing south. Yates County historians report a bronze sword taken from an ancient mound near here. It's supposedly still with a family in the neighborhood, though we've not been able to view it.

Known Native American groups in this part of the world were virtually

Spirits of the Great Hill

nomadic, and not thought to build elaborate stone structures. Even the famed Iroquois longhouse was of wood. We can't rule out the influence of Hopewell and Adena cultures in the Yates County mysteries. Though the Hopewell culture may have been centered in Ohio, it probably extended at least its influence into Western New York. Neither Yates County structure sounds like anything they were known to build, however, and we're left with the impression of an unknown influence in the area.

Antiquarian and scholar Dave Robinson of Swain, NY, compares the earliest descriptions of Bluff Point to all that's usually left by time of one type of ancient European dwelling - Bronze Age to post-Roman British, in the Lake District of England. Others have asserted Celtic migrations to the Americas, but we don't see the need to look that far.

Ironically these ruins were of little interest to state archaeologists who seem to have embraced a "Catch-22" attitude: the Hopewell-influenced groups known to have been in the area were either "too primitive or too far regressed" (others' words) to have done any complex building, and no one else here could have done it. So: Nothing to talk about. Yet the ruins stood.

There's little left of the Yates County ruins. It's possible that a full-scale modern dig would tell us all we needed to know, possibly that there's no mystery in the first place, but our chances of learning something the easy way seem long gone.

Other Council Fires

THE GREAT CIRCLE-HENGE

[Some ancient constructions - like Egypt's Great Pyramid - are so big that they boggle the mind. Some others - like Britain's Avebury monument - are so big that they weren't even rediscovered until humankind could fly over them. That's big. WW II aerial photography revealed the Avebury "henge" to be a ring-ditch so gigantic that it seemed a natural formation to the citizens of the village inside it. That's *really* big. The Western Door has its own giant mystery.]

It would have a right to feel left out. They took its picture, but it was years before anyone noticed it, this Old-World-style monument on New-World soil. In 1980 Peter Tierney, District Manager of the Yates County Soil and Water Conservation Service, was going over some aerial photographs of his region taken in October 1974 when he spotted something too curving and smooth to be natural.

Terrestrial inspection revealed the arc in the upper reaches of Clark's Gully to be an earthen ring, in many places invisible from the ground. Sited partly on a bench on a hillside and partly on gently sloping ground, the Clark's Gully Henge (near Middlesex) is accessible only by foot and was unknown to local folk - those that are talking, anyway - until that sky-high pic.

Only the northern third of it is visible, but the full arc would have been a thousand meters in diameter. At ground-level what you can see of it is about thirty-five feet across and five high; the rest is only a suggestion until you're in the air. It's possible that the henge was never completed, but only a full study could tell. An aerial photo from the 1950s shows a much more defined shape. The rapid rate of erosion between the two shots makes some wonder if this formation is relatively recent, only a few centuries or so old. The elements don't play the same, though, every century; just think about acid rain. The Seneca questioned knew nothing about this mound, and most of us think it's old.

Who made it? Any guess depends on the arc's as-yet unknown age, although the Hopewell culture built earthworks, and Hopewell-style stonework is in the area. Somebody around here was up to something. There are seventeen small stone mounds, and two big ones are near the Clark's Gully arc. One of them on the highest part of the henge is thirty-three feet long and made of three connected parts: a circle ten feet in diameter, a rectangle ten by fifteen, and a square of eight-foot sides. The other eighteen mounds are less intricate and located a short way uphill (north) of the henge.

David Robinson has applied the learning of the Continental geomancers to his own upstate region, deducing (with British earth-mystic John Michell) that, since dragon legends usually involved forts, man-made mounds, or hills, the Clark's Gully Henge is a myth etched in earth, the Great Serpent of the Seneca, "the People of the Great Hill." The image of the arc split in half by the long slash of Clark's Gully gives others the fanciful notion of an arrow in a bow aimed northward. When it was made, only the UFO's were high enough above it to have been impressed. Maybe they can give us the answers, too.

Spirits of the Great Hill

The Mastodon Rider

[The last American elephant should have died over ten thousand years ago. Representations of them on apparently ancient Native American artifacts pose a distinct theoretical problem. Visions of fortified cities, Homeric battles, dying civilizations, and elephant-cavalry charges came to one writer's mind as the result of something he found in a Western New York burial mound.]

Dr. Frederick Larkin of Randolph, NY, was professor of physiology at the Randolph Eclectic Medical College. His medical degree may have been honorary, but his interest in ancient American cultures was passionate. Like many Euroamericans of the middle nineteenth century he set out upon his own freelance excavations. His book *Ancient Man in America* lists his most dramatic find.

In 1859, while exploring some tumuli (burial mounds) in the Red House Valley probably within today's Allegany State Park, Larkin and pals found "a flat piece of native copper, six inches in length by four in width, artistically wrought, with the form of an elephant represented in harness engraved upon it, and a sort of breast collar with tugs on either side, which extended past the hips."

Hold on. Though impressive, even moving images of humans and Ice Age animals have been executed in pigment and bone, by the time people were at the societal level implied by Larkin's plate - fashioning earthworks and crafting copper - the last mastodon should have been long gone. Even more electrifying was the impression that Larkin's beast had been domesticated, conscripted into transportation, agriculture, and maybe even warfare. To Larkin, this and other reported finds indicated that human beings had "tamed that monster of the forest and made him a willing slave to their intellectual power." Shades of *Dinotopia!*

Or Atlantis. But we go too fast. Ranging in size from a Wisconsin earthwork to a tobacco pipe, and in development from a Mayan temple carving to a pecked stone slab, elephant-like images do appear in Native American art. The study of them is a sub-industry in "fringe archaeology," and a few examples should suffice. Author Graham Hancock saw the image of an elephant (with other extinct animals) on the "Gateway of the Sun" at Tiwanaku in Bolivia. Carl Johannessen, Professor Emeritus at the University of Oregon, notes that the image has been discovered in Olmec regions on the Gulf of Mexico, and also in several Mayan sites at Copan, Uxmal and Kabah. To Johannessen these images are distinct enough to suggest that the sculptures "were made under the direction of someone who was familiar with the animals."

"Are they really elephants?" some ask. A few mammals native to these continents - like the tapir - might seem elephantine through the distortion of ancient art, which is never easy to interpret. [Erich Von Daniken (*Chariots of the Gods*), for instance, took the portrait of Mayan king Pacal on his stylized throne to be a UFO-ride.] The Wisconsin mound could be a bear whose snaky schnozz came courtesy of a flooded stream, and other images like the Mayan carvings could be representations of the long-nosed rain-god, or simply ornate motifs.

Others are less ambiguous. A famous pictograph from the Moab seems to be surely some large trunked animal no longer living in the region, and clear elephant-images have been found throughout North America in a variety of inscrip-

Other Council Fires

tions, like Pennsylvania's Lenape Stone and Massachusetts' Hammond Stone. Some of the most convincing sculptures are a clearly elephantine pipe from a mound in Iowa (the main skeptical quibble seeming to be that it lacks tusks), and one of red soapstone (catlinite) in our own Little Valley Museum, where you can check it out yourself.

Of these cases the question is authenticity. Hearsay is never evidence, and it's usually impossible to date a stone artifact isolated from its site. Skeptics object that these elephant-images could be errors or modern hoaxes, particularly the inscribed stones. A range of motives offers itself for forging or reporting archaeological curiosities, a game which seems to have been the rage in the nineteenth century.

Not much can be judged about Larkin's plate from the information we have. A copper artifact might last a long time in the right soil, and it might deteriorate in just a century or so under the wrong conditions. It's possible that the tradition of the elephant-image existed from very ancient times, and that this plate was simply copied from an earlier original, maybe a legacy of them.

Doc Larkin was a phrenologist, deducing from a mere skull the character of its living owner. ("The intellectual and moral regions were exceedingly well developed," he complimented the late bearer of one doughty specimen.) His imagination was also dramatic, envisioning ancient Homeric American battles in our own Chautauqua and Cattaraugus counties, "soldiers driving their flint arrows into the quivering flesh of their victims," and "the tributary streams of the Conewango pouring down their turbid waters red with human gore." Nevertheless, his take on what he and others actually found is pretty pragmatic. He quarrels, for instance, with reports of giant skeletons, and, except for a few apparently pre-Columbian roads about Western New York (which we discuss elsewhere), mentions few oddities. He is the more credible as he describes his mastodon platter.

Though Larkin's elephant may still be preserved in some private collection, Iroquois scholar and archaeologist Arthur Parker searched for it in vain. We could get our glimpse of its subjects another way someday, if, as Larkin fancies, the Last Trumpet sounds, and "Blacksnake, Cornplanter, and all their nameless prehistoric forbears leap forth in their full-fleshed finery." Will the mastodon rider and his violent legions lead the Judgment-parade in the Red House Valley? It will have to wait, the mystery of Larkin's elephant, whose bones "and those of his master are crumbling together in the ground."

The Power Points

It is possible that the ability to perceive these ghosts and elemental creatures, sometimes experienced by mere mortals, could stem from the energy of the earth currents that flow through the ancient sites.

Janet and Colin Bord

The Power Points

THE PEACE QUEEN

[This State Historic Site near Rochester appears on many a list of the world's spiritual high points. Maybe it should be a political shrine as well - the Athens of America. It may be here that the legendary Peacemaker had his vision of the Iroquois union, the grand confederacy that went on to influence that of the young American States. Sacred to the Iroquois, Ganondagan may once have been the town of *Jikonsaseh*, "Mother of Nations," "the Peace Queen," foundress of the Iroquois league. Jikonsaseh (spelling flexible) was the unseen hand behind famous leaders Hiawatha and The Peacemaker. A shrine, a burial-ground, a battlefield - this may be the heaviest site in the Northeast. Let's go back.]

Once the Iroquois nations fought each other. Mohawk leader Deganawidah - Peacemaker - had a vision of the great pact. He traveled among the nations, gathering followers, persuading the Mohawks, Cayugas, and Oneidas to form a confederation. Onondaga leader Hiawatha became the only convert of his nation; the Seneca and Tuscarora were later-comers. The visionary pair traveled west to counsel with Jikonsaseh ("the Lynx"), the Peace Mother, a member of the Neutral Nation who lived near Lake Erie. At this meeting the Great Law of Peace was established, and the Iroquois, the Longhouse People, adopted their constitution. Jikonsaseh also convinced the two leaders to include women in their plan, something that would have lasting implications. The longhouse, with all nations living safely and justly under one roof, was a symbol of the universal peace. It would be tested.

In the late seventeenth century, the French and English struggled over North America, even splitting the Iroquois Confederacy. The proud Seneca had refused French demands for exclusive trade. With sixteen hundred European veterans, a thousand Native Americans (some Mohawk), and 400 colonials, Marquis Denonville landed at Rochester's Irondequoit Bay on July 10, 1687, bent on teaching the Great Hill Folk a lesson. Reinforced with Ottawa allies and even seven Illinois, this was a mighty army for the place and time that marched to the biggest Seneca town Gannagaro on Boughton Hill near Victor. A small but savage Seneca ambush was repulsed, and on July 14 the expedition came upon the main village, deserted.

It was a standoff. The Seneca lurked in the woods where the Euros dassn't go. The French stayed on the field, wasting crops and not living Seneca, then returned to their ships, jeered all the way as "corn-cutters," by their spoiling-for-a-fight Mohawk allies, whose love for their Seneca brothers could be situational.

The following spring the Seneca women returned to see what was left of their homes at the ruined Gannagaro. Nothing but pathos remained, and memories; but overrunning the site like snow-patches, as if a natural peace-offering, was white trillium, delicate, gleaming. "Ganondagan!" they proclaimed, calling to each other through their tears: "Light! Brightness!" The name is thus one of cheer and renewal.

The spirit of the Peace Queen lives on. Legend has it that Jikonsaseh was buried in a blanket of fresh water pearls at a secret site near Gannagaro. Her grave may be in a beautiful, secluded spot still known to the Iroquois, still visited by her faithful. They come at private times, at sunrise or after sunset, to pay respects, espe-

Spirits of the Great Hill

cially in Spring, her special season.

Though it can't be said that the Iroquois nations were matriarchies all the way, like many Native American societies the Great Hill folk showed strong matriarchal features. The clan mothers chose all the chiefs, who held office only as long as they did right. If such things can linger, Iroquois feminist energy could have influenced the Womens' Movement of Seneca Falls, NY, that was so vivid in this segment of the state.

Like many battlefields Ganondagan is regarded as the classic "vortex," a confluence of natural-spiritual energy which, as we see, shows itself in a variety of ways. People of all races claim mystical experiences here, including sessions with the spirits of the corn, the staple crop of so many Amerindian cultures. "This place sizzles," says one source. People hear faint chanting and drums in the distance, all of it inspiring. Sometimes they're too delirious to speak to the staff.

According to historian J. Sheldon Fisher, every house bordering the site has some story attached to it, and one we'll repeat. As a family raked leaves outside their house, the mother noticed an odd human-sized gust, a mini-tornado, approaching. It carried dust and leaves and moved purposefully toward the open door of their house as if an invisible wizard walked within it. It entered before the family could reach it and close the door. The house was still, and nothing had been disturbed, but the climate had changed. In the coming weeks the family was troubled, and psychic phenomena broke out all over the house. A Seneca elder visited them, and at one point his dog bristled, terrified by an invisible presence the people could track through his gaze. The elder reacted immediately, commencing a ritual to banish the force, whatever it was. Soon the house was again at peace.

Ganondagan is a powerful, spiritual place, but not all Whites have positive reactions to it at every visit. The night after her first tour, the youngest daughter of a medical professor had an unsettling dream, of an old, grey-haired Native American climbing the porch outside her window, intent upon entering her room.

The Power Points

ONTARIO ATLANTIS
[Do the Great Lakes have their own lost islands?]

When the French explorer Samuel de Champlain scoured the northeast, he was looking for the fabled "northwest passage" to the Pacific, a water route to China through the North American continent. As expected, through surrogates he mapped much of what he saw. Unexpectedly, some of what he mapped is no longer there, like the two islands, one very large, in Lake Ontario. One is to the north, near Coburg in Canada. The other is near the Niagara and the American side, probably just north of present-day Olcott, NY. Each island was apparently sizeable enough to fit a city the size of today's Toronto. What gives? There are no such islands today, nor were there fortysomething years later when the explorer Louis Joliet did his work. Because of the accuracy of Champlain's other maps, this is interesting.

The Native Americans were asked for their take on the matter, and offered some of their own Lakes legends of lost civilizations on island "cities of light." Could a mini-Atlantis have existed in these parts of the Great Lakes? Hydrographic maps surely point to shallow areas in the areas of Lake Ontario corresponding to the supposed former "islands."

Lake Chautauqua may have something interesting of the sort, though vanished communities may not be involved. The notes and papers of Chautauqua County historian Norman Carlson offer some stories about Lake Chautauqua's reputed "Grass Island" about which there are direct references starting as early as 1875. In 1931 Henry Strunk's little genealogy mentions Gideon and Aurilla Sherman taking their kids out to Grass Island to swim, probably in the early 1800s.

Grass Island may even have held a fortress whose ruins were visible in recent times. In a 1923 newspaper article, a citizen of Jamestown and later Falconer recalls a story told by William Fenton, possibly a member of the Governor's family. When Fenton was ten or twelve he observed a stone fortress on this island, appearing only at low water. It was circular, single-story, and large, and most of its stones, he reports, were taken by more recent settlers for their own buildings. There is lots of recycled mileage on this one. Some even claim to know the French expedition (that of de Celoron) that built this fortress, possibly for the burial of treasure. Trouble is, there's almost no hard record of a Grass Island, and only conjecture about de Celoron's route. The whole thing may be a myth.

It's interesting to think of the "Atlantis" legends repeatedly associated with The Bermuda Triangle, and the underwater cities recently found (2001) off the shore of Cuba; it's also worth observing that the Great Lakes have their own ominous, disastrous triangle (see *Shadows*), and that we now see their legends of lost islands. Time for a video of some of these lake bottoms.

Spirits of the Great Hill

The Angel's Mountain

Even for those who haven't read *Shadows*, the motif is familiar. A Vermont farmboy moved with his family to upstate New York and believed an angel led him to his visionary "Golden Books." Burrowing into nearby Cumorah Hill (possibly into a Native American earthwork), he wrote a Bible of his own, with tales of ancient American civilizations, lost tribes of Israel, climactic battles, and Biblical allegories. Within only a few years his inspired supporters had formed a new religion, and Prophet Smith (like Another) was killed by a mob. His devout followers suffered persecution, migrated into the wilderness, and built their New Jerusalem for one of the world's great young religions. This tale of fantastic achievement begins with a serious mystery.

Few but the Mormons believe Joseph Smith (1805-1844) truly met angels or set postscripts to the Judeo-Christian Bible, but few of any stripe doubt that he may have found something in Palmyra's strange Hill Cumorah. "This is a special place," says Salvator Michael Trento, the Oxford-trained "fringe" archaeologist and author who's made a study of North America's sacred places. He sees this as one of the energy points, which he's studied from many perspectives, including the technical.

"As one climbs to the top of this hill," he notes, "the total magnetic field radically changed from 500 milligaus units to over 900! The angle of incidence also deviated from its baseline reading of 55 degrees to well over 80 degrees." Trento asks three main questions of Hill Cumorah:

- *Did Smith find artifacts of the "Lost Tribes" of Israel?* Objects are found all over the Americas allegedly from Phoenician wanderers, certainly Semitic folk. Smith's "buried cavern" sounds suspiciously like the stone chambers found on hilltops throughout the Northeast. There are two centuries of reports of buried stones and inscribed tablets, many from Western New York.
- *Why did Joseph Smith - who spent his boyhood among central Vermont's strange stone ruins - see things here that no one else did?* Could he have recognized something about upstate New York?
- *Why did Smith find something on that particular hill?* Many doubt that his engraved tablets were material objects. Was that hill a classic "vortex" that would give anyone visions? It would not be lonely in Western New York.

Tests of ancient monuments worldwide have revealed electromagnetic anomalies, as if their designers were able to detect and harness this power in the earth. Their purposes in doing so are unknown. Paranormal folklore also flocks to such sites and nearby regions. A grab-bag of effects has been reported in the vicinity of Smith's hill: UFO sightings, apparitions, and even witchcraft-inspired murders. Despite the sinister ring, the pattern is familiar. The energy of the paranormal is just that, energy, as neutral as fire or water; it's also strong here, surely making it one of North America's hotspots.

The Power Points

THE SPIRITUAL SPRINGS

[In *Shadows* we wrote about Harmonia, the dream-community southwest of Jamestown in Kiantone, NY, which for a time was actually called "Spiritual Springs." Here we focus on their energy source.]

It all started, of course, with Spiritualism, the religion spun off the poltergeist effects of March, 1848, in the Fox sisters' Hydesville, NY, cottage. A craze of seances swept America, in one of which (in 1850) the family of Kiantone blacksmith John Chase heard some interesting things about their home region. The spirits reported that a prehistoric tribe of "Celtic Indians" had settled the Kiantone Creek valley. Their society was perfect, thanks to "free love," the abolition of marriage, and two "magnetic springs," one positive, one negative, with the power to cure all ills. An attack by "barbaric hordes" destroyed their culture and covered over the spring.

Aha. This rendition certainly touched most of the bases of nineteenth-century speculation about ancient North America. Still, holy fountains and "Celtic Indians" were slightly unusual things to infer without the benefits of the twentieth century's Barry Fell and his book *America BC*. The area around Kiantone had been important in Seneca legend, though, and who knows how long before that. The warrior Cornplanter (1736-1836) was said to come here before and after campaigns, and the site was sacred to the old and the ailing. Kiantone actually means "The Planted Fields" in some early tongue, seeming to imply that there were traces of habitation when the Iroquois arrived.

The blacksmith's team of spiritual adventurers soon included debonair Chautauqua doctor William Brittingham. They dowsed with a witch-hazel wand, bored fifty feet into the earth, and came up with their healing springs, which became a source of income. The water was boiled down and the residue - a white powder - sold. (When the distilling was slow, the Chase boys, Dwight, Oscar, and Gilman, dipped into the ample blue clay bank beside the creek.) Samples of the water were sent to the leading spiritualists in the East. One impressed was John Murray Spear, whose spiritual advisors (naming themselves "The Association of Benificents") directed a model community in Kiantone. The valley would be bright with color, commotion, and curiosity for decades to come.

Spear and his community have come and gone, and all that remains of their "stately pleasure dome" are few half-buried foundations, an earthy circle round a stagnant pool, and a door in a hillside. (Right out of *The Hobbit*, it keeps the tunnel, its buried spring, and who knows what else from the legions of would-be mystics.) Still, believers say the spirit around Kiantone Creek runs high. As recently as the 1960s a local cottager heard a fumbling at the side of his house and found a strange woman, a New England medium, sleep-walking. She'd been driving by when the Kiantone force hit her, threw her into trance, and aimed her toward the site of old Harmonia. Glowing stones, spectral Native Americans, and fireballs hurtling up and down the creek figure in the recent folklore. There has to be some energy left.

Spirits of the Great Hill

Garden of the Gods

[The chert - a glassy rock, ideal for tools and projectile-points - was mined here and traded across the continent. The space near it had to be a shrine to somebody. Our name for it may be only a century old, but the spot was important long before. Maybe you can still get a little of its feel - if you can find it.]

As the crow flies, Ontario's Point Abino is about twenty miles south of Niagara Falls and twelve or so west of Buffalo. This limestone promontory forging a mile and a half into Lake Erie has dunes so high and old that they seem mountainous, and marshes, meadows, and sandy tracts lie behind them. In one of the last, within the private Point community, is a shrinelike natural space named "The Garden of the Gods." It's easy to see how it got its name.

Amidst the leafy wood stood a sandy area of thin evergreens. Pyramidal Arbor Vitae mixed with columnar red junipers, some of which grew in natural rings. Circular patches of ground juniper made monuments of single trees around which they sprouted. In the warm seasons special flowers bloomed and livened the space differently each week. Some great Architect must have crafted the central formation, a natural ring of trees. Surely He - perhaps in this case, She - arranged for the natural *feng-shui* ("fung-shway"), even to Western eyes, a harmony.

To generations of American summer-settlers its sanctity was proverbial; the lore of it is far older. It's on or near the ancient burial ground of a Native American society wiped out by the Iroquois. To Native American nations uncounted it was a special place, a site of worship and vision-quest. Ceremonies have been held in it living memory; who knows what revelations marked its past?

In 1988, historian Earl Plato and naturalist Tim Seburn made a pilgrimage to the Garden of the Gods. A short walk along the Sandhill Trail through a deciduous forest brought them to a special spot that only those in the know could find; this, at least, was the same. A dive into the underbrush and more hiking led to an elliptical opening where the Point meets the mainland. They had trouble recognizing the sacred site.

The outcropping limestone ledges were still there, but the circles of ground juniper and other trees had died. A landowner had dumped garbage on the edge of the special spot, and a batch of rusting cans affected the mood. An ice storm from 1969 had finished the job, decimating the cedars and red junipers that had made the central ring-formation. Most were broken and decaying. At one point the men stopped and stared at each other, realizing that the scene lingered only in memory.

"We can't always understand the laws of nature and why things have to change," wrote Plato of the experience. His friend and mentor Bert Miller had taught him that mankind was given dominion over the natural world, but with that power came responsibility, to nurture and protect the beautiful spaces. Ah, for the Garden of the Gods, so long here, so quickly gone. Surely one can find the exact spot by communing near it long enough.

The Power Points

THE DEVIL'S HOLE

["A fit place for a demon dwelling," wrote Orsamus Turner of the panic of water and wind, the deadly chasm and glacial cave at Devil's Hole. The *Field Guide to North American Hauntings* is more direct, noting "shrieks and moans from within the cave," and a tradition of deaths, murders, and suicides near it. Those who explore Devil's Hole "do so only at tremendous personal risk." Only those ghosthunters who have "nothing left to lose should even attempt to study this site."]

It impressed the Seneca, in whose legends even its creation was an act of rage. In a bout of displeasure the Good Spirit drove the great Falls back up the Niagara. When his Seneca beheld the cavern three miles north of the cataracts, thunder and groans issued forth, as if it were the gates of the evil dead. One young Seneca entered the cave fully armed and never came out. He may have been accepted as a sacrifice, though, because a voice boomed prophecies of the White men, generations to come. Legends gathered about the haunted cavern, but in spite of them, another brave went in, to come out white-haired and raving. His wits may have been another offering, and prophecy the return gift. The Whites were near.

The Whites may have starred in Seneca prediction, but more of them should have listened to it. In 1669 explorer La Salle saw Devil's Hole, out of which Iroquois words boomed: "Go back, to wealth, honors, and a long useful life. Go onward, to misery, and a treacherous end." He entered nonetheless, possibly thinking the legends guarded treasure. He may have had there a mystical moment like Bonaparte's in the Great Pyramid, but there is no record of it impressing him. The Seneca were not surprised to hear of his many disasters and his murder by his own men. Mighty spirits had been offended, and they called many living ones to join them in the Devil's Hole's famous massacre, naming the creek near it Bloody Run. The most credible account may be Turner's (*History of the Holland Purchase*).

By 1763 the English had won control of the northeast's water routes, and thus the rich fur trade. The Seneca porters on the route round the Falls were downsized in favor of wagons. Unwise. In September 1763 the English were shown the Seneca version of a wildcat strike.

Twenty-five wagons and fifty English soldiers nearing the Devil's Hole were virtually wiped out by a single volley, fired from cover by about five hundred Seneca. Some of the wounded jumped to their deaths into the gorge as the Seneca swarmed with knife, club, and tomahawk. There were two survivors: a drummer boy whose drum-strap caught on a tree, and leader John Stedman, who spurred his horse at the first onslaught. A rescue force from the Fort blundered into more of the same medicine.

The twentieth century saw its own disasters. President McKinley toured here hours before his 1901 assassination. In July 1917, the trolley derailed, shooting one car and fifty passengers into the howling gorge. "Since the 1850s, countless people have lost their lives in freak accidents near the cave," claims *The National Directory of Haunted Places*. "Nearly every year someone is killed by falling or drowning." Testimony even features them returning, like old Hamlets, to replay their deaths. An eerie amphitheater, this Devil's Hole, whose dead become instant thespians.

Spirits of the Great Hill

The Valley of Madness

"The Valley of Madness" is the region about the Kanakadea Creek in which SUNY Alfred and Alfred Tech are located. Its name is no exact translation of anything, and versions range from "Valley of the Mad" to "Land of the Insane." They point to the same thing, though, the sense of an age-old suspicion and even dread to this valley. The lore may predate the Iroquois, and it doesn't let up there.

The name *Kanakadea* is said to mean "where heaven and hell meet earth." Who knows what that meant to the Iroquois, but it may have led to the region's nickname. An ancient Seneca burial ground is reportedly covered by the "dead-ended" valley holding both Alfred campuses. People hike and hunt in the woods, and sense strange "things" in the trees at dawn and dusk, strange sounds at dawn and twilight, strange images at the eye-corners. After dark some say you can see spectral figures carrying their dead to the sound of deep drumming. Others observe that ghosts here would be natural, since battlefields are sites of spooklore, and, they maintain, the area saw action during General Sullivan's Revolutionary War campaign against the Iroquois. Something must be behind it all.

Allegany County Historian Craig Braack observes that the folkloric bedrock here is especially shifty ground. For one thing, there's no earthly peculiarity about the region of Alfred University. It's a creek valley, but with no dead-end. The area's hilly, often steep. Its soil has a high clay content, and is marginal at best for agriculture. While you can't rule out scouting and skirmishing, there was no battle here in 1779 nor at any point in Sullivan's campaign. The army did march up the Susquehanna, but it split at or near Elmira, and its engagements were elsewhere. The Native Americans' grave-sites are always likely to be near where they lived, as they did in this area, but Braack doesn't know of any burial grounds in the town. There were, however, many ancient earthworks in the region. Visible from Braack's Belmont office is a house situated on top of a mound. Bones were found when its foundations were laid.

Passing near and possibly through this "Valley of Madness" is "The Forbidden Trail," an ancient path not fully mapped today, of eerie repute to several Native American nations. The tales of it could have been manufactured for reasons all too material. This shortcut track had military uses, and there was a deadly penalty for transgressing, especially for Whites. The gory lore could have been part of the plan to keep it secret, and surely its valleys would have been vested with the same fearful talk. But maybe it's more than talk. Ominous visions have long been reported along known parts of this trail.

We've heard it suggested that "The Valley of Madness," like much other Alfred folklore, is just the invention of college pranksters, possibly no older than the 1970s. We often see that the merest hint of such a thing is enough for materialists to declare victory and stop questioning. We've made at least reasonable efforts to track this one down, and don't sense that we're at the bottom of it yet; but a rumor-cycle so strong and prevalent at least deserved mention in a book on the area's mysteries.

The Power Points

THE GREAT HILL

[The head of Canandaigua Lake is a region of ancient significance. A large mica-flecked stone was found here, deeply cut with symbols never explained. Here a Seneca-Onondaga army defeated a fierce nation whose name (*Massawomeck*) means "Great Snake." What else awaits?]

It's little wonder that Arthur Parker of the Cattaraugus Reservation achieved so much. The great-great grandson of Seneca prophet Handsome Lake, Dr. Arthur C. Parker (1881-1955) was also a great-nephew of General Eli Parker, "Last of the Six Nations Sachems," who served on Ulysses Grant's staff and wrote surrender terms at Appomattox. In 1905 he was appointed the first New York Archaeologist, and in 1925 became director of the Rochester Museum of Arts and Sciences. His work tells us much of what we know about his ancestors.

The origin tale of the Seneca people gives them their name *Nundawaono*, "People of the Great Hill" at the head of Canandaigua Lake. There are Old World myths like it, about a tiny serpent found, fed and nurtured by a boy, till it becomes such a monster that (like the Fenris Wolf of Norse lore) it turns on its patrons. In the Seneca tale, the boy's queer worm comes from a creek feeding Canandaigua Lake, and grows so fast that the community is afraid not to feed it. Soon it's eaten every one of them but a girl and the boy who found it; their reward is to be dessert. In a dream the Great Spirit tells the boy to fletch his arrows with the girl's hair, a fatal charm that kills the monster with one shot. From these two springs the Seneca nation. Just legend? A giant serpent was often reported in Canandaigua Lake on lazy midweek days with few motorboats about. [Something serious of the sort was encountered on Seneca Lake in 1901 (see *Shadows*).] There's debate, though, about the exact site of the sacred mountain, and no wonder; the story may have 63 forms.

Seneca historian George Abrams believed that the great snake's legend was set at South Hill, at the foot of Canandaigua Lake. Arthur Parker thought that the events go from there to Bare Hill, at the lake's head. (There's some debate as to which is the real Bare Hill.) It was said, though, that Parker came to believe that the true spot was a valley or two over, and was in no hurry to correct the misapprehension. Maybe some things should be kept for the people who own them.

In the 1930s the Parkers bought an old farmhouse on Parrish Hill near Naples, high over the valley legendary as the birthplace of the Senecas. Beyond the site rises the expanse of South Hill, and this summer home became their residence when Parker retired from the Rochester Museum in 1946. Parker built a cabin at the foot of the hill down which the serpent rolled, its death-throes felling all the trees.

When the death-owl hooted days by his cabin-door, Parker knew he was near his time. Never feeling fully accepted on the Reservation, possibly because of his half-White blood, possibly because of his integration with White society, Parker went and made his peace in the old Seneca fashion, then returned and ended his days at his people's most sacred place. O, lucky man, to know it. O, Reader, where is yours?

On the Spirit Way

When you come, as you soon must, to the streets of our city,
Mad-eyed from stating the obvious...

>   Richard Wilbur, "Advice to a Prophet"

On the Spirit Way

CHAUTAUQUA: BYZANTIUM BY THE LAKE

[There has long been the sense in America that a community should not only house its inhabitants, but also serve their spiritual and mental wellbeing. "Chautauqua," said Pulitzer Prize-winning historian David MacCullough, is "one of these places that help define who we are and what we believe in. It has its own mythic force."]

In 1873 Ohio inventor Lewis Miller and Methodist Episcopal minister John Heyl Vincent took a boat ride on Lake Chautauqua, a hundred miles west of its glacier-torn sisters, the Finger Lakes. Miller, deviser of a reaper ("the Buckeye Mower") whose adjustable arm could adapt to land contours, and Vincent, editor and preacher, had the lofty goal of making lifelong learners of the American people, envisioning no less than an ideal community answering to "a hunger of the mind" they perceived in the American psyche. Their choice of site for this grand design may not have been unnatural.

Folklore may point to this part of the lake as a zone of some sort, and the area had old significance. Ossuaries (bone-gardens), earthworks, and an ancient road were found hereabouts. The lake could have been a hub in ancient water transport between the continent's northern interior and the Gulf of Mexico. It could bespeak some latent energy that could play a hand in Chautauqua's prominence today.

The "Fair Point" campgrounds Miller and Vincent had come to see were unassuming: tents, rough cottages, a grove, a roofed platform, and wooden benches that could seat 2,000. [Someone would later describe the walls of its frontier hotel as so thin that (a la Mark Twain) one could hear the women next door changing their minds.] The pair came to an agreement to lease the meeting grounds for two weeks of August 1874. Ten to fifteen thousand people showed up to see what the fuss was about. What they saw that first summer would have been fairly familiar.

Chautauqua planned to piggy-back on several 19th century trends: "Sunday School" programs designed to educate children who farmed instead of attending weekday schools; the "Lyceum" movement, a series of informative lectures given in many American cities; and the campground experience, "a uniquely American religious expression," according to historian Jeffrey Simpson. (Camp meetings in rural and wooded areas mixed Christian evangelism with theatrics and the opportunity for collective emotional release not available until the development of group therapy.)

By 1878 the official transfer of the land was complete, but the biggest single step in the phenomenon that is Chautauqua was the formation of the "Chautauqua Literary and Scientific Circle," a four-year program of home study, culminating in a degree with full ceremony. Response was amazing. Thousands enrolled, and eight hundred people showed up in 1882 for that first graduation.

The Institution has had four main phases: From its founding in 1874 to the mid-1920s, Chautauqua was a national podium. Its reading club, correspondence courses, and famous speakers made *Chautauqua* a household word. (By 1904 there were nearly 300 summer "Chautauqua Assemblies" about the nation, and even "traveling Chautauquas," rolling troupes of speakers and performing artists.)

Spirits of the Great Hill

The roar of the twenties - mass communication and quick travel - drowned subtle messages, and Chautauqua expanded internally, creating a virtual standing seasonal arts festival. The Depression sent the Institution into a tailspin, and it was saved from receivership by the skin of its figurative teeth. The next thirty-five years had a low-budget tone. Thousands flocked, and Chautauqua's name was still revered, but its buildings deteriorated. The 1970 election of Richard Miller, grandson of the inventor-founder, began its renaissance with a new influx of money and energy, the sometimes-regrettable bottom-lines of much earthly good.

Today the Chautauqua Institution is a collection of about twelve hundred Victorian cottages, contemporary houses, condos, hotels, shops, and meeting halls. Covering 225 acres along the shore of Chautauqua, its splendid buildings remind us of sacred cities like Athens and Jerusalem. The resident population of about 400 goes up fifty times in the nine prime weeks of summer, during which 150,000 people may visit the community's townlike campus called "the Grounds." Illustrious people speak, teach, and perform here; what may be more significant, enlightened ones live here and visit. Chautauqua is one of the world's gems, and it rests in an area seeking its soul.

Founders Miller and Vincent wanted their Chautauqua to reach well beyond evangelism, and we see that they have succeeded. Today's Chautauqua is confined by no "mind-forged manacles" of any sort. Nevertheless, the Christian camp meetings were among Chautauqua's early models, and its first curriculi (which included Biblical geography) would seem pretty religious today. Every year for quite some time a plaster model of Jerusalem was made on the shore of the lake, with its own little Dead Sea and tiny Jordan River, using the actual lake shore whose proportional role was to be the blue Mediterranean. With adjustments in the name of permanence, a miniature Holy Land exists today. It's hard not to suspect that Chautauqua sprang from the energy of the Spirit Way. This energy can be wacky, but it never fails to be wondrous; Chautauqua is one place where it went straight.

While the Judeo-Christian holy city comes soonest to many minds at any mention of Chautauqua, to us it's more reminiscent of Byzantium, the philosophers' Valhalla created in the poetry of Irishman Yeats. Bearing little resemblance to the historic capital of the Eastern Roman Empire, Yeats' mystical city was an afterlife-in-life - somewhere - whose conceptual pillars could as well have been those of Chautauqua's central square: music, art, knowledge, and religion. On the right summer day of its prime one could imagine this is to be as close as any earthly spot could naturally make itself to Yeats' aesthetic kingdom.

The folks you pass along these deep avenues in the tender season have no glow of the unreal about them, but they seem more peaceful, more positive, more reflective than you think people in the street would be anywhere else. Almost every bit of the day, some artistic or educational experience transpires somewhere about the grounds, into which you need merely walk. Out-of-time buildings and elven-gardens seem all too fragile to bear the tossing of the world's winters above. Then a patch of green hill across the ruddy lake comes to brightness from a farewell beam through the twilight, and you see hope even in coming darkness. See if it doesn't seem to you, too, here like a place away from place, a boundary within which all seems to change, memory and meaning, of all that's past, or passing, or to come.

On the Spirit Way

Lily Dale: City of Light

[With a small *S*, spiritualism is a way of looking at things, a faith that there may be another level to it all and that the departed dead may sometimes manifest back. Capitalized, Spiritualism is a world religion, and it may be no coincidence that its largest community is on the Western Door.]

In 1809 first White resident Othello Church set up at the outlet of Cassadaga Lake. Second settler Ichabod Fisher and the first tavern followed in short order. In 1829 a pupil of Anton Mesmer, father of hypnotism, gave eight lectures to the small community and zapped the zeal for matters metaphysical. The Association of Free Thinkers was formed; the energy may have been awaiting it for thousands of years.

Earthworks on the shores of Cassadaga Lake suggest the area as a religious site, maybe even a "City of the Dead," perhaps also a shrine of peace for the living at which Native Americans dropped their conflicts. They may not have been the only ones to see something here. Strange ancient roads found by the first historians may hint at its significance to visitors from other parts of the world. Like Chautauqua, this lake may have been a link in ancient water travel through the continent. It could have had visitors from many places.

In 1848 the Fox sisters set off events that would be seismic for the West's interior life, and a new religion that would be momentous for Lily Dale. (See *Shadows*, "The Hydesville Knockings." The Foxes' original cottage was moved to Lily Dale in 1915 and destroyed by fire in 1956.) By 1855 the census showed 131 people here, and the tradition of "eclectic" thinking was well underway. Doubtless the then-called "Cassadaga Lakes Free Association" held many Spiritualists, but not until the summer of 1873 did it show. Spiritualists from nearby Laona held their first summer picnic in the Alden grove on Middle Lake near today's Leolyn Inn. By the early 1890s even the name of the community was Spiritualist-inspired: "City of Light." This title was apt for one of the first communities anywhere to become fully electrified. In the early 1900s "The Lily Dale Assembly of Spiritualists" was established.

By the 1930s a mediums' league was set up, at last setting some standards for the profession of speaking for the dead. No sort of conformity has ever been imposed upon Lily Dale's speakers to the living, and its programs have always been diverse. It's no proof of anything mystical that Roycroft's Elbert Hubbard spoke here. Susan B. Anthony and other early Feminists appeared here numerous times. (They say that at the start Anthony's message was too radical for anywhere but 'the Dale.') Other Victorian speakers range from Helen Blavatsky, founder of Theosophy and "The Order of the Golden Dawn," to Robert Ingersoll, famous agnostic. Modern guests Deepak Chopra and Wayne Dyer are more inspirational than Spiritualist; then, of course, there's TV psychic John Edward, current (as of 2001) rage of the spirit.

It should be clear that there are mediums at Lily Dale, and that this is the place to see one. Joyce LaJudice, Lily Dale historian, conjectures, though, that nothing mystical need be read into Lily Dale's survival as a Spiritualist community when so many of its early fellows - like Lake George - have gone by the by. As an associ-

Spirits of the Great Hill

ation, Lily Dale couldn't be bought up piece by piece. Nevertheless, it's hard to be sure there isn't some energy to the place. Maybe you can feel it.

Visit Lily Dale today. Fall, winter, and spring are bleaker, but maybe more inspiring than the summer prime. The wind comes in over the lake; trees shiver, and windows shudder. Walk the old streets on glittering nights when the black pools sheen like they hold silver; there's a sheltering quality here, as though layers of something arc over you to keep off the gaping universe. The houses seem voluminous, withdrawing deeply into their crowded blocks. One wonders at the rites, the communications they have held. But in the summers "the Dale" comes to life.

It's the kids who give Summer away. You'll pass teens at a picnic table casting tarots, and sniff an incense sweeter than you knew any could be. Kids hitching to the drive-in may walk with you, talking of witchcraft in their families, generations deep.

Take a daytime hike to the tranquil woods, the Leolyn grove, or the shrine, Inspiration Stump, site of readings every summer noon. Regard the labyrinth of low bushes laid by Vermont (now Glastonbury) teacher and dowser Sig Lonegren. Settle on a single question or problem; forget it as you tread the spiraling path, letting the influences flow; stand in the eye and regard the grove, the trees around you, the sky, the simple realities. Be amazed at how often you leave with progress in the debate with which you entered, often a new direction in your thinking about it.

Watch day pass by the central cafe, by the lake, or at any of the little shrines about the grounds. Human nature will pass you by: sometimes psychic luminaries whose presence doesn't give them away; sometimes on-edge spirits more at home here than anywhere; sometimes illustrious and successful folk from all walks of life who, every once in a while, have to answer a call that the greater society doesn't make. Sometimes life goes too fast for many people; it may be over before they understand it. This is one of those rare places at which you can catch up by sitting still. You may even get ahead.

Maybe you'll even see a miracle, something just-too-wondrous to seem fully natural. Psychic Gwendolyn Pratt recalls a midnight walk to Inspiration Stump just after a rain. In glistening steam and moon-spattered foliage, the bole in the sublime grove was covered with white butterflies. They gave back the moonlight. What drew them all here, only here? Not another was in sight, anywhere. It took the breath away.

On the Spirit Way

"That Place is Burnt"

[One might think a single faith that ruled a society would get soft. A boon came to the Protestant Christianity that ran early 1800s America. The idea started that it wasn't enough to be baptized in a church at the start of life and go back most Sundays throughout it, and that one's faith could stand frequent renewals.]

Between 1833 and 1843 the Western Door may have seen 1,300 revivals. No more impressive religious cycle has occurred in US history. Lawyers, doctors, and real estate agents were in the front row of the saved-again. Taverns became orphanages, and theaters (those dark dens of debauchery!) turned into churches. Roving revivalists hit town and shook Hell out of it, whether it knew it needed it or not. Some staged grand door-crashing entrances, fire-and-brimstoning sinners and disrupting busy businesses. Evangelists, spotting sinful behavior, stopped people on streets with choice comments. ("You are an enemy to the rightful King." "You are going right to the pit." "There is not a fiend in Hell, nor out of Hell, so bad as you are.") Guess the police hadn't been invented yet.

Though not a native of the Western Door, the 19th century's greatest American evangelist did most of his work here, setting his stamp on the Burned-over District and maybe even giving it its name. It was Charles Grandison Finney (1792-1875) who returned from a tour of this upstate region and commented wearily, "That place is burnt."

Born and schooled in southern New England, Finney spent time in his youth on the shores of Lake Ontario. By 1821 he'd returned upstate ("worldly and sinful," he'd later say) for a law career in Adams, NY. To understand Hebraic law, Finney studied the Bible; he found it taking over.

Starting four-hour prayer sessions with country Reverend Daniel Nash, Finney was ordained a Presbyterian minister in 1824. Touring and preaching with Father Nash, Finney converted many in the hamlets of Jefferson County. Soon the folklore styled him a saintly Richard Simmons, driving slackers into faith once again; and, at the head of "Finney's Holy Band," a religious Robin Hood leading peripatetic preachers from town to town, rousting Beelzebub ahead of them. We see, though, that these pious pirates were not an official group, but carpetbagging evangelists after Finney's action, some out for the take.

"We must have exciting, powerful preaching," said Finney, "or the devil will have the people - all the Methodists can't save." (*What!?*) Nevertheless, the mature Finney came through, using classic psychological techniques, including an "anxious" bench in the front of the church where all could see the people waiting second salvation, fidgeting as if demons crawled within them. Finney also became a captivating speaker. When he described a sinner's slide to perdition, half the congregation stood, following his fingers "to the pit below" as if they expected to see it.

"Never was a man whose soul looked out through his face as his did," reported one adoring source, and others called Finney "tall, athletic, and handsome." Neutral parties found him disarmingly plain, noting his weak chin, average height, and country manners. By the time he was famous enough for anyone to write about him, the die was cast.

Spirits of the Great Hill

By 1825 Finney'd started a fire, and calls for the evangelist came from all quarters. He moved to Rochester, a hotbed for his services. His impact on the Burned-over District (and the nation at large) came mostly from two revival tours in 1826 and 1831. He re-converted thousands, winning most of them - Presbyterians, Baptists, Methodists - back to established Protestant faiths. He had disciples by the league.

Citified with success, Finney started to like the days of a star far more than the rough ones of a country revivalist. ("We might get a house in Rome," he wrote to his wife, "but I do so hate a village.") Like an old rock star, as his legend grew, his performance suffered, "losing the soul-stirring appeals to the heart that once brought so many sinners to the feet of Jesus." His confidants saw the painful change. "Your preaching a few years ago was better," one said. "You reason more than formerly." (An old Hamilton professor was more direct: "Brother Finney, when you go among strangers, don't talk too much about yourself. They have an idea that you are a self-sufficient egotist.")

People tried to guide him back to his inspirational roots. We're not sure what they meant with lines like, "Go back to Western New York.... where every blow you strike... is a blow on the head," but it's clear that they saw something on the Spirit Way. ("Once you get that region thoroughly soaked and all Hell can't wring it dry, don't you know," was another of their inscrutable injunctions.)

"Those who can't do, teach," is an adage we defy, because teaching - well - is really doing. Nevertheless, like failed NFL coaches Finney went back to college. At Oberlin he trained generations of clergymen.

We've seen the superlatives of the mature Finney, but few remember his Pythonesque *Life of Brian* start. As Finney groped for religious rhetoric and possibly his own inspiration, his delivery in those early years could be John Donne-like paradoxical. "I have no more religion than your horse," he once said. "I am the wickedest man in all this country," was another utterance, as was, "I do not believe what I preach; and I have told you I did not believe what I preached." His first audiences, eighty or so country folks at a time, were left not quite sure if they'd beheld something marvelous or simply muddled. A rural Universalist minister could only conjecture that Finney was "subject to paroxisms of insanity."

But then venerable, folksy Father Nash, who had "unusual grace with the country folk," pulled them all aside and said something like, *He's a good boy, and this is what he really means.* Finney's gravy-train might never have started rolling without Father Nash at the country beginning. Mentor and lifelong advisor Daniel Nash showed Finney the Godly example whose image at least played so well once the big stage neared.

We have no photos of Nash, already old by the time he showed to history, a saintly man so deaf that he shouted. (His prayers for the sick carried half a mile.) Nash, too homely for the high life, never toured with Finney once Finney had started to live it. Nash remained a supporter, even in the days of Finney's decline, writing letters of courage for his "boy." Father Nash was at last found dead as he had lived, alone, in piety, in the act of praying, "in his closet, on his knees dead before God."

On the Spirit Way

THE MILLENNIAL MILLERITES

For many centuries the Christian Bible has been a book of unutterable import. More than one group of people have believed that, coded within its letters, "the Sacred Volume" holds messages even heavier than its holy lines. "Biblical exegesis" is the practice of interpreting them. Hudson Valley farmer and Biblical "exegete" William Miller (1782-1849) thought he'd used the right cipher and read a mighty message: that Christ would return to earth before the Millennium, and that the sinners had best get ready. The Baptists gave him a license to preach and by 1844 he'd delivered 4,500 sermons and gained thousands of followers. Called "Millerites," their exact numbers will never be known. Their faith, Millerism, spread. Though Millerism was not a localized phenomenon, our own Burned-over District was clearly its center of gravity, and Rochester was a stronghold.

Millerism was another form of millenarianism - the idea that the Lord is coming again and that the world had best prepare. This "Second Adventism" was actually a logical way of looking at things, were a few Biblical precepts taken as given, and Millerism was far from alone in its century. Like other contemporary millenarian ideas, Millerism was preoccupied with images of destruction, and saw earthly society as evil and corrupt. The Millerites were also eager to save those in the world who could be saved.

Some of Millerism's leading speakers believed that the movement's opponents served Antichrist, witting or no. "If you intend to be found a Christian when Christ appears," thundered Charles Fitch, "Come out of Babylon, and come out now!" Some adherents even developed the "closed-door" theory of Millerism, naming pre-millennial dates after which The Big Guy had surely shut the pearly gates on those who hadn't publically repented. You had to join up *before* the sky started falling and take your lumps at the office with every other one of Miller's faithful.

Other things set Millerism apart. Wild-eyed would-be Christs led most rival groups, but Miller - a modest, uncharismatic man - insisted that there was nothing remarkable about him, and that anyone else would reach the same conclusion if they read the Bible with the same system. In an age when most religion-groupies were poor and dispossessed, Millerism was a middle-class movement. Also, the Millerites were apolitical. Later movements like Spiritualism would hitch rides with Abolition and Women's Suffrage.

Of course, the religious and political establishments were downright scornful of Millerism. Word got out that insane asylums were full of Millerites raving about the advent of the Lord. The records don't support it, but as late as 1845 the *American Journal of Insanity* suggested that Millerism was as great a danger to public health as cholera or yellow fever.

Even among fellow upstate Utopians the resentment of Millerism was keen. "They hear the same voice we have heard," said John Humphrey Noyes, speaking of the inimitable Millerites. "God is coming into the world and the day of judgment is at hand. But to them the voice is not clear enough to save them from the delusions of their own imagination."

So far, though, so good. Spirit Way was never the path of the straight and narrow; but Millerism's Waterloo was coming, and probably born of its own piety.

Spirits of the Great Hill

Encouraged by the wildfire success of their sensation and eager to gain ground on their religious competitors, firebrand disciples like Joshua Himes pressured Miller to up the ante and name the actual date Christ would re-arrive. (*That* would fix them.) Miller got out the Good Book, fiddled with his charts, and, seemingly a bit against his better judgement, gave the date - March 21, 1843, or the same day in 1844, or sometime in between - of the Second Coming. Naturally, kingdom didn't come - it has a way of not doing that - and Miller turned to his figures again. October 22, 1844 was proposed as a new date.

Of course, this Millerite deadline passed rapture-less, and for skeptics and satirists, "The Great Disappointment" was the stuff of legend. For Miller's expectant followers, a terrible beauty was born. The most devout had made no preparations for earthly life beyond the fated dates. They'd quit working their farms and businesses, given away their money and property, donned bedsheets or gleaming "ascension robes," and, on the magic nights, climbed hills and high places (even trees!), all to make Heaven-coursing the shorter.

It's easy to simplify things and say that Millerism flopped because it was wacky. Indeed, after "The Great Disappointment," many followers abandoned Miller's cause. In fact, the swoon of Millerism swelled other colonies like those of the Shakers and Associationists. Millerism has survived, but in different forms, most notably as the varied Advent churches.

By 1848 the matter had come full circle. William Miller and his family went back to Low Hampton (near Fairhaven) NY, with a handful of the once-multitudinous followers. They built a tiny white wooden chapel in an edge-wood clearing near the Baptist Church from which the roller-coaster ride had set forth. On the wall behind the altar, nineteen of the still-faithful placed this inscription, still sure that Miller's only mistake had been timing:

For At The Time Appointed The End Shall Be.

On the Spirit Way

"Whosoever Will May Come."

[By the mid-1940s the trucks were topics of discussion. They rolled through many a Southern Tier town, "SHILOH" painted in big letters on the sides. Shiloh has been called colony, community, commune, even communist, but the real C-word - cult - (a four-letter-one at that) seems so far to have eluded print. Should it?]

Business executive E. Crosby Monroe (1880-1961) sensed a crisis around him in the human body and spirit. Ordained a minister by the Apostolic Church of England, Monroe retired in 1942 and bought three farms outside his native Sherman, welcoming all with "bodily and spiritual" needs. Work did for the one and daily Christian services for the other.

First came a dairy farm, with egg-and-butter routes through Chautauqua County. Then came the retail operations, a bakery and butcher. By 1952 Shiloh was a trust whose profits might only be used for religious, charitable, scientific, literary, or educational purposes. By living piously together, the Shiloh folk hoped to create an environment for the rehabilitation of humankind in all aspects of life.

"Whosoever will may come" was their official motto; no one who wanted to join them was denied. Newcomers were assigned jobs that helped the group's welfare and aided with their own "rehabilitation." By the 1960s Shiloh numbered fifty souls. Families shared houses, the unmarried lived in dorms, and even meals were communal, in a single dining hall. Active in civic projects, the Shiloh folks took over the local phone answering service, handling emergency calls 24-7.

Founder Monroe was succeeded as trustee by his son, Rev. Raymond Monroe, who held his post only a year. After his 1962 death in a small-plane collision, he was instantly replaced by Rev. James Janisch, formerly of Long Beach, CA. (Locals griped that the community never lacked a number one-in-waiting.) The business grew into wholesale health food distribution, and soon Shiloh served stores around the nation. The point, though, was still Christian life and growth; the business was just a means to an end.

Reverend Janisch seemed ambitious, showing a reporter a national map with tacks representing spinoff colonies and stores carrying Shiloh foods. Soon the group needed a home base nearer the national heartland, and set up in Arkansas as the Church of Shiloh. By 1969 they were completely relocated.

To some, Shiloh seemed a "unique venture in the rehabilitation of man." Others, though, sensed "lean and hungry" looks on the bread-delivery folks in their driveways. Word spread that those who didn't sell their loads were denied dinner; that Shiloh's "brainwashed" citizens were all ex-convicts and former alcoholics; and that they had deified "Father" Monroe (whom the locals found at once affable and domineering). Shiloh's members were actually from many walks of life, but secretaries did indeed follow the founder night and day, recording his words as if for someday's Scripture. Sounds like they were working on a new religion.

Spirits of the Great Hill

Calvin of Oak Knoll

[This Chautauqua County tale could be mere freakery, but it confirms the Spirit Way's restless, erratic energy. One historian likens its subject more to Jim Jones than David Koresh.]

In 1987 a Cleveland veterinarian filed a petition with New York State Governor Mario Cuomo, asking clemency on behalf of the Humanist Society for "Calvin of Oakknoll," then festering in a federal pen. "It's no crime to be an eccentric," wrote Dr. D. A. Rickards, claiming Calvin a fellow-member. It is a crime to kill someone, though, and the Humanist Society had no records of Calvin. His pardon was summarily denied.

A little history. Calvin Kline (1920-1999) was the proverbial "rocket scientist," a brilliant computer man who'd worked for NASA. At midlife he felt called to found the Religious Society of Families at Oak Knoll, his farm near Frewsburg. Maybe to avoid jokes about the stylish clothier, his name was legally changed to "Calvin of Oakknoll." It's not easy to know what he stood for or what his outfit might have become.

Even the historians aren't sure what moved the man, and his religious *raison d'etre* didn't come out at his trial. His order recruited by word of mouth, and when he sought religious tax exemption in earlier court actions, Calvin could name only a handful of members; few were admitting it in 1987. This looks like a Spirit Way special, nipped in the bud.

Calvin's Humanist sympathizers regard the universe as natural and not supernatural (read, *Godly*). Calvin may have been of like philosophy, thinking humanity should look to itself to solve its problems, offering himself as part of a solution. We gather that Oakknoll's beliefs were granola-crunchy, living a natural life without fossil fuels or processed foods. Calvin despised hunting of any type, and had once sued the state Department of Environmental Conservation for permitting it. He'd also written against the legalization of hunting, and his whole property in the Poland township was posted. Possibly related to this was Calvin's propensity for sniper-shooting his neighbor's dogs, doubtless sensing them part of the predatory process. What shipped him to the Big House was something else.

On the first day of hunting season in 1980, Jamestown barkeeper Douglas O'Kelley came onto Calvin's land. The spat could sound like a duel, but the jury didn't agree that O'Kelley's shotgun was raised when Calvin's bullet struck. Calvin got fifteen-to-life.

Some in the Southern Tier thought that Calvin had acted in self-defense; others deemed him too righteous to defend himself in court. Whatever. Besides a guilty verdict, a $420,000 judgement was levied against Calvin to compensate his victim's widow, "deprived of her husband's earning power," depriving Calvin's wife of farm, property, and all she owned. Community sympathy is strongest for her, loyal to her husband to the end.

They say Calvin believed that people should "self-destruct" at seventy, possibly to save world resources they were no longer producing. To the locals this looked like a suicide-pact. Evidently prison life didn't count, or else Calvin gave himself nine years for good behavior, shuffling off the coil in 1999.

On the Spirit Way

FATHER X OF THE WESTERN DOOR

[The push is justly on to make a modern saint of Lackawanna's Father Baker, but many folks who knew him think the Western Door may have had another miracle-maker. There's a world of stories about the man we call "Father X," and some who don't breathe it half-wonder to themselves if the Second Coming hasn't already come and gone.]

There's an air of mystery to him as if he truly came from another place. Sure facts are few: He was born in Europe in the late nineteenth century and was on the Western Door in the early twentieth, maybe serving at an altar in one of the churches. Later in his life, some tiff with his first faith began; he broke from it and his congregation followed. Near the end of his time here he was ordained in another Christian faith so that his church might have someone to look over it. The tales of him sound so fantastic that they would be hard to credit at all except for the testimony of so many witnesses. Something marvelous - we don't know what - may have been going on. Only his goodness is in no doubt.

The animals sensed it, birds especially. There was that robin whose singing so spelled the church caretaker; the Father stretched out an index upon which it landed. There was the owl often perched outside his window, waiting for him to greet it. There was that parrot that chirped, *Hey-soo* (Spanish, "Jesus") when he came near.

The needy understood. His charity was legendary. Someone could give a large sum to this holy man and find him hungry that night. He'd given it all away to others whose need was greater.

The Native Americans knew. He drove horse and buggy over dirt roads to the nearby reservation, answering the needs he could. The chief told his folk that the Father was welcome day or night, never to be impeded.

Some churchfolk got the picture. An imposing bishop came to his church, and the Father knelt and asked blessing. After watching him preach, eyes as always closed, the bishop knelt and asked blessing back. Why not? People say he could work miracles.

The lore of him has much in common with that of classic saints. Father X studied no music, but could launch the organ into symphonies so celestial that angels seemed to play, and Heaven filled the night-black church. They say he'd hold a Bible in any language, in darkness or with closed eyes, and read from it in the ones he could speak, needing no script to recite Scripture. They say he clapped his hands, and sacramental wafer appeared within them. They saw him sign the cross over ordinary crocks and throw them down so hard they bounced. Never did they crack. Once they say he broke a piece off a cast-iron stove by hurling an unhurt teacup at it. One churchman described the marvelous natural scent he gave off as "a fine incense." Even "bilocation" - appearing in two places at once - was said of him. Others found most startling his unnatural discernment. He could look through you, and see you at your core. Good as you are, it could be alarming. And there were the healings.

Ask those he'd cured or given sight. The number is proverbial, and his congregation today includes people from all over the world. You should have seen that church on an Easter Sunday when the Father was preaching. Even in his life it was

Spirits of the Great Hill

a pilgrimage-site, and today many journey here from far parts.

He harrowed a bit of Hell in his own way. There was that orchard in which apparitions and psychic trouble of some kind had been reported. The Father went for a solo stroll in it one night, emerging battered, but pronouncing it "delivered." Could he have given himself those injuries?

The Father made an impression. He saw his eventual domain first when he was visiting the fields. When the berry-pickers, immigrants all, beheld him, robed, long-haired, holding a staff and a lamb, they quit their work and followed him into town, crying, "Jesus!" To those not in his fold he was an eccentric, "the Monk," resembling George Harrison at the time of *Abbey Road*. Others worried about the wonders; not all were sure who was behind them. The Father never claimed that it was anyone but Christ, but what would you make of a man who struck a dozen box-matches, put them into a lady's apron, gestured over them, then relit them one by one? Others saw him set altar candles alight with a look.

Of course, there were those who had it in for him. His preaching cost the bad guys recruits. Five of them rode up in a Continental one fall day, offering the Father a ride. Though surprised at his new friends, he was agreeable to a sight-see. At a wooded spot they suggested a walk around. A look at God's glory in the leaves seemed wonderful, too; but soon his five hosts faced the Father against the trees. "Say your own prayers," one snarled, and all reached under their coats. Their expressions changed. The Father opened his robe, showing all five pistols. After a stroll and some testy preaching, he was returned to his church.

Someone else with a grudge brewed blackberry wine, powdered with pills enough to send Superman Maker-ward. The Father took a hearty swig, nodding appreciatively. "But you lost something." He reached into his mouth as if testing a tooth and brought forth a pill, intact. "This must be yours."

Why didn't this man with so much power leave something vaster behind? It seems at least partly that he didn't want to. The humblest of men, the Father took no credit, ceding all power to the higher One, all destiny to His design. He disdained publicity of all sorts. Some things, too, may be covered up. We hear there are reports deep in the archives, and that Hell will have hockey leagues before we see them. Maybe there's room for only one Western Door saint.

Buried near the church he founded, the Father is at his rest. He never sought to found religion or sect, and there seems no chance that he will have done so. Almost nothing he taught is kept past word-of-mouth, and those who heard him - his modest, devout congregation - pass, one by one, too, to their peace. It's in respect to their wishes that we have given no details that would serve to identify their beloved Father, and the reader is free to presume that this whole piece is nothing but folklore. Still, the presence of this pious, gifted man among us, of whom so few have heard, fills us with awe.

What would greet the real Son of Man on His second visit, were His first step into our trendy decades? We who did not believe because we did not see, what would we have made of Him, a mystical longhair Who knew nothing of our slang, our styles, our music, our money, Who told us to be better people? Ignorant of worldliness and shy of sex, would He impress us as He ought? What messages around us do we never hear?

Spooks, Spirits, Specters

These spirits are not necessarily the souls of the dead; for other kinds of spiritual beings may exist, and space may be full of them without our ever knowing anything about it, except under unusual circumstance.

Camille Flammarion

Spirits of the Great Hill

The Niagara Frontier

Allentown: Psychic Symphony

[The locals call it "the Millonzi House" after the family who gave it to the Phil, but Allentown old-timers know the majestic Queen Anne brick at Symphony Circle as "the Maytham Mansion." It would have a right to feel schizophrenic, two mirror-image houses in one, split by double walls, fueling folklore of blood-feuds between brothers. Now the Buffalo Philharmonic Orchestra's administration offices, it may be Buffalo's most haunted building. An internal memo even addressed the matter, and though some of the folklore is surely exaggerated, the psychic pedigree of this classic site is thoroughbred.]

The house at 26 Richmond with its conical tower has long had ghostly rumors, surely old when, as part of a Halloween 1992 stint, a psychic couple, one an ordained Spiritualist minister, toured it along with WGR DJ Tom Bauerle. Though Bauerle may be most famous nationally for asking Hillary the type of question other politicians get asked, his longstanding interest in the paranormal has made big contributions to local interest, and for it he may be the area's foremost field investigator.

On approaching the house the psychics had felt a "negative aura" and warned of trouble inside. Through dramatic visions on the second floor, they identified scandals and outrages: trails of blood in the kitchen; a hanging suicide; a male body floating in a crimson bathtub; a female spirit by the second-floor water-cooler who needed help to "pass over"; a spectral butler on the back stairs, still controlling illicit traffic; and a woman nurturing another stairs so that no one tumbles and breaks a neck as did she. The conference room seemed especially negative, and in what were then the marketing offices, a flock of mistreated women and children had died. Angels and ministers of grace defend us!

The third floor, once a nursery, seemed more peaceful, with but a single lingering waif, a seven-year-old in the kitchen awaiting her parents. Even after being told by the psychics that she's dead, she visits, enjoying her moments with the living.

Well. If psychic testimony is all you need, you have your explanation. The home is surely built in twin parts, and has other mysteries. What seem to be entrances to basement tunnels are boarded over, and the inner layout is one of intrigue. Not all historians, though, are sure about that war between the Maytham brothers serious enough to leave psychic markers. Brothels, underground railroads, and crazed tenants are just possibilities.

The architect of the Maytham Mansion is unknown, but historians Chris Brown and Martin Wachadlo think he may have been Edward Kent. Built in 1892 for brothers Thomas and Edward Maytham, owners of a Great Lakes shipping line, this house replaced an earlier one above the pre-1820 Black Rock cemetery, which Native Americans may have been using long before. Its sleeping tenants were thought reinterred at Forest Lawn in 1874, but more were found here in the 1950s. If you hold to the common theory of hauntings, you have a legion of good candidates.

Thomas Maytham died soon after his home was completed, and his wife

Spooks, Spirits, Specters

Ann Elizabeth, known for her work with the needy, stayed until 1900. Two other successful men became owners of 26 Richmond: Tonawanda lumberman Herbert White and Buffalo clothier Edward Hengerer. After a period of transition in which the manse could have hosted freelance tenants like the reputed madam, it became El Nathan ("Gift of God"), a home for poor women, some of whom may have been impaired. Miracles like those of Father Baker (empty larders magically replenished, cash donated in times of crisis) were reported about founder Abigail Luffe.

As of Summer 2001 the Buffalo Philharmonic owns this unique mansion at Symphony Circle. Administrator Amy Manton can't support the rumors of electrical pranks so common that new employees are instructed on the circuit-breakers, but psychic reports are still consistent and strong. An impish prankster disarranges the desks of "neat-freaks." People still encounter the cold spots common to paranormal sites. Apparitions include a little girl at the top of the stairs (said once to be caught on camera), and a stern old woman who answers the door on misty days, peers through the door-glass, and withdraws. Like a high-society bouncer, she has the air of judging the bell-ringer, finding him or her not quite of the right cut, and deeming them unsuitable for admittance.

Odd effects did surface under the the 1992 examination. Normal discussions in the meeting-room took on a strange quality when they were taped, sounding like angry confrontations and barking-matches when replayed. A recommended move to another room with better "vibes" has been all to the good. On other tapes, chanting and faint drumming could be heard, as if the home provided a psychic backdrop just beneath hearing. Some who work in the Millonzi House, though, know nothing of paranormal effects, which is as it should be. Though they may go in cycles, psychic phenomena are not common and seldom dramatic, except that they shouldn't be able to happen at all; and we all know that people are more likely to see what they expect, especially at the Millonzi House, the former Maytham Mansion, the former "Gift of God."

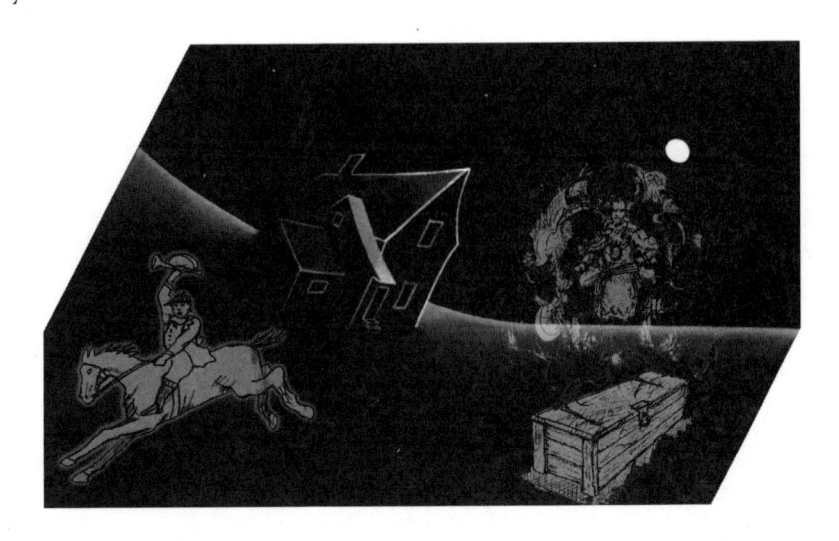

Spirits of the Great Hill

Buffalo: Niagara Square

[In *Shadows* we discussed the mystical features of Buffalo's Niagara Square, including its (and the city's) potentially Masonic layout, courtesy of surveyor Joseph Ellicott. We cited the octagonal shape of the square and its alignments of radiating streets: Niagara (to the Falls), Delaware (to Gates Circle's former mighty fountain), and Genesee (toward a likely earthwork). We mentioned archaeological curiosities found at the Square, such as brass kettles from unseemly depth, and (earlier in this book) an apparently ancient road. We discussed its Art Deco City Hall, designed by Dietel and Wade in 1931, almost certainly a sacred building with mystical symbols set into it. We described the Egyptianate McKinley monument, a white marble obelisk dedicated in 1907. In other cities (like ancient sacred ones and Washington, DC) these monuments are selectively located, almost like "tuning forks" at the circles and intersections of major streets. No wonder if there's a haunting here, a story like Chaucer's Pardoner's tale.]

Nelson, Israel, and Isaac Thayer - 25, 23, and 21 - had moved to Western New York from Worcester, Mass., about eight years before the tragedy that made them famous. Their tenant at their Town of Boston (NY) farm was a man named John Love, unemployed, but far from poor. The Thayers seem to have been moochers, a condition that, one old source conjectures, might not have happened "had they, in early age, given right direction to their thoughts, and instead of attending shooting matches and hanging about taverns, had employed their time at home, and in reading instructive books." They were also irreverent types. Their oxen were named "Jesus Christ" and "God Almighty."

Soon the Thayers were in debt to their tenant, who threatened to foreclose on their land and get them thrown into jail. With a plan, they lured Love into the kitchen of their Boston home on December 15, 1824, a day of pig-butchering. As the others talked, young Isaac was to go outside, aim a rifle through the window, and shoot Love in the head. If still alive, Love was to be finished by the two others. Right enough, blows from a meat-axe were needed. Quite a mess. The Thayers served Love to their pigs, who were, it seems, vegetarians. They tried to bury him under a stream, but the digging was too hard. They planted him too shallowly near it, his toes blooming like toadstools out of the soil. The brothers were soon convicted.

The crowd that swelled the budding city's square on June 17, 1825, has been estimated at 15,000, a mass that could effortlessly have had its will. Some think the cocky Thayers presumed that the mob was there for their rescue, and that the guards were worried. Nobody made a move, though, as the brothers neared the triple gibbet; they were actually just here to see the string-kicking, and the Thayers were the stars of the performance. As it dawned on the three Thayers, one of them gave forth with a steady, bizarre sound, a miserable, high-pitched, whistly squealing, perhaps the imitation of pigs being slaughtered. First one, then both of his brothers took it up; and soon the enormous crowd, for inexplicable reasons of its own, took up the sound as well, and the square reeled with the porcine keening - a surreal scene stilled only by the brothers' final bucks. The sound is reported on occasion today within the magnificent City Hall building. Surely it's the elevator-cables.

Spooks, Spirits, Specters

BUFFALO:
THE MCKINLEY CURSE

[One would have thought the Lincoln assassination - in which one Western Door nastie, Dr. Francis Tumblety, was questioned (see *Shadows*, "The Grave of Jack the Ripper") - would have taught the country to take no chances with its Chief Executive.]

  The Pan-American Exposition was in full swing. In the Temple of Music the world's largest pipe organ delivered a Bach sonata. President William McKinley was finishing his visit, and among the mass of greeters at the 4 PM reception was a short, gazing, blue-eyed young man whose right hand was wrapped in white cloth. Leon Czolgolz, a Polish-American anarchist who had stalked the President all over the city, brushed aside his extended hand and fired the .32 caliber revolver twice.
  Only pandemonium played. The President, whose agonized death would come a week later in the Milburn Mansion, first thought of his wife. "Be careful about her," he told his secretary. "Don't let her know." His next concerns were for his killer, piled beneath outraged citizens. "Don't let them hurt him."
  September 1901 should have been Buffalo's triumph. It led to tragedy, and ominous rumor tracks the cataclysmic event.

- At the President's arrival, a 21-gun salute was fired; his wife fainted.
- The day of his shooting the President toured the cursed Devil's Hole.
- Uneasy before the fatal reception, the President's secretary George B. Cortelyou called it off. The President insisted on attending. "No one would want to hurt me."
- Before the deed the assassin drank at an Amherst Street pub and stole the bar rag that wrapped his pistol. Native American women who cleaned the place in the day considered it cursed thereafter. Members of the family that owned it said the bar underwent unspecified psychic effects until finally purged by a Seneca elder in the 1960s.
- Many sites of McKinley's Buffalo stays are reputed haunts, and the lore assuredly makes the connection.
- The site of McKinley's monument, Niagara Square, is quite significant from occult perspectives which we discussed in *Shadows*. Odd that they put it there.

  Remembered mostly as the site of McKinley's assassination, the Temple of Music was one of the expo's glories. Designed by August Esenwein to recall the Pantheon in Rome, its dome towered 180 feet. Its auditorium seated 2,200 for John Philip Sousa's performance, but, like all but one of the Pan-Am buildings, the Temple of Music was temporary, and torn down after the fair, now only shadows like the Milburn Mansion on Delaware Avenue, site of a President's last breath.
  The Pan-Am expo was one of the first in a string of dubious campaigns (remember "Talkin' Proud"?) aimed at luring positive notice Buffalo's way. Even in the city's widely-acknowledged heyday, the inferiority complex must have been showing. Is this a lesson against all posturing, or on behalf of the invincibility of fate? Or is there no lesson at all? Some think "The Curse of McKinley" lingers over the region still.

Spirits of the Great Hill

Buffalo:

Mark Twain's Buffalo Ghost

[Samuel Clemens, the redoubtable "Mark Twain," lived in Buffalo only eighteen months, (1869-71) while editor of the *Buffalo Express*. We're lucky to have had him. Twain's standing as the droll catcher of the Yankee conscience has never been higher, and in some quarters "Huck Finn" is *the* American book. Unlike many literary heavyweights - Dickens, Hugo, Yeats and James - Twain left little to suggest what (or if ever) he thought of the supernatural. It would figure. Great satirists execute in bold strokes. They need to regard human behavior in relief, the reverse of the indulgence of nuance and ambiguity needed to sift sense from the splatter of the mystico-spiritualist business of any day.]

To great fanfare, in 1995 the *New Yorker* ran "Jim and the Dead Man," a century-old cut from *The Adventures of Huckleberry Finn*. Jim's rendition of a night among medical cadavers sets Huck's hackles arise. Twain may have heard a similar tale from his doctor-uncle, but his other taps at supernature are mostly whimsical.

On April 24, 1910 (the day of his Big Apple funeral) the *Buffalo Express* ran what was pronounced Twain's only ghost story, a dream in which dead skeletons protest their shabby burials and carry their tombstones out of what's thought to be the old North Street Cemetery at Delaware. When he wrote it in 1869 Twain lived nearby, at Delaware and Virginia.

Another Twain tale ("A Ghost Story") stars the spook of something never alive, the Cardiff Giant, a silly concrete titan fooling no one who knew archaeology. Worse, Twain's spook seeks the plaster replica of its already-forged body in a nearby museum. "Confound it, don't you know your own remains?" said the narrator, who sends it, begging that none of this see print, to the proper museum in Albany.

Though the late Mark Twain "spoke" frequently at seances, the living one was no longer around to protest, and the practice of channeling the illustrious dead has an air of humor. For instance, early psychic researcher James Hyslop follows a seance with "Mrs. Chenoweth" (speaking for Twain) with one in which another spook claimed he'd helped the newly-dead Twain give the earlier reading. "It was several sittings before I was able to get his name and identity established," comments Hyslop. "It was Washington Irving." Ah. Nice to have that cleared up.

We've heard some generic ghost stories from the picturesque building on the site of Twain's former house, but none are more recent than the 1970s and its time as the Cloister Restaurant. No wonder there were tales about the Cloister, with its labyrinth of parlors and decorous chaos: street signs, carousel horses, cigar-store chiefs, and legions of famous patrons in photographs on the walls. It was a hall of celluloid stars.

Twain did believe in premonition. In his early manhood he had some sort of forewarning of his brother's death due to faulty treatment after an accident; as the real event took place, he was paralyzed with fear. Dream, event, and responsibility haunted Twain all his life. Huck's creator retired to his daughter's Elmira home where his study was formed in the allegedly mystical octagonal shape, maybe a sign of a late-come tolerance for matters supernal.

Spooks, Spirits, Specters

BUFFALO: THE LOCKWOOD MANSION

[If the building radiates tradition, it should. Jewett Richmond's 1878 English Tudor is another E. B. Greene-designed "haunted" site with all the trappings of mystery: secret passages, spiral staircases, dungeon-like basements... "the works."]

One of the state's great philanthropists, Thomas Brown Lockwood owned this Delaware Avenue manse from 1918 to 1947. At a time when cultured gestures were fashionable, Lockwood collected books, but his interest was far from hollow. His collection was forty years old at the 1935 dedication of the UB library named for him. Lockwood's acquisition of manuscripts and first editions of then-living poets seemed quirky at the time, but it looks visionary now, and it's Buffalo's treasure.

A series of owners followed. Once a manor home for retired priests, the Lockwood Mansion was the source of a flap when owners International Business Machines wanted to flatten it for their new headquarters. Computer Task Group acquired it for its educational center. Though in the shuffle of several owners the building lost frills (like some 17th-Century fireplaces), it's still standing, now the home of Child and Family Services. This worthy not-for-profit started in the late nineteenth century when future president Millard Fillmore and philanthropist William Pryor Letchworth noticed that, though there was a society for the protection of animals in Western New York, there was nothing of the sort for people.

Most "haunted" sites fit a pattern: a slurry of physical effects attributed either to generic ghosts or the most famous stiff associated with the building. This is one of those less common cases in which the "haunter," if we use the word, has crystallized into the apparition of an unknown person, and, notably, not one of the ghostly archetypes like "the woman in white" or the waifish tot. It's a tame spook in the Lockwood Mansion, an austere dame, somberly dressed, hair schoolmarmishly back.

The staff sense her, hearing "vanishing footsteps" in empty halls, hearing her work intercoms and transfer calls at night. Kids feel her, even scoffing ones, like an administrator's boy, who felt something, bolted from the staircase landing, and locked himself in a car. Once she appeared clearly on this landing, in a floral summer-dress or gown, hands folded, as if surveying a gay scene in the marble foyer below. Two workmen saw her, "faded, dusty-looking," not transparent like ghosts in the most common movie-treatment. Then she faded all the way. An artist drew her.

In cases like this it's always tempting to find some late, historic person in the mansion's past and give the current spook a name, but we suggest resisting. This is the "spiritualist" idea of the apparitions we call ghosts, that is, presuming they're the spirits of dead people. We don't rule it out; we just don't know what ghosts are. Even if we lean toward that idea, the spook at the Lockwood Mansion could represent any number of women associated with the old, long-occupied house: a nurse, a servant, a family member, possibly a visitor whose cheery moments were here.

They're proud of their gentle guest, the folks at Child and Family Services, as if they sense her blessing upon their high mission. They have ours.

Spirits of the Great Hill

Lancaster: Lady in Lavender

[There was a death here. A caretaker suffered a heart attack in the bell-and-clock tower, and was borne on his last trip down the winding stairs. He's not the one they blame, though, at the Lancaster Opera House, where the picture is pretty much the usual poltergeist pattern - doors, lights, sounds, and small objects moving to their own sweet will - except for the presence of two well-defined apparitions and one electrifying on-stage event.]

An 1894 fire flattened both sides of Central Avenue from Broadway to Main Street, and out of the rubble stood the Lancaster Opera House, which, unlike a lot of buildings around Western New York, was built to be what it is now. It's gone a route to get back there. By the 1920s, the splendid three-story building was a warehouse and, into the fifties, a Civil Defense map room and backup regional headquarters. A movement to revive the Opera House started in the mid-1970s, and the curtain rose in September 1981 for the first time in over fifty years. Fifty thousand patrons packed shows for the 1999-2000 season, and at least two who didn't buy them have season tickets.

"The Lady in Lavender" is just that. She appears in the balcony stage right as if admiring the performance, then dematerializes. She's not the prankster, though. That's "William," the staff's name for the spirit of a gaslight-era actor. A field reporter for the Psychical Research Center in Durham, NC divined the name when interviewed by WKBW meteorologist Mike Randall. She described William, in period costume, on stage with the TV-man as he played Mark Twain in a one-man show. "He was not harmful," she said; nor was he the man who died in the bell tower.

Actors feel the energy, sometimes while on stage. Cool breezes hit them and move curtains, though there's no wind, no fan, no draft, no explanation. Custodians have to relock certain doors after someone somehow unlocks them. ("William, will you please let me get out of here!" one shouted.) Small objects are relocated. Papers on desks are often resorted into chaotic piles. Doors open and close as people watch, sometimes very gently, as if admitting a stealthy invisible presence. The elevator runs itself after hours. "It's just William," they say. He's the real actor.

Experiencing the pranks of the two resident spooks has long been considered an initiation. "I guess I've finally been accepted," said a new administrator once. "William has been moving my things around all day."

Nothing tops the display that came during the July 1988 performance of "Play it Again, Lulu." As the male lead crawled toward a TV on the stage, preparing to turn it on with his teeth to prove some point within the script, its stand gave way. Instead of hitting the floor as expected, the set arched high in the air, hurtled across the footlights as if punted by a titan, and landed before the first row. Strangest of all, the TV worked as well as ever. This is a gentle zephyr, for sure, or a playful poltergeist.

Spooks, Spirits, Specters

Orchard Park: Team Spirit

[We think of the stadium curse as one only the Bills' foes despair, but read on.]

By 1972 War Memorial Stadium, "the old Rockpile" on the city's east side, had fought its last good fight. Work commenced on the new stronghold of two-time AFL champs the Buffalo Bills, today's Ralph Wilson Stadium. Soon something seemed rotten in Orchard Park.

Households on the edge of the country tract reported outbreaks of poltergeist phenomena. These events are usually as neutral as the wind, but families felt targeted, talking of curses, blaming the budding stadium.

Workers clearing the former farmland rediscovered the tiny graveyard of the Joseph Sheldon family, second owners of the property. Dating from 1820, it was abandoned by 1924, and reverently restored in the early 1970s. These weren't the only troubled rests. Smokes Creek curls through the stadium plot, and along it had been much ancient Native American habitation. Their burial ground was here, too, which some say moaned when it was dug. Those were the days when the ravage could be kept under wraps. Word got out that this was the root of the psychic activity.

"That's about what oughtta start happening,'" said Algonquin Michael Bastine when told of the circumstances. "Little stuff going wrong around the house. Cats running away, dogs shying away from certain spots in the house and yard... People getting spooked, turning to drugs and stuff, even families breaking up. Lotta people don't realize that sometimes these things aren't coincidental. Sometimes they do have causes."

"Things only act up when our ancestors are disturbed," said Joyce Jamison of the Cattaraugus "Res." We don't know who called them, but we've heard from many people that Seneca elders came to work a rite of blessing and ease the offended spirits. Graves may have been resanctified or moved, and peace returned.

Doubtless some can be found to scoff at this rumor-cycle, and the tale as a whole has been strangely hard to track. Some Seneca representatives recall nothing of a ceremony. Written records aren't in likely places; the Bills' Beverly McClellan sought them without success, as did reporter Mike Vogel through decades of *Buffalo News* files. Our late friend Orchard Park historian John Printy had no memory of the matter in October 2000. In the community, though, there's the strong sense that this rendition is in the main true; and some Native Americans are sure a ceremony was done. There's also talk that the curse was merely shifted, and lingers still above all Buffalo professional sports teams, tantalizing them and us with short-term success, snatching ultimate triumph as it's within sight.

Three decades after their fitful frolic, the stadium graves are at rest, and it's hard to claim that the winningest NFL franchise of the 1990s is star-crossed in any sense. There are those Super Bowl losses to consider. Still, we think there'd be no talk of a curse but for a single kick (outside its kicker's range) in the first Super Bowl, or just one 300-pounder on the defensive line in the other three. Four straight AFC Championships, one as a wild-card? The biggest comeback in NFL history? What kind of curse is that? But fearing hits as hard as a Tom Sestak sack and cursing of all sorts, we mastered the impulse to call this tale, "Wide right."

Spirits of the Great Hill

West Seneca: The Imaginary Friend

[The old Ebenezer territory in West Seneca (see *Shadows*) seems a rich field of ghost lore.]

A boy of four started surprising his parents at breakfast with wonderful folk and fairy tales he'd learned overnight, seemingly in his dreams. The more diverse and clever the tales became, the more the parents wondered. From references to elves, dragons, landscapes, artifacts, and words the boy could not have known, the parents recognized these as old German folk and fairy tales. Though occasionally sharing motifs with those of the brothers Grimm, their son's tales were never identical. It was as if they were the originals from which the Grimms wrote. And there were many more.

Since it was obvious the boy was not sleeping normally, they often listened outside his room. One night they heard a deep, melodious voice and sensed an intruder. They rushed in, turned on the lights, and beheld only their son. "Don't do that," he said. "You make my friend go away. He wasn't done with his story." They decided to ride with this one as long as it ran.

One night when the boy was about five he woke his parents in the middle of the night and told them that a fire was just starting in the apartments in back of theirs. His "friend" told him that it would kill the two young women upstairs if no one acted. Suspecting that this was another fable but persuaded by the young boy's manner, the drowsy father checked on the building and saw that his son was right. Two lives were saved by the warning.

After this, the parents were more curious than ever about the boy's friend, and eager for the influence to continue so that the story might be solved. But after that night there were no more stories or appearances.

Years passed. The family moved to East Aurora, and the matter remained a charming "How about that...?" from their former home and their son's childhood. While entertaining some of their West Seneca neighbors, it was revealed that an earlier resident of their house had been an old German whose wife had died before him. He was so grief-stricken that he refused to care for himself or even eat, and thus his death was at his own hands.

Those who told this tale conjectured that, to whatever extent the boy's story was true, it was at least consistent. Odd fates are often rumored for suicides. The old German may have been cursed to haunt his home until he did a good deed, liberating his spirit from the waystation of its own purgatory, winning his passage to the next life. The saving of the girls had surely qualified him.

It was thought that none but children could see the old specter, but years later, a grandmother who'd sat for the children confessed that, one night as she'd dozed before the television in that very house, she'd seen a man passing through the room from the staircase behind the TV. No harm was done, and it had seemed impossible anyway, an image moving so silently, then vanishing, so she'd kept the matter to herself. The trespasser was a swarthy old European fitting the descriptions of the former tenant.

Spooks, Spirits, Specters

East Aurora: The Lemon Angel

That December night in 1956 would be fateful. Joyce and Charles Roof waded through waist-high snow to a Blakeley Road home, the 1901 hunting lodge possibly designed by Roycroft architect William Roth. Restoring it would be a job. "You could throw a hat through some of the cracks," Joyce recalled; but the deal was made, and a classic inn reborn.

Today's Old Orchard was a summer place for Buffalo's prominent Dr. Barber. Son Marsh kept it as a weekend retreat, but family fortunes crashed with the market, and he and wife Marian moved to Blakeley Road. Marian ran the lodge as a seasonal tea room, offering its signature Lemon Angel pie from the early '30s.

The Orchard gets in the blood, if it gets any hold at all. The Barbers kept eager eye on its progress, visiting often. Two girls from the family that ran the farm worked here 17 and 25 years. "It was good to us," says Joyce, here forty, most of them (after the tragic loss of Charles Roof to an accident) with second husband Jack Waterhouse. Many Arts & Crafts buildings seem to have spirits, and it may be no wonder if some on the other side of life feel the lure to this one. Maybe the energy was here. There was surely curiosity.

Just downhill to the east is the Cazenovia Creek and its ancient Native American trail. Just across it is Route 16 and its old farms, in which someone digging his basement reported finding giant human bones. Within walking distance was an odd creekside burial, thirteen Native American skeletons in rare positions, sitting or standing round a cache of ceremonial objects. Some think an ancient battlefield lies under the overpass just down the road. Today a freeform group of psychics meets at the Orchard frequently after hours, possibly tapping into something.

They've lost a lot of night people here; those who last long accept the surprises, the feelings, the possibly psychic effects. The freezer slams its door, or something else makes the same sepulchral sound. Lights and radios work themselves in funny ways. Someone rearranges silver already set. Once a salad plate blew into "ten million pieces" in one waitress' hand; another server notes after-hours effects in the small "South Room" past the bar. "When you work nights, things move," says an old timer.

Sometimes they say a shadow drifts by the ovens, and a woman in light garments comes down the stairs. She could have lived or worked here, now still tending particulars, maybe the silver. A phantom diner now and then sits for service in the main dining room, as if savoring its legacy of fine meals. A pipe-smoker appears at the bar, then vanishes. The overnight baker of the famous cinnamon rolls regards them all as comforting friends.

Now owned by Buffalo restaurateurs Jim and Jeanne Romanello, the Orchard hasn't lost a beat, and a new century of wholesome Yankee cuisine has dawned. The Lemon Angel's still rich, and the trademark red silo, the ducks, and their sheeny pond are sights from a Rockwell painting. The fall ridges peak into harlequin glory, and pines, snow, and lights make a Christmas scene into which people often say they'd like to retire. "Retire to a restaurant!" Joyce Waterhouse laughs, having given it forty years of weekends and holidays. "It ends up being your life." Or thereafter.

Spirits of the Great Hill

Niagara Falls: Clet Hall

[Niagara University was founded in 1856 as the Seminary of Our Lady of Angels, in what was then the town of Suspension Bridge, the northernmost part of today's American Niagara Falls. The alleged haunt is on Monteagle Ridge, the highest point on the Niagara Gorge. Given such sublime vistas and medievalesque atmosphere, it's little wonder that stories would fly about Clet ("clay") Hall.]

In the conflagration of December 5, 1864, the unfortunate Thomas Hopkins, a seminary student from Brooklyn, met his maker a few decades early. A fast-moving fire broke out at 2:30 in the afternoon in the philosophers' room of the Seminary, which was the forerunner of Clet Hall. According to the *Lockport Daily Journal & Courier*, the fire started with a stove pipe that passed through the ceiling. Dry and made of wood, the afflicted wing was entirely destroyed. The ever-zealous young Hopkins had been too devoted in his efforts to save property. He should have thought about saving himself. He was buried under a collapsing wall.

Niagara County historians have heard of the famous haunting; direct experience of it is more or less a rite of passage for Niagara University freshmen. "Hopkins lives inn the attic," Clet Graduate Hall Director Marty Bourke told the *Buffalo News*. The business administration major noted poltergeist phenomena like faucets turned on in totally - as in summer - empty buildings. More trademarks of the friendly spirit are footsteps in the halls and doors opening, sometimes to laughter. Nevertheless, Bourke points out, "It's eerie." The spook seems to have the run of the building, sometimes, according to the folklore, moving from room to room spooking people. Outbreaks of Hopkins' hijinks seem to happen all over the building on the same nights. Clanking sounds - like the proverbial rattling chains - come from below the theater. Clet Hall custodian Don Hathaway confided to the *News* that he has been frightened.

Other students note lamps in their dorm rooms seeming to turn themselves on and off. It's the usual poltergeist checklist, different - if at all - in the faith of the believers. There is a surprising lack of apparitions. We don't doubt there may be some reports, but we've heard of no instances in which the resident spirit has made himself visible. This may be a poltergeist, not a ghost, for all the folklore.

On the grassy knoll between Clet Hall and Route 104 is a simple white stone obelisk, the monument to poor Thomas Hopkins, once (according to an old account) the most promising of the 180 seminarians of his day. If his persistence is any sign of anything, he displays that promise to this day.

Theaters and college campuses are the two most commonly haunted categories of buildings in the United States. We could probably have turned up something allegedly psychic about any theater in the Western Door, and it seems as if every college campus anywhere has one alleged haunt. Like St. Bonaventure's fabled Devereux Hall (see *Shadows*), Niagara's Clet accommodates a theater, fulfilling both of the whimsical profiles. Either you believe all the folklore, find a middle ground, or presume that the general occupation of being a college student is less superstitious than only the profession of acting.

Spooks, Spirits, Specters

Lockport: Tale of the Tailor

[Lockport tailor William Shaack was admired in his Spalding Street neighborhood. No one suspected his family of staging the uncanny effects reported in two papers of the day. Few Western New York tales match the strangeness of this 1867 encounter.]

One Thursday evening in early December the family of William Shaack returned to find windows in the front of the house broken, and parlor carpet and woodwork smeared with something the papers delicately called "filth." (It was of the intestinal variety, we suppose, and upon that presumption, we'll call it "IVF": intestinal variety filth). Shaack's nine-year-old daughter and a young German woman had been in a room in one wing of the house. Neither had heard anything.

Suspicion included human agents, since furtive IVF-ing had happened before in Lockport. Things were calm for a stretch, but at around nine in the morning of the following Saturday a shrill whistle in the parlor summoned the family to find that the clothes folded on the sofa before ironing had been thrown about. No human could have done this and escaped notice. Wonders were to come.

Later the family gaped as the kitchen pump handle flew up and down as if a phantom worked five-minute bouts. The pump was in good order and the cistern full, but the spout was dry - a wonder, to say nothing of the demon-plunger.

As they peeled potatoes in the kitchen, the German girl and the family daughter saw each other's dresses in tatters, cut without their notice "in diamond shape," according to the *Journal*. As they rushed to tell the mother, they saw a black animal "in the shape of a toad" on the cover of the dinner pot. It vanished as they neared it, but when they raised the handle, the dinner had been IVF'd. A new hat and a fine dress were found upstairs, removed from storage and laid on a bed, the feather from the hat cut in two. They were put away, but found later in a different room, the hat mangled inside-out, the dress cut in shreds.

One girl went to the clothesline and came back crying that her finger was cut off. There was indeed a deep cut, but it never bled, healed quickly, and caused her few problems. The garment from the line, though, was cut in pieces. The papers allude to half a dozen more incidents from between 9 AM and 3 PM, untraditional hours for ghostbusting. After that the visitations seemed over. The ruined articles were put on display.

Lockport papers the *Union* and the *Journal* commenced a roaring word-war, gleefully correcting each other on minor details of this story that could have hurt neither's circulation. The *Journal* article ended with a snipe at its rival, crowing that, as demand for their article was higher than their supply, they were reprinting it in the weekend edition.

This tale is astoundingly similar to the devil/possession tales of Europe. That's the easy part, at least folklorically; the sewer-spewing toad is little other than a familiar, possibly a caco-demon in tamer form. What other factors could there have been? What was that girl's background in Germany?

Spirits of the Great Hill

Lockport:
The Cold Springs *Whatever*

A panic-stricken woman, a visitor to Lockport, almost staggered into the doctor's office. Out of breath, she asked the whole waiting room if anyone had heard of a ghost on Cold Spring Road. A young woman had simply "appeared" in front of her car before she could stop. She looked in her rear-view mirror, expecting to see either a crumpled form or the plain air of day. The woman was still there, standing on the road. The car had passed right through her.

Along Rt. 31 in Lockport near the Cold Springs Cemetery and De Sales High School there are many reports of the Cold Springs manifestation. The folklore is far richer in renditions of her than it is in ideas as to just what - witch, ghost, "vanishing hitchhiker" - she may be. She may have been a girl who lived near De Sales Catholic High School; maybe she was killed by her boyfriend near a well-known cemetery lover's lane, reappearing often at the same time of year, looking for her murderer; maybe she was even one of the Harrisons, the prominent family that started the General Motors plant here, haunting the street that led to her home.

Some report her as an old woman who disappears as the car approaches, evoking a host of classic images: the fate-hag, the Morrigan, the banshee, the washer-by-the-ford. To others, though, she's the proverbial "vanishing hitchhiker" who even specifies her destination - "the white house on the hill" - and disappears from the car just outside it. Some call her a witch. Maybe she's just an honest ghost.

One very good 1973 report of her, replete with identifiable witnesses, features her as a phantom hitchhiker or the like thereof. A pair of drivers picked her up along Cold Spring Road during a spell of ghost reports and found her an old woman who didn't know where she wanted to go. She mumbled as they drove, had them stop near a house they would not identify, then vanished as she moved up the walk in the headlights. According to the rumor mill, a deputy sheriff once took her in and had a similar experience, though the Niagara County Sheriff's Department spokesman would not confirm the account for reporters.

Another couple cited essentially the same figure, one who vanished from between them in the car as they drove over a bridge. This lends an unwholesome cast to the picture. In old European folklore it was traditional for beings of the negative kind - witches, malevolent ghosts, ill-meaning fairies - to stall before running streams, which were thought to represent either the baptism ritual or symbolic thresholds, "changes of state" often forbidden to such baddies as a condition of their power on earth. They need assistance to cross such features, and they are often found waiting by them for well-meaning citizens of earth, unlettered in folklore. There are plenty of them today. See Coleridge's fine fragment "Chrystabel" for a shot of one of these beings in action. Or, evidently, take a drive on Cold Spring Road.

Spooks, Spirits, Specters

Clarence Center: Spirit-Sisters

[Former ski racer Jeff Koso-Graceffa and inveterate world traveler Kyleena Falzone first saw the building in May 1998. By August, the Clarence Center Coffee Company was in business, and today serves 3,000 souls a week... give or take a few who don't show up in the receipts.]

There's energy at these corners; drive through in October, and you may feel it yourself. Once these crossed roads had been "Vantine's Corners," but the sense of them being the nexus of something took over, and Clarence Center they became. They may have their own karma.

A fine restaurant here bought the building next door, booting a group of dames and their emporium. The dear souls had to liquidate, and the restaurateurs expanded with a cafe of their own, thinking - how could it be otherwise? - to upstage the still-young coffee house across the street. The newest-comer soon vanished, and, sadly, later even the restaurant closed. Nothing but good, however, seems to come to the Clarence Center Coffee Company, which may have its own spirits on guard.

The marker outside tells the story. Built in 1829 by settler David Vantine, ten years later the building hosted the first Town Board meeting in Clarence, and in ten more became Erie County's first post office. Folks in the neighborhood had warned that it was haunted, and the list of potential haunters is vast. First owner Vantine (there's a family sandwich at the CCCC) may have had fifteen children, and the building's seen many incarnations: home, market place, general store, the Clarence Center Inn... There were two nineteenth-century fires here, and here two Vantine daughters may have died. Maybe it's their spirits that play. Most people sense that the energy here is gentle, and female; "Mary" is the name they give it.

The first signs of her (or their) presence were the strange, subtle voices. On several occasions, working late before opening, Kyleena heard a pert little presence say, "Excuse me..." as if inquiring the business of someone in that corner of her home. After a few weeks - and no talk of ghosts - Ky approached partner Jeff, who stopped her before she could speak: "Was it a young female voice?"

No full-formed apparitions are reported, but many sense motion at the eye-corners. "We never feel alone here," Jeff smiles, and no one feels threatened, either, though employees have flipped at some of the events, like a row of syrup-bottles springing their shelf, falling six feet to the hard floor. Wondrously, none broke, though when coffee cups act up, they don't just drop, they shoot. Ky's favorite mug, a tawny 20-ouncer, was found one dawn in a trail of pieces, yards from its wonted hanger. A basement trapdoor stuck as if it were held till someone asked "Mary" to let up.

"Mary's acting up again," they sometimes hear when Jeff and Ky call in from another adventure in the jungles of West Whatchadoonhere. But why do people think spirits here only come singly? Those of the three sisters Falzone are lively enough to go around; what wonder others wake in their presence?

Spirits of the Great Hill

The Left Side of the River:
Fort Erie: The Dollhouse

[The Mildred M. Mahoney Dolls' House collection was assessed at a million and a half 1981 smackers. The former "Bertie Hall" housing it has quite a past.]

Scottish-American innkeeper William Forsyth was a venturesome rogue oft in trouble with both his neighbors and the law. His 1822 hotel by the Horseshoe Falls, Pavilion Hall, was called "the first tourist trap in Upper Canada." Forsyth was also the builder of Bertie Hall (1826), the storied mansion so involved in the seminal events of the Niagara Peninsula and one of the main whistle stops of the Underground Railroad between 1828 and 1865. Named for Scottish duke Sir Peregrine Bertie, backer of the 1791 Canada Bill, Bertie Hall's many owners included the Fenian Raiders, who commandeered the landmark for their headquarters during the 1866 siege of Fort Erie. In 1981 John Kilbridge sold Bertie Hall to the Niagara Parks Commission. Now a dollhouse museum on the Niagara Parkway, it's a likely place for spooklore.

This "rare example of the Greek Revival Style" surely suggests the Greek Golden Ratio and other aspects of sacred architecture. Its grandeur lasts still, a Classical entrance of white Doric columns, Italian marble fireplaces, glorious woodwork, and black walnut beams. Cut out of the bedrock, the mammoth lower floor supposedly covers a tunnel to the river whose entrance led to a landing just below the Bertie House.

Much of the ghost lore harks to this tunnel, its role in smuggling and human traffic. People alive in the twentieth century said they'd seen this passage in the nineteenth, but no one's found it since. Touring school kids still seek it, tapping brick walls and scouring the riverbank. Forsyth children were rumored drowned in or near it, and two river-deaths are known - Rodney Forsyth (14 in 1842) and Isaac Brock (31 in 1850). Immigrant Chinese issuing from the other direction may also have met their ends.

Dollhouse lore features few apparitions, but the notion of a haunting is long-settled. "David" is a little boy allegedly drowned in the tunnel. "All he wants is attention," said one of the staff who named him. Psychics gave another ghost a dramatic profile: that of a young multiple-rapist who'd simply "hung around" too long after being stabbed in the heart and hung from a rafter in the basement. Yowie.

Psi reports include rapping sounds and electrical pranks, even a video camera inexplicably malfunctioning in the basement. One sweet effect involves a lilac-smell, sometimes after the stairtop apparition of a woman in Victorian dress bearing a flower-basket. Other effects are ambiguous. Displays are torn up overnight. Neighbors describe noises, even laughter, coming from the empty house after dark.

Some trace the spookery to just one dollhouse - the 1924 Pink Colonial, often moved overnight from its last location. Others narrow the focus to a single spot in it, the living room, whose furnishings include a tiny Ouija board. Many think it's all just David, out for a little fun.

Spooks, Spirits, Specters

BLACK CREEK: THE LIGHTHOUSE
[Site of the bloodiest battle in Canada's history, Fort Erie would be a natural for spirits.]

Settled by United Empire Loyalists in the late 1700s, Black Creek's real growth started with a saw mill. By the mid-1800s the town had expanded, hosting blacksmith shops, ferries, stores, a cheese factory, a grist mill, and six taverns. By the time of the American Civil War a railroad line ran through.

Where the Black Creek feeds the Niagara River under the Niagara Parkway is the restaurant named for its cupola with three large lights, a beacon shining out on the water, at night visible for many miles in this low country along the river. Built in the early 1800s, the two-story building has been an Underground Railroad station, a lumber mill, a jail, a pub, an ice cream bar, and an inn (to which American President Grover Cleveland brought his mistress in the late 19th century). An owner in the 1870s applied for a liquor license for "The Lighthouse Tavern," and it seemed a good name to current owner Kevin Smith.

When Smith opened The Lighthouse in Spring 1997 he was hoping for something special to offer his customers. When the first of them started telling him about "Stella" (evidently an old rumor) he suspected it was already at hand. From the start, stubborn and unusual maintenance problems made it seem that something was at play. Some lights don't work no matter what people do; others dim themselves so gradually that it takes patrons by surprise, finding themselves in dark. The heat cranks itself to full blast, and objects move themselves all the time. The effects alone don't instill absolute conclusions; the apparitions may make a different story.

There are lasting presences. They call the psychic hour here "Stella Night" after the keeper of the Inn, a nurturing influence who may well have company. One apparition they call "George" may have been a soldier, most likely a guard or watchman, who comes running with his musket when accidents occur, as they do too frequently on the tricky, scenic parkway. In 1998 there was a collision to the right of the Lighthouse, toward which most patrons turned their attention; but two women stared off to the left, at a British soldier in 1812-era garb, apparently George, still on call. He trotted off as if to summon help, then vanished.

There are the passing presences, entering with natural guests, no longer visible once past the door. Customers often report them after parkway accidents that let loose several new souls. A tall Black man arrived thus, vanishing within. An American looking like him had just lost his life in a wreck nearby, and psychic Gwendolyn Pratt was sure he'd been drawn to the lights. Other presences come in with people who had been special to them in life, waiting for an environment in which to reach them. ("Most of the time all they want to say is, *Goodbye*," notes Gwendolyn Pratt. "And, *I love you*.") And there are spirit-children; you hear them laugh in the breeze.

Today this restaurant-pub on the river is a designated port, maybe a port-of-call for more than mortal boaters. "They come to the first light they see," sums Gwendolyn Pratt. "From here they find their way home."

Spirits of the Great Hill

Niagara Falls:
The Niagara Poltergeist

[One of the world's most stunning psychic events began in 1970 with the newly-formed Toronto Society for Psychical Research. The goal of "The Philip Experiment" was no less than inventing its own ghost. Devising a personality right out of a Harlequin romance, an English Cavalier from the 17th century, a group of researchers met weekly, thinking hard about "Philip" and waiting hours round a table for anything to happen. After months came the first rapping sounds, seemingly within the table. Something answering to "Philip" met their expectations, tapping answers to yes-or-no questions but posing new ones about life, afterlife, and human (and possibly extra-human) potential. Iris Owen tells the story in *Conjuring up Philip* (1976). Through the *National Enquirer*, "Philip" researchers Iris and A. R. G. Owen held a contest soliciting Canadian paranormal reports. Below is one of the winners, from an unidentified St. Catherines woman who'd lived in Niagara Falls, Ontario, between August, 1975, and April 1976.]

From their first day in it the old Drummond Road farmhouse made its noises. The small family and their boarder blamed their nerves. On the second morning the mother dressed her two-year old and noticed another peering through the rails on the bannister. This little girl was not hers.

It was just the start. There were voices, even muffled conversations between a man and woman. Never were they intelligible. People thought they heard themselves called, sometimes in heavy whispers. Once the boarder paled when he realized that the woman hailing him could not have been anyone in the house. Saddest was a child calling, "Mommy," lost in some unimaginable psychic wilderness. There were more sounds, often of doors opening and closing. Late in their brief stay came a crash so violent that the house seemed ready to implode. Once even smells manifested, the most dramatic a scent of spicy flowers.

Physical effects seemed to crest and subside. Doors opened and closed themselves persistently, often while being watched. Once a bathroom door locked itself from the inside. Twice a day for a week the toddler's bed was found disassembled, sheets hurled and mattress tumbled. A painting made by the five-year-old daughter threw itself off the wall and onto the floor, surprisingly undamaged. Never were there material explanations for any of this.

Animals, especially cats, are thought highly sensitive to "presences," and the family dog and two cats reacted. Once they refused to go with the mother upstairs, the source of most of the noises. The big boxer whined and stood fast, and the cats ran away and hid, as if all sensed energies gathering. In half an hour came another enormous crash, but again nothing was broken or even moved.

In the spring the doors and footsteps acted up with a new frenzy. The last straw seemed to be the feeling of "something totally evil" entering the bedroom one night when the mother was reading. It held her down for ten minutes. She ran out when she could. The family tried to break their lease, failed, then just moved.

Spooks, Spirits, Specters

Niagara Falls: Houdini's Halloween

The greatest illusionist and escape artist of his time, "Harry" Houdini (Erich Weiss, 1874-1926) was almost as famous for his interest in psychic phenomena and the question of life after death. Houdini was a skeptic celebrated for his rightful debunking of fin-de-siecle fakes and his duels with Spiritualist and Sherlock Holmes-creator Sir Arthur Conan Doyle (1859-1930). Houdini's interest in legitimate psychic communication was sincere and passionate, however. He wanted to be convinced. He'd vowed to escape even from death, were it possible, and make a statement back into life. Some have even taken the great escapist's failure as proof that the trip may be a one-way ride. Without cell phones.

Less well known may be Houdini's connection to many Western New Yorkers - the Brothers Davenport among them (see *Shadows*) and, according to unconfirmed rumor, Roycroft's Elbert Hubbard, and possibly this author's grandfather Mason C. Winfield, Sr. (1886-1966). In family folklore, magician and manufacturer somehow became friends and were said to visit whenever paths neared. Whether the chats had any connection to the esteemed gent's deep Masonic affiliation - he was a "Shriner," a modern Templar - is a matter for speculation. Our concern is the very public 1974 seance in "The Houdini Magical Hall of Fame" on Clifton Hill in Niagara Falls, on the day - November 1 - of Houdini's death, the day of the dead in the old Celtic calendar, a century after his birth.

The medium - Mrs. Ann Fisher from Albany - had evidently no sensitivity about preserving herself from exploitation and mockery. Famed debunker James ("The Amazing") Randi was on hand, as well as Walter Gibson, creator of radio's *The Shadow* program, and mentalist Joseph Dunninger (with whom Houdini had coauthored a book and devised a code for calling home from the undiscovered country).

As the group attempted to find its spiritual focus, the irrepressible Randi broke the ice with a few tricks, like one with computer cards, and Houdini's "Milk Can" escape. ("Dumb," said reporter Mike Healy.) The group eventually regained its composure, and, at a solemn moment, all psychic energies stretched to the max, the medium asked for a sign. A bouquet fell off a bookshelf behind the 13th chair, left empty for the spirit of Houdini. Randi coaxed others to examine the marvel; in the flowers was a book open to a page with a poster of Houdini which read, "Do Spirits Return?" It seemed clear that the indefatigable Randi had pulled the prank.

The group recovered its form and the medium did her channeling, but no one spotted Houdini's code, and the great magician cannot be said to have shown himself in any recognizable form. The evening ended with a thought-transference experiment in which the crowd at the Niagara Falls site tried to communicate a specific card (the Queen of Hearts) to one at The Magic Castle in Los Angeles, also on "Houdini Night." The phone lines were tangled, and reporter Healy was too riled and bored even to stick around for the results. It was understandable. It would be hard to imagine that real psychic phenomena would find this environment encouraging, and the situation seemed an opportunity for silliness.

Spirits of the Great Hill

Niagara-on-the-Lake: The Buttery

[Winston Churchill declared Niagara-on-the-Lake the most beautiful place in the world. By all the signs, it appeals to the spirits, too.

"The ghost of a murderer once haunted The Buttery," declares Rosemary Ellen Guiley in *Atlas of the Mysterious in North America*. "Lloyd Burns, who abused his wife Kate, was killed by her and her brother. They threw him down the stairs from the second floor. Kate was so upset over the crime that her ghost remained to create poltergeist-like disturbances. It was supposedly exorcised in 1981." The theory's as good as anyone's; not sure about the facts behind it. Here when they turn out the lights, lock, and bid him a cheery good night, the staff call him "Philip."]

The town had its stories, of course, but owner Margaret Niemann's first suspicion that she might have something "extra" in The Buttery came in the mid-1970s. A self-professed psychic walked village streets, drinking "vibes" and seeking buildings with "presences." One would think she'd have trouble missing them in Niagara-on-the-Lake, reputedly the most haunted town in Canada; but at The Buttery, she paused and lingered. This was the only village site whose owners she approached; she asked to hold a seance.

Recruiting villagers, this latter-day Sibyl held her sitting, believing she'd reached three troubled spooks with whom the psychic activity in the Buttery may start. A classic love-triangle brewed when the hub (the one they nickname "Philip") grew jealous of the wife's ministrations to his own invalid brother. A double-murder-suicide was said to be the result. This may be the source of Guiley's impressions, but the situation feels murky. It's hard to be sure whether the psychic's revelations were echoes, origins, or confirmation of village rumors about the place.

Now cheerfully-themed after Henry VIII (England's rotund, wife-killing gourmand), the building housing The Buttery is only thirty or so years old. At least two others preceded it on the spot, probably dating to the late 1700s. We know of nothing in the site's architecture or history to associate it with haunters, but even without the village's battle-lore, any site that old would have ready suspects. Those here test guests and newcomers. These are reports, not rumors:

◉ A new steward saw a man duck into the Mens' room and presumed he was from the tour bus parked outside. He yelled when it started up, then went in. No one.
◉ A new manager lived next door, and through windows could see The Buttery's upper floor. "Who is that walking every day through the hall?" he asked the owners. No one, of course. Margaret confessed to hearing footsteps, often at the same times the manager reported them.
◉ "Is this place haunted?" a guest asked waitress Kim McQuhae. The woman had passed through a cold spot that had made her hair stand up.
◉ A new waitress folding napkins upstairs saw someone cross the room and pass right through two closed doors. The girl's terror would have been comical had it not been serious. It was a simple ghost, for God's sake, if anything at all. You'd have thought Godzilla had looked in the window. ("Well... I gave her brandy!" said Margaret.)

Spooks, Spirits, Specters

Niagara-on-the-Lake: The Angel Inn

The Angel may be the oldest still-operating Inn in British Canada. The hand-hewn beams and heavy plank floors set down in 1815 "still echo to the sounds of the British soldiers and townsfolk who two centuries ago gathered here for food and drink," says its brochure. The Angel has hosted some serious luminaries, like Irish National Poet Thomas Moore, explorer Alexander Mackenzie, and Prince Albert. Something was here before it, however: "The Harmonious Coach House," built in 1789, frequented by historic figures like John Graves Simcoe, first lieutenant-governor, and Colonel John Butler, revered as a town founder. (A Loyalist hero, to the Colonials Butler was infamous as a slaughtering, roughriding, "White Indian" terrorist, leader of "Butler's Rangers." It was he and his war-hound whelp of a son Walter who, among other atrocities, may have presided over the Mohawks' "Torture Tree," a Revolutionary War incident on the Western Door starring two reluctant members of the Boyd-Parker mission. It was said of the Butlers that they could "out-savage the savages.") The Inn did well, but in 1813 was set alight by the retreating Yanks (to the sacrifice of Butler's famed and prized pewter beer mug). It was rebuilt by John Ross as The Angel Inn, named in reference to his wife. The old softie. It's prospered ever since.

There's a ghost rumored here since the 1820s, thought to be that of Captain Colin Swayze. When last in the flesh the resident specter may have delayed fleeing the town to rendezvous with a sweetheart, and been killed in the fighting. Word got started that he was tortured to death in the Inn cellars by American soldiers. That's not common Yankee practice, though it's hard to be sure some improvisation couldn't have been made if they could just have got hold of that Butler... Rumor has it that it's Captain Swayze still walking the Inn late at night.

The employees buy it. Some of them won't enter the building alone at night. One called another upon arriving for duty at 1:30 AM, finding the place unexpectedly dark and empty and fearing to go in solo. Sometimes the phones get into the act, ringing sporadically, with no one speaking at the other end. Sometimes the doors shake, seemingly on their own. Footsteps, distinct, sharp, and sometimes heavy, can be heard, usually in the basement named for Captain Swayze.

Sometimes the noble captain shows himself in the apparent flesh. A pastry chef came in early to prepare for the day and saw someone in English Colonial-era army garb walk into the lavatory she was (ahem) using. He walked in, turned around, and walked out. A gentlemanly spook, that. Lucky for her it wasn't Butler. Of course, when you think of how easily any spook could spy in a disembodied state on anything it wanted and never be spied in return, you wonder if Swayze merely returned in a condition of translucence. It could get a body creeped out...

Impression runs that it's this single spirit behind the haunting. A basement room is named for him, and it's believed that, as long as the British flag flies over the Inn as it does now, the apparently chivalrous ghost of Colin Swayze will do no harm. No other ghost in the world seems to do harm, either, but that's by the by. So far the guests (who are encouraged to report sightings) have suffered no ill, and the charm of "the Union Jack" might seem to hold. Now try the trick in Belfast and see what you get.

Spirits of the Great Hill

Niagara-on-the-Lake: The Kiely

Niagara-on-the-Lake's splendid Kiely Inn was built in 1832 by Charles Richardson, lawyer and Member of Parliament for English Upper Canada. In 1837 Richardson moved to Toronto with the law society, but the spacious wooden house continued to serve as his summer residence.

The building was eventually transferred under "power of sale" to Colonel Grant Suttie, an evident rascal nicknamed "Foxy Grandpa." At his death, the silver fox willed the house to his niece Mrs. Kathleen Drope (nee Gooderhan), who restored it as well as other historic homes in Niagara-on-the-Lake, a community undergoing a renaissance into a trendy summer resort served by rail and lake steamer. Mrs. Drope's daughter Jane Kiely took over in 1986, at which point The Kiely Inn was born. In two years Ray and Heather Pettit bought the property, setting up as the Tapestries Dining Room. Inn and restaurant they sold in October 1999 to Upper Canada Hotels, which installed new ventilation and fireplaces, and in general did a major renovation.

A building over a battlefield two centuries old would have numerous candidates for haunting, but we haven't uncovered a folkloric cycle at the Kiely. So far the staff are mum on the subject, and they're the ones who should know, if they feel like talking. They may mistrust either strangers claiming to be authors or the sheer subject of ghosts. There is, of course, another explanation: that the Kiely isn't haunted. Not many buildings are; but one senses there may be more to the story in any old, prominent building in this village. As one of its historians points out, "You can find a ghost story about any building in Niagara-on-the-Lake." The Kiely may be one of those rare sites at which we have actual evidence of... something.

A former night manager was an amateur psi buff who believed the Kiely was haunted and took many photos during his term. He caught no formerly animate images, but he did get several pictures of the effect known as "orbs" - small spheres of light often thought to mean a psychic manifestation not yet developed enough to seem an apparition. Not every cold becomes pneumonia, and not every "spirit manifestation" congeals into a recognizable human image. Sometimes what we have is an unexplained, biomorphic blob of light, even invisible to the human eye. Sometimes these orbs are all that show when people point their cameras at apparitions. In some circles they are as good as ghosts. Shy ones, though.

"Spirit photography" has long been one of the most controversial subjects in parapsychology, a controversial discipline to begin with. There have been some famous debacles - like the case of the Cottingley Fairies, one that fooled even Sherlock Holmes' creator Arthur Conan Doyle. There have been some provocative successes, few of them well-publicized.

Some modern ghosthunters use gear of all sorts - infra-red cameras, motion-detectors, high-frequency tape recorders, temperature-gauges, and others - to detect influences they take for signs of spooks. Whatever you make of this - at least in theory reducing the spirits of our dead to metaphysical animals or even predictable natural effects like weather - in the days of Adobe Photoshop pictures are proof of little unless the circumstances of the taking are controlled. The case isn't clear at the Kiely, nor is it closed. Drop by for a visit. Maybe you can settle it.

Spooks, Spirits, Specters

ROCHESTER AND REGION

ROCHESTER: POOR TESSIE KEATING

[Real parapsychology is considerably less dramatic than many people would presume. Vengeful ghosts and accusers from the grave are usually just features of folklore. Usually.]

On November 20, 1900 a beautiful brunette looking for a job knocked on the door of 127 Davis Street near the railroad tracks in the center of Rochester. The next morning behind a billboard was found the beaten, defiled body of twenty-eight-year-old Theresa Keating.

More than sixty suspects were interviewed, some based on the flimsiest of connections. One of them - Hobart Fuller, a 17-year-old Canadian working as a janitor in the Sixth Ward Republican Headquarters - had entered the list of suspects because a Canadian coin had been found in the field near the murder-spot. It could have been dropped under any number of circumstances, including during the stampede to view the tragic site. (It's thought that 25,000 people may have visited, destroying whatever real evidence was to be found.) The city was in a vengeful mood, and vigilante justice was not too far in the past of the Western Door. Maybe Fuller thought his odds were better in battle.

Master Fuller fled to South Africa and joined the British forces in the Boer War. Anyone who knew the ferocity of that conflict would, in hindsight, rather have taken his chances with a trial. We know no more of young Fuller, except that he was almost surely innocent. Even had he been tried and convicted on the basis of the flight, another voice would have had her say.

In 1903 an immigrant farmhand, a Belgian named August Russell, went to his doctor with a complaint. He couldn't sleep, he said, because of strange sights and sounds in the night. He heard voices and footfalls, and felt as if something was coming for him. He reported that he saw images, too - of a young, dark-haired woman. Under more questioning, he acknowledged that he knew the woman he saw at night - young Tessie Keating - that he had been her murderer, and that he would get no peace until he admitted to it. He had confessed long ago to his wife, even threatening her life if she dared speak, but that wasn't enough, and there was no need to conceal it further. His life was useless to him under the interrogation of the indignant specter, and earthly accusers could do no worse.

If Tessie Keaton made a malevolent ghost, she could have had her way. Her apparitions could have brought forth her killer and saved him from the hangman of a materialist world which could only presume him insane, saving him for a full life of her torment. Russell spent the rest of his days in the Matteawan prison for the criminally insane, possibly his own deserved hell on earth if still visited by Tessie.

Russell must have been hideous to do what he did, but he had to have something decent in him to repent it. We curse those who can know themselves guilty and love their lives to the end, fearing only the world's justice. Maybe that of another world is waiting.

Spirits of the Great Hill

Rochester: Hill of 1,000 Ghosts

[Rochester's Corn Hill is so-called for its latter-day grain transactions, but commerce of another sort made it "the home of 1,000 ghosts." That's doubtless a misapprehension. A world record for SPSM ("spirits per square mile") would have been set here. This section, though, and Plymouth Avenue running through it, was a virtual Bethlehem in its early days for the Spiritualist religion (discussed in *Shadows*). Every service of that young faith involves a period of speaking for the spirits; it would be natural journalistic shorthand to write that they were also seen.]

From the first night in their new home John and Margaret Fox were troubled by mysterious rappings, sounds that came from the very walls. On the last night in March, 1848, daughters Margaret and Kate (fifteen and twelve) noticed that, whenever they knocked, the sourceless sounds seemed to reply, and they followed the girls wherever they went. To the forty-something earthbound souls, mostly peppermint farmers, of Hydesville (thirty miles east of Rochester), this portable poltergeist show was wondrous strange, and to us it's stranger still to think that it could found a new religion; as a stranger, though, give it welcome.

Like most things, Spiritualism had a regional genesis, but it's gone so far beyond its origins by now that one might as well speak of "radiation" or "communism" as things that need location to be relevant. Though the sisters hosted houses-full of their suspicious Hydesville neighbors and even, as the proteges of P. T. Barnum, showed New York City audiences what "the spirits" could do, the faith's real coming-out (thus that of the Fox girls) took place in the Queen City of the Genesee, at sister Leah Fox's Plymouth Avenue home. Regularly visited by spirit-rappings, it hosted customers eager to pay to observe otherworld communications into this one. Photos of the graceful columns suggest sacred architecture, and this mansion once at 167 Plymouth was rumored to top a number of tunnels. Such passages, often associated with the Underground Railroad (also figuring in paranormal rumors), are reputed beneath some northeastern cities. Either the rumors are false or mystery is here. Who dug them?

Even more impressive was the Plymouth Avenue church, raised in 1855 as a Congregationalist fane. Soon adopted by the spirit-talkers, it became a shrine to Spiritualism, and would have been a scene of numinous devotion. The impression of the thousand ghosts came from the great Spiritualist activity in the region. It's important to point out that apparitions - ghosts - are unexpected at Spiritualist services, which resemble Protestant worship more than anything else, interrupted, of course, by a break for speaking "from spirit."

Alas, the fine church and the famous Fox home were leveled in 1954 on behalf of the Inner Loop Expressway. It's hard to suspect that the racing cars sense spirits, or that any one walking hereabouts would be metaphysically inspired. Ah, city planning at its finest. At least it wasn't a world-famous Frank Lloyd Wright masterpiece or a Frederick Law Olmsted landscape-design, done in in the name of nothing. Leave that to Buffalo, whose ever-morphing system eats billions in taxes and can't afford the treasures it already has.

Spooks, Spirits, Specters

ROCHESTER: OF WIDOWS AND WINDOWS

[The house that became the Brighton once overlooked the Erie Canal, and the widow that may be its ghost stared out her days down its course.]

Built around 1854 as a canal house, today's Brighton restaurant and pub is at least the second-oldest operating food-and-drink establishment in Monroe County. It's been altered over the years, but its outer self today is about what you'd have seen of it in its earliest photo. A residence for most of its life as well as an owner-run Inn and tavern, the Brighton is a cheery place, not the craggy, voluminous ruin often associated with ghosts. Its setting on busy East Ave is neither isolated nor tree-shadowed. Nevertheless, some of the Brighton's employees are spooked. Few who work here spend time in the offices upstairs after dark, especially in "her" special room.

There's more than one story about "our lady," as they call her, the Brighton's gentle, mournful spook, still keeping watch of the vanished canal. The daughter of the innkeeper, she was, they say, a young woman whose lover, boyfriend, fiance, or husband stepped out and embarked down the torpid sheen, probably to the infinite west, and never a word did she hear of him after. That vein at her doorstep must have seemed passage to the endless possibilities of the young nation, yet her lover's course down it ended all her own. She seemed sustained by the faith that this injustice was too great, that he'd return as he'd left. She stared out her window hours each day, maybe gazing onto the sluggish waterway that beckoned him, maybe to the tender cemetery across it beckoning her. That looking, at least, was constant. Soon faith was both thirst and drink.

Even the canal abandoned her, though not in her mortal lifetime. Once an aqueduct of the Genesee River following today's Rt. 490, the canal was routed farther south of the city and its remaining bed used as a subway. As if a life wasn't enough of looking, she likes her view even from afterlife. The rocker's still kept for her in the room overseeing the once-canal. They say that if someone moves it, it's always found at the window when next anyone checks. Whatever moves the chair is the likely suspect for whatever else takes down the curtains, which, if left impeding the view of the former waterway, are often found parted the next morning.

The Brighton undergoes the usual run of possibly paranormal effects involving lights, sounds, and small objects. One was even radical. The lady's window exploded outward, and none of the glass was ever found. There may even be more than one spook. An older gentleman has been reported, walking down the stairs with a cane, disappearing once seated like that old canal. Those booths are only decades old and could hardly seem familiar to a witting wight from Canal days. This spirit must be a newer-comer, if there is anything to the reports at all. Maybe the lady's love returned for her after all, righting old wrongs. Let those spirits here comfort each other.

An odd way to ebb life, staring down a canal after a lost love, neither anymore where it should have been. May this short-lived, artificial river have seemed as fervent as the Nile, as daunting as the Amazon, as primal as the God-formed Ganges, anything that would reward the life-gazing.

Spirits of the Great Hill

Greece: Mother of Sorrows

[One of the Western Door's most storied haunts is a National Landmark in Paddy Hill, a legendarily haunted region of Rochester's northeastern burb of Greece.]

Steeped in psi lore like so many sacred buildings, the former Our Mother of Sorrows Church is now the Paddy Hill Library. One of the staunchest ghost tales of this early nineteenth-century Romanesque structure is also an old one. A janitor tended the furnace fire every night so the church would be warm in the morning. Most nights at eleven he heard footsteps overhead, as if someone rose from prayer and came to the altar. He presumed it was the priest, but thought it strange for him to be in the church so late. One night at the outbreak of sudden footsteps he rushed from the church to the rectory nearby and found the priest in his study. From then on, the furnace took its tending an hour early so its tender might avoid the phantom feet.

Another tale concerns a pretty little girl who knocked on the rectory door, begging the priest to come to her ailing mother. She led him through the fields, but vanished just as he neared a small house. He knocked on the door all the same, and the childless woman who answered looked quite hale. The priest recognized the little girl he had just met in a picture on a table. It was the woman's daughter, who had been dead for three years. Puzzled, and suddenly very impressed, the priest gave her confession and left. The woman died suddenly before the morning.

As part of a Halloween 1986 experiment, *Rochester Times-Union* reporter Amy Wilson and historian Shirley Cox Husted put to the test the old church, testing as well as a psychic, Reverend Lydia Samuel, an ordained Spiritualist minister. Rev. Samuel toured the site, receiving images of one of the rumored ghosts, a known priest called Father Maurice. Historian Husted confirmed this detail, as well as impressions of another former priest. The psychic's sense - of "repressed sorrow here" - seemed supported again; the historian noted that this was likely an Underground Railroad station. Even the strong-minded Husted reacted with visible disturbance when the psychic spoke of a girl killed here in a fire. The tragedy is true, and the girl was Husted's niece.

Even living schoolchildren get into the act. In 1993 several snuck out of a sleepover and visited the library at midnight. They heard phantom steps and an eerie bell, then looked in a cobwebbed window and saw pale, spectral people reading and socializing. They ran back whence they'd come, but their party was no longer of the "slumber" variety. Other neighborhood kids claim that ghosts from Paddy Hill's graveyard roister in its former church, clanging on pipes and creaking floors.

Psi lore seems to gather in "zones," and this immediate area has centuries of it: ghosts, phantom lights, fairy sightings, and maybe even the fearsome Seneca child-eater "High Hat." "Ghost lights" are thought common in swampy terrain, as this was, but it's hard to believe those described here - and everything else - have such simple explanations. Either the reports are fabricated or we need other insights.

Spooks, Spirits, Specters

ONTARIO: BUMP-AND-RUN

[As part of a Halloween 1996, promotion, the *Rochester Democrat & Chronicle* asked its readers for stories about haunted houses. This is the winner.]

  The three-story Victorian on Furnace Road in Ontario stands out on its street of ranch houses. It was about eighty years old in 1995 when its new owner moved in; it took just a few days to reach the conclusion that it was haunted. Eleven months later she wrote to the *D&C*, and reporter Sheila Rayam was interested enough to visit. She found that its owner, a quarter-century employee of Xerox and a manager at the Webster site, held a chemistry degree from the University of Rochester. She was not your average flake.
  It started with the talking, the lady scientist said: murmurs, impressions of the hum of conversation, even single, distinctive voices. At first she disregarded them; a TV in another part of the house, even the radio of a passing car, could be to blame, to say nothing of simple imagination.
  Then came the real sound effects, at first a pair of loud bangs, like doors slamming, at exactly four in the morning on separate nights. She was alone in the house. They had to be paranormal. They woke her from a deep sleep.
  Next it was the lights, ones dimmed that she knew she'd left on, ones alight that she knew had been off. Soon doors opened and closed themselves. It was the banging that finally convinced her. The voices and pounding occurred on so many nights that she could no longer presume all was natural.
  Just twice she thought she saw her spectral guest, her "spirit sister." Once it came when she was in the yard. "I looked at the house and saw a curtain move in the back and a figure withdraw." Another time she was in the kitchen, and developed the familiar impression of being watched. She turned quickly, and believed she saw - or saw - a white cloud, like a spectral person, drawing up the stairs.
  "Spirits remain on earth for one reason," said Barbara Konish, a psychic consulted for the *D&C* article. "Their work isn't done." The activities reported of the Ontario spook were typical for haunted sites, maintained Konish, a medium from Brighton's "Visions Unlimited." "Spirits can manifest in physical forms: sounds, a cold breeze - that's very common - cold chills and dampness. They pick stuff up and look at it."
  The house's owner isn't sure of the entity's point in sharing it, but she's sure it's a benign spirit; and she may have found out whose it was before "crossing over." A member of the previous owners' family told her that a younger sister had died in the house at the age of twelve.
  As if there could be a cause-and-effect relationship between any earthly event and something so mysterious as ghosts, a death at a house or site puts many in mind of the unrestful dead. Maybe so, if you presume that the things that appear to us as ghosts are indeed spirits of the human departed, but consider: there should be a legion of them at the emergency room of every hospital, and who has heard that rumor? (Though it's a buzz in a few paranormal circles that some hospitals are indeed very haunted, the point holds.) For sure, though, the Ontario occurrences seemed too numerous for the lady scientist to rack them all up to chance or imagination. Too much happened there, for too long.

Spirits of the Great Hill

Lake and Lakeside Wights:

Flying Dutchmen

The most famous "ghost ship" in the world, *The Flying Dutchman* may be only the nickname of a Dutch East Indian captained by boastful Hendrick Vanderdecken, setting sail from Amsterdam to an Indian port in 1680. (In other versions, "Vanderdecker" was the ship's name.) Loading the *Dutchman* with loot of his own, the captain planned to be rich on his return. Beset by a storm, he scorned turning into port and took the Devil's wager to race it around the Cape of Good Hope. His crew never made it, but he and the *Dutchman* sail the world's seas until the Judgment Day, sort of a nautical Jack-o-Lantern or watery Wandering Jew. The Great Lakes have their own lore of the sort.

Unless phantom Viking or Phoenician barks are spotted - which we haven't heard - the oldest Great Lakes ghost ship is undoubtedly the first Euroamerican one, the *Griffon*, a small galleot, seventy feet or so long, with a tubby hull, a high stern, and two or three masts. On Aug. 7, 1679, famed explorer Rene Cavalier Sieur de La Salle's ship put out from the entrance to the Niagara River (likely near Cayuga Creek) in Lake Erie and set out to explore the Lakes. Named for the mythical animal with a lion's body and eagle's head and wings, it was said to be the first vessel to sail above the Niagara. Native Americans last saw her heading into rough seas on Lake Michigan, but nothing has ever been proved about her disappearance, and apparently only the writings of pioneering Jesuit Father Hennepin contain even the name of the ship.

The Lakes' most famous ghost ship is the *Edmund Fitzgerald*, lost in 1975 on Lake Superior and immortalized in Gordon Lightfoot's ballad. The largest carrier on the lakes (711 feet), the *Edmund Fitzgerald* should have been a dreadnought, but everything seemed to point the wrong way for it from the christening. [The champagne bottle took three tries to break, the boat launched awry (splashing dockers and damaging itself), and a heart attack killed a witness at the scene.] Things didn't get better afterward. Rare and hellish waves - nicknamed "The Three Sisters" - may have struck it on its final voyage during the late autumn storm called "The Witch of November." Its curse may have followed it into the lightless fathoms. Even an objective writer such as Frederick Stonehouse mentions paranormal phenomena reported by those studying the *Edmund Fitzgerald*'s wreck: a remote vehicle exploring the hulk lost power several times; surveillance equipment inexplicably failed; "ghost lights" and other manifestations beneath the waves have been observed on the ship, 530 feet down. It heebie-jeebied Jacques Cousteau's *Calypso* team into cutting short their dive.

The best-documented candidate for a Great Lakes' "Flying Dutchman" may be Lake Superior's *Bannockburn*, a steamer loaded with grain at Port Arthur and lost on November 21, 1902. It's still reported on stormy nights near Caribou Island, searching for the lighthouse.

Spooks, Spirits, Specters

THE BLACK DOG OF THE ERIE

One of the lakes' most fearsome goblins, "The Black Dog of Lake Erie" is so potent that its disasters spill into its eastern cousin Ontario. This notorious bogie has been implicated in many wrecks on the eastern lakes, such as the *T. G. Jenkins*, the *Thomas Home*, the *Mary Jane*, and the *Phoebe Catherine*. Calamity always seems to follow when sailors see the mordant mutt nonchalantly walk their decks in the dim hours.

The canal schooner *Mary Jane* was being towed from her wharf in Port Colborne, Ontario, when the Black Dog put in an appearance. Elevator workers noticed a big Newfoundland with "eyes like coals of fire" on the port side of the deck. It walked across the top of the load of cedar posts and leaped ashore, vanishing when it hit the wharf. The *Mary Jane* never reached her destination, lost with all hands. No good explanation of her loss has ever been given.

In November 1875 the three-masted schooner the *T. G. Jenkins* was on her way from Chicago to Kingston, Ontario, loaded with grain. One lovely night the helmsman roused captain and crew with a tale of the nefarious Newfie, climbing up from the Lake Erie surface across the deck, over the other rail and back down onto the drink. Either it walked on water or had dematerialized. A quick search of the old salt produced moonshine, and he was booted when the schooner reached Port Colborne. As his mates went down the Welland Canal, he bellowed from the bridge that they should leave the ship or change their course.

The *T. G. Jenkins* made for open water, and something went wrong somewhere between Dalhousie and Oswego. Tugs sent out to search found nothing, not a body nor a single piece of wreckage. The Black Dog had worked his evil well. However, the night the schooner was missing, a farmer at Sheldon's Point (west of Oswego) claimed to have seen a strange black dog come ashore. Its hair was matted and bedraggled, and its hindquarters trailed behind it on land as if it were paralyzed. It looked a little satisfied with itself, though. It trucked along for a spell, then just vanished.

Once a shipboard fight went too far and a captain killed a mate. The Dog appeared outside his cabin, gnashing its teeth. The ship's next voyage was its last.

The Dog was so fearsome that its very mention was trouble. A drunken mate of the *Azimuth* became displeased with one of the captain's orders and cursed, "May the Black Dog of Lake Erie cross your bow."

The captain knocked him to the deck. "Take it off, or your own mother will never know the look of you. If I told the boys you'd called down the Dog they'd tear you limb from limb."

The sufferin' spaniel was rumored to be the ghost of a natural Newfoundland that had fallen off its ship and drowned in the Welland Canal. "To such a good saltwater swimmer," the soon-to-be-sorry sailors laughed, "a little sweetwater should do no harm." When the schooner stuck tight in the lock, though, its crew broke their backs to get it loose. The dog's body was the obstacle that had stuck them, and its hellish howling came back to them on stormy nights.

Spirits of the Great Hill

The Phoebe Catherine

[This nautical "House of Frankenstein" sounds like it never had a chance.]

The schooner *Phoebe Catherine* suffered from a double-whammy of the Black Dog and something known as "doubling" - when a sailor on his midnight watch found that a shadowy form was stalking him, imitating his motions on other parts of the deck. Evidently it was undoing some of his work, because cabin doors wouldn't keep shut and few hatches would stay locked.

The *Phoebe Catherine* may have had her own complaints, though, unattributable to dogs or doubles. Though outwardly a lakeworthy schooner, she bore a bad-luck rep. In her second sailing season (1865) she ran aground near Wellington, Ontario. Nine years later she gave the same service to Manitoulin Island in northern Lake Huron. Her captain died aboard her when she was icebound in a Manitoulin winter.

Even "the woman in white" (or some such archetype) haunted the *Phoebe Catherine*. On a late-night drinking and gaming binge a member of the crew looked up once to see his landbound wife - in a sheet - looming above them. He took the pledge. Scared sheetless, might we say.

The Point Charles Marker (Ontario)

[It's an old rumor that ghosts have a reverence for the resting places of their physical remains, and at least one resident of Sodus, NY, believed he had it proved to him.]

In the spring of 1857 the body of a dead French-Canadian sailor was found on the bar connecting Point Charles with the mainland. His name was reportedly tattooed on his arm, but it does not come to us. A simple stone marker shows where he was buried not far from the spot, about twenty feet south of one of the largest cottages.

In late August of 1917 a party of three were having a midnight snack in a house on the Point not far from the sailor's grave. They heard intervals of rappings on the wall that seemed to be communications or messages. This kept up so long that the two men investigated, going different routes around the house till they met at the likely source. A little later, one of them saw a white form on a bench between the cottage and the shore. He called the others. All three of them swore they saw the white shape stand, walk to the stone marker, and disappear into the grave.

George Carson was the caretaker at Point Charles for the cottage association, and by earthly accounts had a relatively uneventful term. One day (probably in 1921) he was getting the lawns of the point ready for the summer season when he toppled the simple stone marker the ghost had designated as his own. It found its way with other debris to a rubbish heap. During his evening stroll that night, Carson was "scared stiff" by the sight of the old sailor ghost, pacing between the bench and the grave. He shouted a hearty "Hey, there!" and the apparition retreated to the grave and descended into it "with uplifted form." The first item of the next morning's business was the restoration of the marker to its original site. All was well on Point Charles thereafter.

Spooks, Spirits, Specters

"Wherever you can place your eyes" (Ontario)

[If the house spirits are angry, they could well be those of the British Victorians whose displaced charity had built it.]

Pious James Craggs raised money in his ancestral land for converting Native Americans; immigrant James Craggs had his stake in Yankeeland. By 1870 Pultneyville's opportunistic miller was in his fine home - "'arf mansion, 'arf castle," it was joked. It passed from his daughter to Mrs. Jennie Stell, whose love of the house overcame her foresight. She bought her would-be B&B on the doorstep of a poor decade for leisure travel. The Great Depression sent her home into foreclosure, one of whose oddest fallouts was an ambiguous note she left with the new owners as if they were fate's movers rather than its agents. The letter's arrival - Columbus Day, 1939 - may be a pun, either on the supposed ancestry of her clients (the family of Francis D'Amanda) or one likening her own plight to that of the original Americans in 1492. In light of her suspected haunting, the note may have other implications.

"Where ever you can place your eyes," she writes, her spirit will be found; only she, she maintains, found the sunshine in this property, and her spirit will always be there. As of 1995 the third and fourth generation of D'Amandas were in the house, and, as many maintain, so is Mrs. Stell.

One senses that the four-year-old D'Amanda boy (who'd developed a terror of anyone white-haired and wrinkled) had some experiences with manifesting crones. Despite this and the ominous letter, Mrs. Stell seems no nasty haunter, and she acts up only when there is change: renovation, redecorating, guests.

The painters were convinced. One fell off a ladder the first day for some reason he associated with the supernatural and never came back. Another was attacked by a can of spray paint. A third had so surely heard someone in the third-floor room Jennie Stell claimed as her own that he presumed one of the owners was home. Of course the painters were alone in the house. A rash of flats struck cars driving to the James Craggs Mansion or parked in its driveway. A painter summarized the slurry of effects as "spook central."

The family most concerned, however - the D'Amandas - feels no malice, but rather even a sense of peace. In 1995 the owners recalled awakening on several occasions, sometimes to the sounds of something falling. Always they reported "feeling not alone" and sensing a presence in their room. Then a sensation came over them which they described as comforting - "not unlike a hug" - and they always returned to sleep peacefully. Mrs. D'Amanda sensed "presence" in the nursery upstairs and on the third floor. Several times at night she went into the baby's room to find her up and awake, as if listening to someone.

Others found these events shocking. One night a sitter heard the baby cry. On the monitor, another voice in the room cooed, "Oh, it's all right. It's all right." Either the malice has faded after three generations or it was never there; either a ghost has grown more reasonable, or it was at first misunderstood.

Spirits of the Great Hill

The Fyfe and Drum (Ontario)

[Many battlefields are thought to be haunted, and Youngstown stands over a big one. If that's not enough reason for it to have spirits, nearby Fort Niagara has enough to spill over.]

Youngstown's colonial history might be said to have started in 1670 when French explorer LaSalle built a small fort just north of today's village. In the Colonial wars this region at the American side of the Niagara's charge into Ontario was swept by European, Colonial, and Native American armies, and was the scene of several engagements.

Much of the 1759 siege of Fort Niagara was launched from what would be today's business district in the western end of Youngstown. Inspired by the Christmas 1813 burning of Canada's Newark (today's Niagara-on-the-Lake), British and Native American forces made a return gift, singeing a swath from Youngstown to Buffalo, sending towns and homes up with the smoke. The peaceful rebuilding took place gradually, but by the 1840s Youngstown was a place of shops, businesses, and homes, some of them splendid. The harbor played a role in this growth, like the soil that proved marvelous for fruit trees.

Little stands from before the burning period in what would be today's Youngstown, but the house at 440 Main Street may be one of them, and there was surely something on the site before. There could be a horde of angry spirits in the region, but today's Fyfe & Drum, an atmospheric colonial pub, seems to have harnessed only the placid - or the puzzled. There's no accounting for the signs of them here - the usual low-key poltergeist grab-bag, as it sounds - but it took a psychic to give faces to the many reports.

"Rudolf" is a little boy they think may be from a family of German immigrants. He appears in either knickers or lederhosen. He may have died of scarlet fever, and remains with us because he "wasn't ready." Like many spooks, he may not know he's dead, and has no idea what space or time he's in. At the moments he wakes into our world, he's fascinated by modern conveniences, especially the lights.

"The Judge" is a pleasant, distinguished man who appears in back of the Fyfe & Drum tending a garden. He arrives pleasantly enough, expecting to indulge his hobby, but at times seems baffled by the look of the lot he sees.

The pacing "Anna" awaits a love gone long, a young man who may have set out upon lake or war and never returned. The real Anna must often have paused in her housekeeping and grieved; in this image she appears today. What psychic imprint or "eidetic image" would make a woman return to this place in just this guise, from this point in her life? Why does any ghost do what it does?

We should not forget the proximity of the Fort in any theory we have about paranormal activity in the vicinity of Youngstown. As *Shadows* pointed out, this was a region of ancient mystery even deeper than its colonial antiquity. A series of forts, Euroamerican and otherwise, dating almost to the time of Christ have been reported beneath the site of today's Fort Niagara, and signs of some ancient disaster - hundreds of burned Native American skeletons - acknowledged. If you believe in paranormal zones, this ought to be one of them. Thank God the spooks use the energy here to be friendly.

Spooks, Spirits, Specters

THE BOX OF RED JACKET'S BONES (ERIE)

[What about Irving encourages originals? First settler Amos Sottle (1773-1849), pulled his canoe into the mouth of the Cattaraugus Creek in 1796 and became an inveterate collector of curiosities. Proclaiming Chautauqua County "the world's wonder corner," Irving's Everett Burmaster (1890-1965) followed in Sottle's footsteps. His own oddity-file included a fiddle made of a horse's skull and a bow from its leg. It played, but its music must have been ghastly. Word holds that the set was presented as a gift to Abe Lincoln, who wisely declined it. It may also have been demonstrated to Handsome Lake, and perhaps was what inspired the otherwise rational Iroquois prophet to blast fiddle music with such fury in his "Code" that founded the Longhouse religion. Burmaster was a volunteer archaeologist for the Buffalo Museum, to which he willed his notes and papers. Two of his interests came together in this spook tale from the lakeshore Reservation.]

In property disputes like divorces, the Iroquois sometimes divided things in the Solomonic sense, breaking them literally in two. One house so treated on the Cattaraugus Reservation was "the old Stevenson place" where relatives had pulled away the kitchen-ell. Ruth Stevenson, the step-daughter of Red Jacket (1750-1830), had lived here, and in her arms the great Seneca orator had breathed his last, thanking the Great Spirit that he had lived his life as a Native American.

One foggy night in his youth, Everett Burmaster and a pal he calls simply "Parker" were on their way to visit Parker's aunt. They heard a strange rustling as they passed the old Stevenson place, and a mass of mist from behind the disfigured house moved toward them. Floating like fog, it neared the missing part of the house and became a man in a long dark coat and beaver hat. The boys watched it drift through a fence and vanish behind a tree. They noted lace-like cuffs over its hands.

They gasped out their tale at the house of Parker's aunt. White guests laughed, but an aged Seneca was understanding. "It's old Red Jacket. You've seen his ghost, that's all. He's been seen there many times. Ruth Stevenson kept his bones in a little coffin in her house so that grave robbers wouldn't steal them. It's a warning."

The grown Burmaster determined to obtain that box. He pulled all his strings and at last beheld the small split-covered cherry coffin. When Red Jacket was taken from his first rest in South Buffalo, an undertaker hid the remains to keep them safe. The Two Guns family heard of the matter and hurried to Buffalo to save the honored bones from the ever-present danger of trophy-hunters. These were kept in the fabled coffin on the lakeside Res until 1884 and the great ceremony of their reburial in Buffalo's Forest Lawn Cemetery.

Some Seneca chuckle that the bones under Red Jacket's imposing statue may not be his. Many Native American cemeteries were relocated about Western New York, and the quality control was, let us say, lax. There is even the suspicion that the contents of many ancient graveyards were mixed with roadbuilding material. Native American bones could be beneath us as we walk or drive about our streets. Still, we think one coffin may have been well-marked. Somebody looking like Red Jacket is widely supposed to walk now and again on the Cattaraugus Res.

Spirits of the Great Hill

Flittin' on the Dock of the Bay (Erie)

In 1805 Nathaniel Titus bought 320 acres of Blasdell land for five bucks, and built the tavern and inn on the lake called "The Willink Hotel." In 1815 Zenas Barker acquired the spread and humbly renamed it "Barkersville." It hosted a short-lived post office. In those days the bay was deeper and nowhere near as rocky as it is today. That made it a major thoroughfare in times of war, and the inn here housed many a soldier.

Today's Dock at the Bay has a little something for everyone. A lakefront reef-and-beef eatery and banquet hall, it's one of the county's older buildings. Summer volleyball and sunsets over the waves appeal to those on this side of the daylight; who knows what appeases those on the other? Maybe they just like to slip in between the lines.

One of the spooks they think is haunting the place tried it when with the living; it earned him his ticket into spirit. Captain James Byrd fought alongside Admiral Perry on the Niagara River in the War of 1812. Perry's ship anchored in the bay in 1814 and Byrd's girlfriend waited at the Willink Hotel; Byrd slipped overboard to visit her, a nocturnal swim as risky as Leander's for Hero. After a few hours and a double shot of his baby's love Byrd came back, but was court-martialed for desertion and shot for real in Erie, PA, and buried in nearby Hamburg. They get damn serious about this war business.

James Byrd's cousin Amos fought in the same war in the naval battle of Black Rock (now Buffalo). His grave is in nearby Bayview, but a piece of his tombstone is reputedly part of today's Dock at the Bay. In the mid-1800s a scuffle spilled outside and went ballistic. In the fighting the owner's front steps were destroyed and a piece of Amos Byrd's tombstone shot off, allegedly refashioned into a doorstep of the inn that would be today's Dock at the Bay. No wonder Byrd family spirits are restless. Who knows when the rumors started? Written ghost reports date from 1932.

As the millennium dawns, the Dock at the Bay seems blessed with a mess of festive spirits. Few members of the staff lack some story or other, and they are encouraged to be forthcoming. A hostess calls the spooks "my friends." A bartender hears them calling his name in faint, artificial voices. We advise a field trip to see for yourself, but do not expect a lineup of spirits. They seem generic, though merry, and there may be too many to count. McKenzie's War was ongoing in 1837 and 1838. On the New Year's Day between them, a band of Americans gathered at Comstock's Tavern (now the Dock at the Bay) for their invasion of Canada. Their foray should have taken much whiskey to launch. It may have been ill-planned and abortive from our viewpoint, but it's given some members of the Maple Leaf nation sixteen decades of cheerful crowing about their victory over the United States... a few hundred of its guys with hangovers, anyway. Roll over, Napoleon, and tell Pizarro the news.

Spooks, Spirits, Specters

CHAUTAUQUA-ALLEGANY SPIRITS:
ELLICOTTVILLE: BOOS AND BREWS

The Monroe Street building that houses today's Ellicottville Brewing Company had a rough start, psychically speaking. Built around 1865, it did a good long stint as a funeral home, which always puts people in mind of the returning dead. Following that was its service as a church, which, as we see throughout this book, is also connected with paranormal folklore, if not the presence of the spooks themselves. An altar still stands upstairs. There's tragedy here, and maybe mystery.

In 1994 the young, hale owner of the building was found hanging in a room upstairs. Between death and discovery were days of summer heat, and the sign that launched the search was said to be blood and fluids, dripping through a ceiling. The police ended their investigation with the verdict of suicide, and there the matter stands, but there are still grumblings in the town that there may be more to the situation. *The man was found dead and hanging* is the only statement to which everybody will agree. The sense of something unsettled began attaching itself to the site.

For a few months after the death, EBC employees would not stay in the building alone. Water was found running in the morning when people showed for duty, seeming to have turned itself on overnight. Sinks in the restrooms still play the same game. The room in which the hanging victim's body was found was later used for storage by the coffee house next door. Many of its employees were spooked to enter it, even those who didn't know of its past.

So far the spookery still hasn't resolved itself into sightings, which isn't all that strange. Ghosts - apparitions - are only one form of psychic phenomena, and they don't always manifest at psychically active sites. There is the usual poltergeist play here at the EBC. Sometimes an apparent computer glitch takes place, and the kitchen gets phantom orders no waitress has punched in. The staff joke that it's the former owner, ordering his favorite take-out, showing a fondness for the EBC steak focaccia. It would figure that we'd all be vegans in the afterlife. May those imaginary delicacies be savored.

The Lily Dale people pick up some energy here. On one occasion psychically-connected folk on the way to or from this mystical mecca stepped just inside the door, then could go no further. Among psychic professionals that's an unusually dramatic reaction to spirit-presence, and, fortunately for the business, a rare one among people of any stripe to the Ellicottville Brewing Company.

There's nothing gloomy about this Monroe Street pub, the home of fine food and spirits of the comestible kind for half a dozen years. Seeming the personification of laughter and life, the EBC is cheerily alight on the many festive weekends of the year and whenever nearby Holiday Valley Ski Area - visible from many Monroe Street porches - is in season. Behind the complacent veil, however, after the lights are dim, in the hours-later echoes of conversation, in the private places and when the living least are looking, there may be another level to its activity, as if some other presence is crying out as it can another message.

Spirits of the Great Hill

Chautauqua: Fatal Bellman

[Beginning with Civil War hero Ulysses S. Grant and including Teddy Roosevelt, nine presidents have visited the Chautauqua Institute. Some of them, including luminaries like Marian Anderson, Susan B. Anthony, Amelia Earhart, Thomas Edison, Duke Ellington, and Robert Kennedy, have graced the Institute's Athenaeum Hotel. Other guests of the 1881 Athenaeum may not have entered their names in the register.]

Though the first hotel in the world to have electric lights, Chautauqua's magnificent Athenaeum is a proud throwback in almost every other respect. Its architecture is like that of Victorian-era resort hotels like those in Saratoga Springs, NY, and its decor within is classic. In scale, the Athenaeum reminds us of Gormenghast, Mervyn Peake's fantasy castle-city. It is voluminous - cyclopean - surmounting a shady hill overlooking Chautauqua Lake in the southwestern corner of the Western Door. The Athenaeum winds in, around, and upon itself as if it could somehow contain greater space than the sum of its outer dimensions, and greater intrigue than its age and inhabitants could justify. It could accommodate a world of mystery.

In the community all around Chautauqua is the feeling that this illustrious old hotel has piled up a number of haunters in its 121 seasons, and a variety of manifestations. At the Athenaeum itself, though, there seems no public tradition of ghosts, and it's no wonder. Surely any native spirits who linger here would observe Chautauqua's stately discretion, and, accordingly, the guests seem completely untroubled. Some of the longest-returning know nothing of ghosts, among them one ninety-year-old former high school principal who has been coming to the Athenaeum since her girlhood. This doesn't prove that the building is not haunted anymore than one report would prove that it is. It isn't unusual to find a wide divergence of opinion upon almost any subject of paranormal interest, even at the heart of some persuasive cases. In one of the most famous and developed poltergeist outbreaks in the twentieth century, some living in the troubled house itself doubted anything untoward. The staff are the ones that seem to know it at the Athenaeum.

A "cold spot," one of those potentially psychic earmarks that are so telling to researchers, has been reported within the Athenaeum, as was, at least once, a robust poltergeist. (A young staffer found his bed shaking under him a whole night, costing him any hope of sleep.) One of the oldest traditional tales concerns a tiny girl who lost her life in the hotel, probably in the early part of the twentieth century. On the day when an elevator was under repair, the story goes, the doors on one floor were yawning open. To the toddler on her trike exploring the wing the open shaft seemed a cave of mystery, to be toured on wheels. She plummeted to her death. They say her plaintive bell can be heard, faintly, as if even she wishes not to alarm. It comes in many parts of the broad hotel; perhaps she's still exploring.

Generations of guests return each summer, some whose grandparents brought them here as children and who bring their grandchildren in return. The Athenaeum seems to inspire such spirit in its mortal guests; little wonder that some might return after-life, even those who merely worked here, ensuring others' comfort. One reported apparition is of a former manager, evidently approving his Athenaeum stint so much that he keeps coming back.

Spooks, Spirits, Specters

LIMESTONE: NEW IRELAND

"There won't be much there," warned teacher-historian Paul Lewis, driving the old gent through Allegany State Park that May day in 1998. "Even its foundations are hard to spot. You'll see, though, why it was such a shrine." His passenger already knew. The memory of the turn-of-the-century Irish settlement in the trees was almost mystical to those whose families had left it. Before his death he wanted to see it again.

This "New Ireland" - his grandparents' first home after leaving the old one - had flourished from the 1860s to the early 1930s. A school, houses, farms, and community were here. Some of its folk came straight from Ireland and some from New York tenements, but the green hills must have reminded them all of the land whose famine and despair they'd fled. They worked in lumber, tanning, and the new oil industry. Always, though, they kept the farms; that call from the land was ingrained. Oil and acculturation sent their descendants to far parts, but none forgot; so many lived and died to get here. For a long time the twenty-five acre site was lost.

The first sight of it shocked Paul Lewis and his passenger. The long, one-lane dirt road teemed with cars and people. By an incredible coincidence, another old man had gone into the hilly Allegany woods a day or two earlier on his own identical pilgrimage; the hundred-plus party was here to find him.

Near Thunder Rocks Charles Sheets, 82, had entered the vast verdance seeking his former home. His children had tried to dissuade him, as did the locals - the rugged tract holding New Ireland is 25,000 acres - but since his wife had died, his life needed this one last thing. Equipped with little more than a metal-detector for the bag of coins he'd buried as a child, the California man seemed convinced that, once near the spot, he could find his childhood home by just the numinous energy many forbears' lives had vested it. There may have been logic in this; there must be something to a site associated with so many psychic events. Here are three:

* A woman who couldn't have known rode her horse through "Little Ireland." A feeling took her. She dismounted, sat, and sobbed uncontrollably. A witness confirms the event. The deaths, 'the sorrows,' the trials... Had all this been what she had felt?

* A hunter waited game in "Little Ireland." At the eye-corners he sensed motion; he turned to see a man in a dark suit and an old-timey bowler hat cross the path as if on an errand and vanish into the trees. In the 1880s this would have been a street that the apparition had just walked.

* A research team sought a "Little Ireland" headstone among hundreds in a Limestone churchyard. Well-weathered, few read easily. One of the dogs circled a certain grave, barking, hackles up, eyes on a single spot as if it was a living being. The stone was Jeremiah McCarty's, the one they'd sought, as if dog and spirit had colluded. It was eerie; napes tingled. The other dog quivered and wouldn't near it.

As for Charles Sheets: At the rectory of St. Patrick's, the Limestone church at which he'd asked directions before his last hike and talked to his last person, his children prayed to find him. They did, near a slope where he may have slipped, then rested, then... They blinked tears, then gave thanks. Why not? He was home.

Spirits of the Great Hill

Ashford: The Ashford Hollow Witch

[A few yards off of a hilly road is a stone whose inscription reads: Lewis Disch, 1794-1882; Salome Disch, 1798-1862; Sophia Disch, 1833-1909.]

There must have been a sense of otherness about "Sophie" Disch. Her stone - and that of her tiny clan - sits apart, near no other graves, near nothing standing but trees. Maybe nothing's odd in this. People liked their space back then. They also tended to get their lives set early and keep them that way. Marriage, kids, family... If you were a woman, you had a slim window. The stock of gents around here, marriageable or no, would have been thin in the mid-1800s, and always looking for that crop of females younger. Miss the cycle, and... in the next life, maybe.

Maybe Sophie never got the time. Her parents were old for the day - 39 and 35 - when they had her, their only child - that also was odd - and she'd lived with them until their deaths. By the time she was of marriageable age, her folks might have needed some taking care of. She'd have been the one to do it, and that high farm would have been endless labor. Her mother died at 64 when Sophie would have been 29, and if her father - who could have fought in the War of 1812 and made it to 88 - had been in the slightest infirm... Even before her life was her own it must have been too late. Well, that was her life, except for the last 27 years of it, scratching an existence selling dairy products, likely milk, to a cheese factory. Maybe she liked it that way, alone. Long-living in the woody hills could gnarl a personality as much as the elements did a countenance. From somewhere it got started that she was a witch, one whose power and emanations manifest still.

West Valley Central teacher Gary Philips set out to track the story of the Ashford Hollow Witch. He found an old-timer, a girl during Sophie's life, who'd lived all her own in East Otto. They'd treated the old woman poorly, she said, when her parents passed away. She had a witchy appearance and a big dog. When they found her dead at her house, possibly of a heart attack, in the act of chopping wood - at 76 - she was wearing thirteen petticoats, doubtless to keep warm. The poor soul. Thank God this was no witch-persecuting century; thank another for the persecutions that have been. Something about Sophie draws rumors nearly a century after her death.

The Otto old-timer who recalled this tale has since gone on to her peace, sorry with how she and the other children had been to the Ashford Hollow Witch, maybe then knowing age from within. On the early spring late-afternoon we visited her grave, deer fed in the high fields, twilight casting their shadows in stalks across the road. April's reviving waters seeped underfoot, and, the young sun every day bolder, we could sense life and power returning to the season. It seemed a long way from darkness, magic, and rough, solitary lives. Still, an old photo of the witch's grave showed an odd path beaten and ringing it, leading from the trees, not the road. There was the hint of an arc in April 2001. What procession comes to it from the woods? Who or what dances here midnights?

Spooks, Spirits, Specters

FREDONIA: THE WHITE INN

[If the pair of maples fronting Fredonia's Inn are ever willfully felled (the story goes), the property reverts to the heirs of the White family who planted them in 1825. There's no proof they're that old or that the contract is in force, but The White Inn's owners put time and energy into keeping them hale, as they are in Spring 2001. A White heir may have already foreclosed.]

The original home was built in 1811 by Mayflower descendant Squire White, Chautauqua County's first medical doctor. In 1868 son Devillo replaced the original wood frame house with a solider Victorian Second Empire, the core of the structure standing now. In 1919 daughter Isabel sold the mansion to Murray Hill Bartley and, unhappy with its conversion to an inn, was said to scowl from a rocker on the porch next door all through the course of the Classically-inspired addition on the front, that is, the Main Street side. Many presume she's the haunter - one of them, anyway - most fond of "her" room, #314. Today in the back Concord Dining Room the Inn keeps a picture of Miss White, her sharp, intently gazing profile framed by light. It does no discredit to either eagles or her gaze to style it "aquiline," that flinty silhouette.

Route 20 was once a major east-west thoroughfare, and for decades The White Inn prospered. In the 1930s it was "discovered" by Duncan Hines and listed in his fifty-strong "Family of Fine Restaurants." Most are gone, but (like Philadelphia's Bookbinder's and New Orleans' Antoine's) The White Inn thrives. It was touch-and-go in the sixties and seventies after the construction of the Interstate-90. In 1980 a pair of scholars, David Bryant and David Palmer, began a thirteen-year renovation. Today's splendid White Inn is the result.

The Inn is composed of 1868 and 1919 wings. The older undergoes the psychic reports, but for one: In the men's room of the bar, a urinal flushed itself manically on several occasions until an owner simply addressed the spirit. "I know you're here. Now please stop." We agree with the respectful approach.

It's natural that many gifted visitors pass through Fredonia, only six or so miles from Lily Dale. On three occasions, professional psychics have told owner Robert Contiguglia that his "presences" are benign, though an actual murder-suicide in the late 1960s has fed speculation that at least one spirit here might be troubled. One owner, a severe alcoholic, took up a shotgun and ended his own despair, taking with it two lives, his wife's and his own.

Psychic sightings persist. One wedding-guest on the third floor saw the apparition of a young girl, thirteen or so years old, in gauzy white apparel and with long auburn hair. She just stood, arms out and palms uplifted. The witness turned back into a room to call for others; when she glanced back into the hall, the girl was gone.

One of the most dramatic events recorded at The White Inn involved a night of sounds, like furniture moving violently, in the extra room of the Presidential Suite. The guests opened the door, expecting to see the results of a nocturnal upheaval that sounded like the Mike Tyson honeymoon special. The only sign of motion was a light, a rotating globe that had turned itself on.

Spirits of the Great Hill

Jamestown: Little Lucy's Theater

["All self-respecting theaters have their ghosts," says Pat Brininger, Director of Marketing at the Lucy-Desi Museum. Clearly, "The Reg" has no problem of self-image.]

Jamestown's original Palace Theater was a vaudeville and movie house built in 1923, state-of-the-art and magnificent for that decade. In later ones it would decline. Today (with the Lucy-Desi Museum) it's enveloped by the multi-use Reg Lenna Civic Center, renamed after local industrialist Reginald Lenna ("Le-*nay*"). This owner of Blackstone (washers and dryers) Corporation gave the first million of the three-plus needed for the 1990 renovation, in whose course were some natural curiosities.

One of the "Reg" theater's most distinctive features is the "dancing ladies" on the friezes of balcony and box seats, pale Classical bas-relief figures on deep teal, a striking effect reminiscent of Wedgwood porcelain. Little wonder that, over the years, many were missing or damaged; once rain fell through the roof onto late singer Harry Chapin, mid-song on stage. The Cleveland company that had made the originals still existed and summoned up replacements. Near the end of the overhaul, the volunteers climbed scaffolding and wrote their names on the dome's inside rim, to be found at the next renovation. Two days before the October 12, 1990 grand opening, there was not a seat in the house, and locals were commencing a steady freak. The Canadian company to which they'd been sent for restoration had never missed an event, and counseled patience. Sure enough, all went well for the full house that included many arts-and-politics dignitaries.

"The Reg" is not the Jamestown theater named for illustrious comedienne Lucille Ball. (That one - the remodeled Allen Opera House, now the Lucille Ball Little Theater of Jamestown - is a tiny walk around the corner from the Reg which takes up most of a block.) Jamestown's most famous daughter frequented the old Palace as a child, thus we call it "Little Lucy's"; and it may have several recognizable spooks. Folklore of course presumes the two women, two children, and a Black man were killed in either of two late 19th century fires, one at a hotel or an earlier theater on the spot, another at the nearby Allen. Folklore also supplies a scandal, presuming them a wealthy woman running off with her lover, her children, and their nurse. Tours and rehearsals seem to bring them out.

Unexplained children's voices have been heard in the dressing rooms, and a tall Black man in top hat and tails is reported in the private box aside a bejewelled lady. Seen near the orchestra pit is "the Gypsy," a scarved, trinketed shade, possibly the aforementioned nurse. A woman in white seemed to watch one closed rehearsal from the box; at another, a racket started in an empty balcony whenever a rehearsing soloist came to a certain song. A woman leading a tour told a little boy by himself to hustle up and rejoin the group. He smiled, ran down the hall, and vanished.

At every theater a starry "ghost light" stays on at all times, usually thought to be for stagehands entering the vast dark space. At the Reg they joke that theirs is for the ghosts' content. Thus they can enjoy the inspiring dome, the "dancing ladies," and other glories of the renovated Reg, all to themselves, all the dim otherside of day as the earthly sleep.

Spooks, Spirits, Specters

The Western Finger Lakes:
Penn Yann:
Portrait of the Grey Lady

[Penn Yan's Oliver House surely deserves its own ghost. From the sounds of things the one it has may be linked to a painting within it.]

From *Shadows* we might be familiar with "pioneer prophetess" Jemima Wilkinson (1752-1819), founder of a community around Penn Yann and the Y-shaped Keuka. She may have been charismatic and at times comical, but the only thing sure is that she was controversial, this "Publick Universal Friend of Mankind," whom "the Mouth of the Lord hath named." Some think her literary treatment was harsher because of her sex, but we wonder; no possible contemporary punches could have been pulled against male Western Door community founders like Thomas Lake Harris, John Murray Spear, and Elbert Hubbard.

It may be no coincidence that the mystical "Friend" was drawn to this region of strange ruins and ancient wonder. A historic curiosity hangs to this day in the Oliver House, seat of the Yates County Historical Society. The notion of a spirit attached long ago to this unflattering portrait of the Friend. Ravishing in her youth, by the early 1800s she was aged and ailing, and we could see her self-respecting spook wanting to screen the manly portrait for simple vanity. (It makes a tolerable Thomas Jefferson, or maybe a more current Ed McMahon in an Elvira wig.) One of Jemima's devoted young followers recounted her marital troubles to the picture as if it were the living Friend, believing it gave counsel back. Word has it that, as a stricture of its gifting to the society, no reproductions of it, including photos, were to be made. There's a story also that no one could, and that folkloric disaster struck all who tried.

A reporter and photographer from a Rochester paper allegedly came to the Oliver House to defy augury. The ever-protective staff refused the attempt. The pair plunked down, skimming Wisbey's *Pioneer Prophetess* and plotting their next move. A lens fell from the reporter's new specs. "The Friend has spoken," said one of the staff.

As the reporter talked to one elderly dame, the photographer edged around her and took aim at the Friend. The flash failed. Another camera, the same snidely strategem. "Did you sneak a picture?" the writer asked his mate as they left. He thought he had, but it never developed.

Two other reporters from a northwestern state couldn't understand why their camera, too, misfired when pointed at the Friend. "We calls that witchery," one said after repeated failure.

Some Oliver House staff dismiss the idea of an enchantment upon the portrait, but there may be other tales of the Friend. Arch Merrill recalls regional lore about her frequent return, the spectral "Grey Lady." She's a historic specter about the lakes, woods, and hills, a patroness of lost children and hurting hikers, leading them to help or help to them.

Spirits of the Great Hill

Elmira: Seth Roberts
[This august Western Door spirit is one of the world's most famous.]

Before her first psychic experience in 1963 - the arrival of her alter ego, the now famous "Seth" - Jane Roberts (1929-1984) had ambitions as a writer. Though she had published poetry and fiction in national magazines, a legendary career did not surely loom. A native of Saratoga Springs, NY, Roberts had attended Skidmore College and married a painter, Robert Butts. The couple lived in Elmira, NY, at the eastern edge of the Spirit Way, scene of virtually this entire episode.

Like many, Jane Roberts commenced her psychic ventures with the Ouija board, disdained for various reasons by many professionals. Soon, though, Roberts found that she could speak for the other side without the need of aids. In brief fits and starts the personality of "Seth" - a wise man so old he doesn't fit into current pictures of history - began to resolve itself, first from various other entities who claimed to be communicating, and then through different means of divination to the final one - channeling (speaking in trance) through the inspired Roberts.

Roberts went on to compose several books of Seth's direct teachings, as well as novels and poetry inspired by them. The Seth material is basically a recycling, with a spiritualist "take," of many fairly familiar New Age ideas. The personality of Seth comes across as a benevolent uncle, and the books done in his name have found a wide and passionate audience. While the Seth dialogues are certainly long and imaginative, they do not seem to represent truly astonishing instances of psychic phenomena or prophecy. Seth does not speak in languages unknown to Roberts, for instance, nor are the few cases of clairvoyance or precognition involved in his transmissions very convincing. The whole business could be fantasy-wish-fulfillment on the part of their creator, Jane Roberts. Other factors, though, complicate the case.

People out for fame and money do not usually balk when both are in sight. Though the general effect of the Seth material did no harm to the author's ego or finances, Roberts never attempted to capitalize as she might have. She never sought the huge audiences, major cash, and mega-tours that could have loomed, nor pondered exercise videos or a marriage to Ted Turner. Most channeling sessions were in her home with small gatherings.

Also to be reckoned is the sheer formidability of the Seth material; it seems within the range of the unconscious mind of a bright, educated adult, but just barely. Most of the very long dialogues were turned out extempore. Furthermore, there were psychokinetic experiences in Roberts' file. Though she seldom condescended to experiment with such abilities in public, she was once observed levitating a table. Roberts may have been one of the most gifted psychics the Western Door has known.

Sadly for this world, an illness sent Jane Roberts from it to join her confidants at a relatively young age. Yet she left behind a body of work that made the world a different place for many receptive to her message. How few of us do more.

Spooks, Spirits, Specters

COHOCTON: MESSAGE FROM MEHITABEL

In her last year of teaching at Genesee Valley Central School, Fran Ambroselli bought the rundown, 17-room Italianate villa (1860) of Samuel Fitch Woodworth, planning to restore it to a Victorian country inn. It would be work. Nature and neglect had rusted the plumbing completely. For ten years the only tenants had been raccoons, gnawing the electrical wiring to shreds. The local teens who used the house as their hangout did no harm to it or themselves. With help from family and spot-duty pros - plumbers, electricians, carpenters - the work commenced in August 1998. It didn't stop until the night before the first guests were due.

Soon to be on the National Register of Historic Places, the Villa Serendip is now a thriving B&B. Near a river and a day's walk from an Underground Railroad station, the Woodworth House may have been one itself. A trapdoor, crawlspace, and false basement were found. While not known to be haunted by any named apparition, there is something about it. "Maybe there are spirits here," says Ms. Ambroselli. "Whenever we need help, it shows up in the walls." This she means.

In the long and all-hours pro-am restoration, needed tools and items so often simply "appeared," falling out of opened panels in walls, that it became proverbial. Once when Ambroselli was scraping woodwork and wishing for a chisel, a pack of new ones "came out of the wall." At other times it was matches, aspirin, a sharp knife, and even a fold-up table.

At first Ms. Ambroselli rationalized. The former owners went on hardware-store shopping-sprees, leaving supplies in the attic, from which, in theory, they could fall through the hollow walls of the house's "balloon" construction to any level beneath. Still, this doesn't explain the timing. "The things that come through the walls are always the tools we need - just when we need them. Maybe there are spirits here." Maybe.

The house's first owner was Samuel Fitch Woodworth, a thrice-married farmer whose family came to the Finger Lakes in 1835. His three granddaughters loved the home so much that they wanted to turn it into a tea room; it would be hard to think of them leaving it. Samuel was descended of Walter Woodworth, prime ancestor of most American Woodworths, who was born in 1612 in Lancashire and landed in Massachusetts Colony in 1631. Walter and Elisabeth Tyson Woodworth had six daughters, one named Mehitabel. "A witch's name," says Ms. Ambroselli, "just asking to be burned at the stake." Records show that this girl, Sam Woodworth's great-aunt, was indeed among those accused of witchcraft, and she died afterward, though we aren't sure she was executed. She may have been epileptic.

So... does some essence of Mehitabel linger? "She was probably a good witch," says Ms. Ambroselli. "This house is watched by good spirits." Here they're known mostly by their sounds. Civil War veteran Henry Paterson Woodworth may be the one whistling riffs from a sprightly old ballad every summer during blueberry season. The baby that cries and coos may be Samuel Woodworth's daughter who died at three months. She's the most touching; she seems the most pleased to see all the guests, whom neither she nor any other spirit here ever alarms.

Spirits of the Great Hill

Canandaigua:

Eliza of the Trackways

[Eliza O'Brien lived by the railroad in Canandaigua, caught up in all the excitement of fast travel (for the day) and people from far parts. She had a normal-enough life before the Civil War, as her tale begins.]

As wood was loaded on a diamond-stack locomotive, a statuesque young woman named Eliza passed a debonair blade named O'Brien. He did no service to his sex. He married Eliza, then soon vanished along with a good share of her money, doubtless along the tracks by which they'd met. She had reason to despair them, if something besides her judgement was to be blamed. Big, strong, and bent on revenge, Eliza now-O'Brien launched herself down the tracks, scouring cities and towns, never finding the bounder who'd done her wrong. Soon her untiring anger encompassed all men.

She wouldn't ride trains if men were engineers or dine where men were cooks. She waited by schoolhouses and pulled girls aside, chiding them on evil male natures. To women's groups she declaimed upon the "perfidiousness of men." The public knew her as the woman in hoop skirts, walking the tracks in all weather.

There was sympathy for Eliza, addled and wronged, even among the men she reviled. By her cross-tied highway many families gave her lodging, and the Fishers community was her second home. Railmen, though, feared her temper, and she was blamed in at least one head-on accident near Fishers. A witness reported an old woman running on the tracks at about the time a main switch was opened. No one could file a charge, but she became a sort of living totem, as if she could cast ill-luck.

In June 1893 Eliza of the Trackways was laid to rest in the Catholic Cemetery of Canandaigua. The passage over may have mellowed a fell spirit. Thereafter, many appearances of the track-ways Eliza were associated with good and salvation. One stormy night at the century's turn, a shadow-figure in billowing skirts darted ahead of a train full of Irish immigrants. She was surreally fast, but still losing ground, and the engineer blasted the whistle. At last he slammed on his brakes, then ran out to check. No skirted woman was found, but the train rested at the edge of a huge washout, saved from a disastrous plunge into Irondequoit Creek.

At other times it's the old Eliza. In summer 1918 the crew of a train stopped near the station and dined at the Fishers Hotel. The train took off by itself and ran out of steam near the Pittsford canal. The only witness reported an old woman near the engine just before its solo venture.

That same war-season, troop trains passed to and fro. Tracks were carefully patrolled for fear of sabotage, and no one was allowed under the bridge by the Auburn tracks. The guards near Eliza's old haunts were especially jumpy. Some nights they saw a figure under this bridge who never responded to challenge. Shots were even fired, but she came again. Then they heard about Eliza O'Brien.

The branchline haunted by Eliza's shade has been closed since 1960, and used since only by cyclists and hikers. One of them may take nothing, and leave not even footprints.

Spooks, Spirits, Specters

Genesee Country Ghosts:

Le Roy: The Legend of Buttermilk Falls

Vermonter Isaac Scanck had a beautiful daughter, and hoped to make a good match for her. Alas, her heart went out to Moses Tull, a dashing rogue and maybe the handsomest man in the Champlain Valley. He was in no hurry to make up his mind about marriage, and in any case was hardly a model farmer. With daughter Anna in tow, the family set out for farther parts, but a Green Mountain boy followed. It was Moses Tull, his own heart, perhaps for once, the one smitten. He followed them to the Genesee Valley, rough country in the late eighteenth century. Here he set up his own homestead, and set out to do right. The young couple begged old Isaac to give his consent to their marriage.

Having listened enough, the father gave his judgment: his daughter could be married to him when Moses Tull, by his own efforts, was able to support her in reasonable style. For a while this seemed like it might come about. Moses Tull worked harder than he ever had before; but by the spring, Ezra Watkins and sly-eyed sister Ina arrived in the valley. Ina was as darkly beautiful as Anna was flaxen-fair. Ina, too, was captured by the silver-tongued Moses, and for at least once the blonde had less fun. The prospect of matrimonial days and nights with his betrothed was forgotten in the name of afternoon dalliances with Ina.

While the responsible men - Ezra Watkins and Isaac Scanck - cleared land and farmed and Anna did household chores, Moses did service of a different sort in the woods with the captivating Ina. One day as she was at her churning, Anna gave over to her despair and went walking in the woods alone. She came to the bank above the falls and looked over the sheer wall. What did she see in this state of mind but the two lovers by the deep pool, lost in each other? Anna dragged her half-filled churn to the edge, tossing it and its creamy contents into the stream, thinking doubtless to disrupt the lovers. It went over the falls and struck Ina, killing her instantly. Moses, broken-hearted, followed her into the grave before long.

Anna, fed up with Colonial inconstancy, ran off and married a Seneca chief. Isaac and Ezra - perhaps each consoling the other over moonshine - were killed in a fire that burned the former's house.

Legend holds that on the right sunset of a warm spring day, two phantoms are seen about the spot of the tragedy, just glimpsed in the eye-corners at the crack of twilight, that old Celtic time of magic, the instant between night and day. Their identities are unclear. Are they Ina, the dark-headed, and Moses, fickle at love in life, learning a noble constancy in death? Or are they Anna and her Seneca chief, come to mourn - or gloat - at the scene of her impulsive act? One constant remains, though. In the cascade and trough of the falls the creamy white of the original dump remains, as if it had taught the Buttermilk Falls how to churn.

Spirits of the Great Hill

Groveland: The Abell House

The shadow-town by the forks of the Genesee was a trading post and tavern when the man who'd give it his name first set his eyes upon it. Hired in 1792 to subdivide the Genesee Valley, Charles Williamson was a manly man, a frontier Clark Gable who'd had affairs with at least one doe-eyed disciple of "pioneer prophetess" Jemima Wilkinson. In two years Williamsburg was a would-be city laid out into avenues, boasting stores, houses, smithy, still, and track.

Geneseo and Mt. Morris left no room for another Yankee metropolis, and Williamsburg ebbed after fifteen fitful years. Today only farmers and hunters tread its fading streets. The ghost-city though, so neatly laid-out, made a fine spot for mansion-building, or so thought Colonel and State Senator D. H. Abell.

Built in 1860, the brick Italianate villa on Mt. Morris Road had no equal in the valley. A paper of the day prays that its owner and his estimable lady "long be spared to enjoy... the many comforts and conveniences so fully demonstrated." As if the Colonel needed any encouraging. He hosted Valley society "jovially and lavishly" into the 1870s. In his last illness, his doctors conferred at his bedside. He asked his nurse the verdict. "You're sure to die," she replied.

The Colonel, an avid gamer, raised himself up and said weakly, "Bet you a fifty I don't." But he did, and now rests in the family plot uphill from his manse, one of the oldest White burying-places in the Western Door. Its pines shelter names famous in the history of the east: Major James A. Birney, first Abolitionist (later Republican) candidate for president; a cousin of Charles Carroll, one of the Declaration signers; a first cousin of Robert E. Lee, his only relation fighting for the North; and veterans of many wars.

The Abell mansion passed to W. A. Wadsworth, then to fox hunter Captain Martin. It was never tenanted after 1902, but ghostly rumors come from the late 1800s. A peddler was said killed with a rock nearby, and the house was plagued many nights by materializing versions of the murder-mineral.

A local minister used the vacant manse as a trysting-place, and Mt. Morris youths came to drink and play cards. Local jokers in sheets rushed in on the lads to teach them a lesson, and the gamers ran home in their fright. The papers reported apparitions and other weird effects, and soon no one would buy or rent the old place. By 1925 the *Rochester D&C* called it a "haunted structure" with no disclaimer.

On the old Seneca path, the site had its mysteries and omens. An ancient town had stood near, and the Boyd-Parker mission (1779) spent its night before destiny at Williamsburg, if not on the site of the mansion. One of its members killed a young Seneca whose skull and scalping knife may have been those found in the 1830s. His mate spread word to the Iroquois and British combing the area.

In 1933 the Abell House was taken by a fire of unknown causes. The *Livingston Republican* hoped it "burned 'to death' all the ghosts - if there is such a thing as death to a ghost," and that the site "would not be hoodooed by the uncanny and eerie stories that served to leave the old Abell place untenanted." It's said, though, that on the right midnight, Charles Williamson in a tricorn hat still gallops by on his pale charger, coursing the phantom avenues of his former village. We say it's the Colonel riding his dearest filly down from the family plot. Bet you a fifty.

Spooks, Spirits, Specters

CALEDONIA: FLOWER OF AVON

[On the north side of the road is a heavy boulder with a plaque, next which a lonely American flag is placed every Memorial Day.]

The old State Road between Caledonia and Avon was once the main thoroughfare between the Great Lakes and the east, and troops used it constantly in the War of 1812. One Saturday a group of American soldiers had camped along it on their way to Buffalo, and (as it was payday) two privates had caroused so rousingly that they were left where they lay, expected to rejoin the troop by the next evening. This sounds like a casual war, though one of its sergeants - Hamlet's fell one - was surely stricter in his arrest. His call would be coming soon.

About three the following afternoon, a woman living nearby heard a gunshot in the direction of the former camp. She didn't make much of it; there was, after all, a war going on. The old timers reflected, though, that the moon that night had come up over the Genesee Valley with a reddish tinge as though blood was on it, and wind and crickets had held an abnormal peace. Someone from the Hosmer household visited the empty camp and found the body of a soldier, shot in the forehead. Word was quickly sent to the commanding officer.

The two privates left behind - John Alexander and William Comfit - were indeed missing. The dead man was Alexander, but his pal Comfit was not to be found. Comfit was soon apprehended in the act of fleeing, and as he had twice the sum of his own pay - and poor Alexander's wallet was empty - he was tried for murder, convicted, and hung. Alexander was buried by the road, a short way from the site of his murder.

In the spring an unusual plant of a single stalk was noticed on the grave of the murdered soldier. At harvest time, it was a waxy lavender flower. Over the years more shoots formed a hazy outline of the grave and never spread beyond it. No one in the Genesee Valley had ever seen this type of flower, so the marvel grew.

Like others, Buffalo's George Clinton (called "the Honorable" in an old article) had often wondered about the curious little bloom on Alexander's fabled grave. In the summer of 1817 he found it - "False Gromwell" it was called - all over Alexander's home town of New Haven, Connecticut. How it came to shadow his Avon grave is a mystery that has never been solved. Perhaps the natural elements and whatever spirits within them stand for justice and compassion have this as their way of easing unfair passage, or at least tributing it. "False Gromwell," indeed; the first blossom should be named again so that this subtle shoot can be rechristened something true.

Decades later a monument was dedicated on the site of the tragedy, inscribed with the following lines from "The Faded Coat of Blue," John Hugh MacNaughton's song to a different American war:

> My brave lad he sleeps in his faded coat of blue,
> In his lonely grave unknown lies the heart that beat so true.

Iroquois Spirits
A. The Charmholder's Bundle
&
B. Miracles of Mad Bear

Man also possesses a power by which he may see his friends and the circumstances by which they are surrounded, although such persons may be a thousand miles away from him at the time.

Paracelsus

Iroquois Spirits

A. The Charmholder's Bundle

Seneca Witch-Belief

In the early twentieth century Arthur Parker stated that no understanding of his own Seneca people was possible without taking into account their witch-belief. (In *Shadows* we recalled the 1821 killing of a witch along the Cazenovia Creek near Buffalo. Iroquois law had pronounced the sentence, but the outraged Whites put Tom Jemmy, a Buffalo Creek Seneca, on trial for murder. Red Jacket's speech in his defense is a classic, and was largely responsible for winning the day.)

In the Iroquois nations of Parker's day we'd have found considerable faith in the power of certain persons to turn themselves into animals and cause bad dreams, injuries, and even death to others through spirits or charms. The Iroquois called sorcerers of both sexes "witches," and thought all charmholders capable of magic. To ward witches away from home and person many Indians bought "witch powder" from their medicine people. It mattered not whether the Native American was Christian or traditional; many followers of both Christ and Handsome Lake kept the faith.

What may have escaped all but arcane history is the extent to which the Whites of an earlier day, like many in ours, believed in witchcraft, too. The hex signs and "superstition" of many Dutch and German immigrants should need merely to be mentioned, and the nineteenth-century religious movements for which Western New York - "The Burned-over District" - was known certainly had their share of occultism. Even in the early twentieth century many Iroquois admitted that some Whites knew more than their share about the dark art. A White doctor on the Tonawanda Reservation used to have a great reputation for diagnosing and curing victims of witchery.

Today we have terms like "psychokinesis" for the work of apparent magic, and "psychosomatic healing" for the successes of the traditional healer. Though customs seem to have changed significantly, belief in what we might call "magic" (including witchcraft) has not been completely erased on the Reservation by the advance of pop culture. Today's Iroquois aren't quite that literally "superstitious," though some of them will occasionally give you a savvy glance and refuse to deny the possibility of "more things in Heaven and earth..." than many of us will accept. They may know someone, though, who says... They may also be guarded; it's never been good form on "the Res" to talk much about witchcraft; to know too much about it may be to be accused of practicing it. We don't know too much about it, either, by the way. We're just telling what we've heard.

Spirits of the Great Hill

The Wailing Spirit of the Genesee Flats

On an early evening in February of 1807 one of the locals walking from Leicester started to cross the Genesee Flats toward the western shore of the river. About halfway across, he was shocked and then terrified by a strange noise, human screaming and wailing, seemingly from above him in the twilight clouds.

He hustled home and told his neighbors, a handful of whom came with him the next night to the same spot. The gusty shrieking returned, but this time there were several witnesses. The phenomenon seemed reliable, and word spread. People came, sometimes from far parts, just to hear it. Sometimes there were as many as two thousand, it was reported, and for every night of two weeks no member of the ever-increasing crowds was disappointed by failing to be scared silly.

This prodigy needed an answer, and someone thought of consulting the Native Americans - a remedy we'd recommend today for many American problems. Those dwelling at nearby Squakie Hill - doubtless Seneca - held a council and came to the conclusion that this was the spirit of one of their fathers who had died a little while before. Apparently it had lost its way on the journey to "the Happy Hunting-Grounds," the Iroquois heaven, and was caught in this sort of nether-land. To help the disoriented soul, a hundred warriors were chosen, armed with rifles, and placed as directly under the noise as possible. At a signal, all of them fired their guns at once into the air, apparently toward it. This doesn't seem like a friendly gesture. When the echoes faded, the wonder was no more.

This is a crazy tale, but the evidence of it is about as strong as the place and time could have provided. Besides the multitude of country spectators, several prominent and educated gentlemen ("very aged and very reliable") were present, and they, too, vouched for the phenomenon.

Though we have no other understanding of the mysterious noise, it was not reported again after the Senecas' ceremony, so maybe their explanation of it was the best. It wouldn't be the first time.

Catching a Blood-Bone

One night three men came to the home of a healer on the Cattaraugus Reservation. One carried a spade, another a lantern, the third - a Tonawanda witch doctor - a response to a story of trouble.

A Cattaraugus family had been plagued with bad luck. Mysterious ailments had taken several children, and the affair had the taint of the supernatural. The Cattaraugus healer had been asked to do something about it. He'd called in the Tonawanda witch doctor.

The four walked into the the woods and swamp. Now and then the witch doctor stopped, took a forked stick out of his bag and held it like a dowsing rod by the two ends, one in each hand. He pointed it in various directions, seemed to study it a moment, and then tucked it away again. Once, though, the rod took on a subtle glow. They went the way it indicated, trying to keep it trained on its target as they negotiated the paths and trails, always following its glow, until they converged on an old stump. When touched to it the forked stick glowed almost like it was red-hot. Its holder tapped the ground between two roots. "Here we dig."

The shovel-bearer set to. At the sound of spade hitting stone, the witch doctor took over. The lantern was lit, and they uncovered a cubical box made of thick slabs from the creek bottom. "It's there," he whispered. He put some white powder on top of the box, then covered it again.

The party went back to the house of the troubled family and dug a hole at the corner of the woodshed. Into it the witch doctor put a five-gallon crock with a large piece of silk weighted at the corners covering it like a drumhead. He made a small fire, threw medicine powder into it, and chanted, commanding the witch bundle to come from its box through the air into this crock. After a while they saw a ball of fire hurl itself across the night sky, and arc down toward them. They dove for cover, all but the witch-doctor, who saw it pass through the silk without burning it.

Inside they found a bundle of rags soaked with blood, and in them a sharp bone, bloody red: the *otnäyont*, the cursed bone that had been drinking the blood of children. The witch doctor made off with it. The last ill child got well and there were no more mystery ailments.

These witch-bones can be laid in an area to curse it, and they'll siphon the blood of children until seen to in the traditional way. No wonder the Iroquois hated witches. At least it wasn't a bomblet in the shape of a toy; Hell awaits too the deviser of that one.

THE HAIR-BONE TOKEN

A strong, healthy man sickened. He saw doctors, took medicine, followed advice, and got worse. By the time he quit work and went to stay with a friend, he was in bed most of the day, and could hardly eat.

A witch doctor from the Tonawanda Reservation made a poultice of unspecified stuff and put it on the sick man's belly. He covered it carefully with rags and moss and studied the operation. Those who touched it found the poultice hot; the sick man groaned as if something were being drawn out. At a moment he seemed to be waiting for, the witch doctor grabbed the poultice, ran to the kitchen, and threw the contents into the ash pan of the stove, from which he pulled a small sharp bone wrapped in a white hair - a traditional witching-token. Jaws dropped. The healer communed with the quirky object for awhile and voiced the feeling that a certain neighborhood widow was behind the witching. Friends and family had a hard time with this; she called every day to check on the man.

"Just see what happens next time she visits," said the witch doctor, tucking the hair-bone token into the patient's absent hand.

There was no quick improvement. The sick man tossed, covering himself with the sheet and mumbling. Was he becoming a witch himself? But by the next dusk he was coherent, and, as he held the bone-and-hair token, sounded as if he was narrating a surveillance video. "Here she comes. She's leaving her house. Now she's down by the well. Now she's on the road... crossing the bridge, the gate, the path... She's by the apple tree. Now she's at the door...." There was a knock.

"I couldn't sleep last night," said the crone when the introductions were done. "I worried so much about our sick friend."

"You're the one!" the sufferer yelled from under the blankets. "Leave me alone or I'll kill you!" Feigning pity, the dame took her leave.

That night the patient talked to the bony trinket, mumbling phrases and

Spirits of the Great Hill

verses from a language none knew. At the end he wrapped one of his own hairs around it and yelled, "Go back to her, and stick in her heart!" He threw it at the wall, and everyone heard it hit. It vanished as if it had flown right through.

The next day the sick man's friends went to see the potential witch, to find people gathered outside her house. They found her dead with the bone in her chest. Those who knew the situation were sad about it, but not much for its true victim. "She had no business witching people," said one of the sick man's friends as if spitting splinters.

The Stealer of Childrens' Hearts

An old village woman seemed especially solicitous when it came to helping with children's funerals. One night another woman walking by her house saw a peculiar shooting marshmallow of light fly out the chimney and head toward the graveyard. This was a "witch-light," as the Longhouse folk would call it, in which some especially powerful witches were thought to fly. "So," she said to herself, "The old girl must be up to it."

Soon another child died and the same woman came to help, agreeing to sit with the corpse. However, the neighbor who had seen the witch-light told her husband to keep an eye open. Sure enough, at midnight when the dame thought she was alone, she took a knife, cut the heart out of the child, and left the house while everyone slept. She went to her cabin, around which the neighbor's husband kept watch. In a while a ball of fire flew out the chimney and streaked to the cemetery. Frightened but game, the husband followed it to the oldest section of the yard in which many graves were sunken. He saw the witch-woman put something into a hole and cry out. "There! I've got you another. Now you're my friend again, and you'll have to show me where I can get money." The neighbor's husband had seen enough, and took off as quickly and quietly as he could. Soon the light soared overhead and back into the witch's chimney.

The next day he went to the father of the dead child and told him what he'd seen. They could find no marks on the child's body; the witch had healed the cut. At the cemetery, though, they found the grave the neighbor's husband had marked, with signs of fresh digging, a small channel of new earth going into an old grave. Working through it, they came to a corpse, its peculiarly fresh and contented face covered with blood, a tender heart in its teeth. They came back at twilight with a witch doctor, poured kerosene down the hole, and set it afire. At the old woman's house they saw bloody rags on a table. They found her at the funeral.

"You're nothing but a witch!" the bereaved father stormed. "Now I know why you go to all the funerals. I should kill you! Admit it!"

She burst out crying. "I never hurt the children. I gave their hearts to my friend after they were dead. My friend in the ground was my friend in life, and she makes luck for me now. I'd starve without her."

"You should have told us you were in need," said the father. "You can do without luck like that. Go home, and quit this business."

A witch doctor made a charm above the heartless child so that she might rest in her grave. The witch woman died soon after, so maybe her time was due.

Iroquois Spirits

MAKER OF THE FALSE FACE

[Among the wonders in Mad Bear's cabin was the False Face on the wall. Its nose, cheeks, chin and lips were gnarled; yet to the Iroquois who believed it was in some sense a living thing. However much he'd learned to respect Iroquois custom, writer Doug Boyd found this hard to accept. Yet over the years of his acquaintance with Mad Bear, he could swear that the yellow, wispy shocks of fiber hanging from the mask dipped closer to the floor than last time, as if its mane grew. Even its grin seemed to broaden.]

The Iroquois have their own child-scaring bogie, masked cannibal-clown "Longnose." He's not to be confused with the False Faces, a healer's cult of which there are two sorts of origin-legends. One stems from the creation-myth, in which a rival to their Good-Minded-god rubber-necked too quickly, bashed his face on a mountain, and was deputized the patron of healing. Others involve mortal hunters, taught through encounters with this first False Face or his misshapen minions.

Rather than portraits of random goonies, the Iroquois Faces are mythological beings, gods of Disease or Wind. There are two classes of them: ones that imitate the crook-faced god, usually red or black, always long-haired, with the broken nose and jaw of the mountain-collision; and Common Faces, of all miscreated sorts. The latter-wearers seem a ramshackle, straggling lot for all their power, chanting, stalking, and rooting about the sickbed, begging offerings of corn mush and tobacco. They choose their moment, shake rattles, cure with a puff of soot, and depart. As recently as 1940 Iroquois False-face healers were seen handling hot ashes and coals, even rubbing them on human bodies safely.

Old masks, veterans of many rites, are passed through centuries. Lesser masks, seasoned with generations of ceremonies and tobacco, can ascend into the ranks of Great Doctor masks. To use any mask irreverently might curse the bearer, or whoever he looked at while wearing it.

A new healer is called to join the Society of Faces; a dream or a seer speaks, and the hearing is lifelong. When he inherits a mask, it's given away with a ritual, telling it of its journey. Otherwise he carves his own. He enters the woods and waits for a living tree to pick him. If it's morning as his tree calls, the mask will be red; if evening, black. He does the features, then strokes notches above and below, chiseling out the face in a block and working it at home. The mask never breaks and the tree never dies, perhaps because he's offered tobacco. It can't be left half-finished, though; it's a more-or-less living thing, with sentiments and power.

In the 1980s an old Seneca from the Tonawanda Reservation broke this taboo, leaving a face on a live tree. Friends tried to talk to him, but for whatever reason, he refused to work on it any further. Then he had a stroke. His features distorted until he resembled the face on the tree; there are said to be pictures (before and after), attesting to the marvel. Finally he relented, and removed and ritually destroyed the mask. His appearance returned to normal before long, but his walking-stride never recovered.

Spirits of the Great Hill

A Witch's Bag

They thought the old woman was a witch, and her Erie shore house sat abandoned for a long time before anyone neared it. Finally Irving historian Everett Burmaster - no slouch with the spooky - found a bag in it and listed its contents. Like Macbeth's witches' gorge-gauging grab-bag ("fillet of a fenny snake," "eye of newt"), these ingredients are macabre but mundane, gross, but easily glommed or made: tiny weapons and dolls; sacks of animal hearts; thread; dried snake blood; a bottle of "eye oil"; various powders; hair in many shades; packs of nail clippings, wet blood, and a small sharp bone; various greases; a dried finger; and the skins of snakes, a black calf, and a big dog. (Hmm. Filet of snake would look like fettucini.)

This lakeshore witch could transform herself, they say, and lived much of the time in a nearby pond as the consort of a huge black snake. We're reminded of the Olympian Zeus who amused himself by getting it on with his conquests - usually mortal women - in the forms of different animals, sometimes even transforming them as well, to deceive his jealous wife Hera. We have no Classical record of which animal does it better, but in Seneca country the snakes must have had the mojo. As if a testament to her eternal flame, when the witch died and was buried a "witch light" (*gahai*) was seen over the very pond. We think we know where it is.

The Charmholder's Bundle

For each craft there's a counter-craft; and for those who'd undo malicious witchery, no charm-bundle's complete (according to Seneca Edward Cornplanter) without: scales or blood of the great horned serpent; a round white stone of the Little People; claws from the death-panther or the fire-beast; castor of the white beaver; an *otnäyont*, a sharp bone; a corn bug; a small mummified hand; hair from the "Flying Head"; a monster-bear bone; an eagle-wing bone whistle; anti-witch powder; sacred tobacco; claws or teeth from wild animals; tiny mortar, pestle, war club, arrow, bow, wooden bowls, spoons, and a doll; "eye-oil" (a potion giving the second sight); and feathers of something called "the exploding bird."

If these or substitutes exist, they're in ancient burials and museums. And this is just a generic list; master wizards would have had their own tricks and ingredients, and no bundle was broken in unless it was "sung for" in the charm-holder's societal ceremony. Great power, though, could be the reward. The holder of the magic bundle could overcome a sorcerer's blight, or determine which offended spirits were behind a problem. It could heal, it could work blessing, it could turn a curse.

Just putting together the Charm-Holder's Bundle would be a quest of sorts. Neither mighty horned snake nor fierce monster bear would part eagerly with scale or bone. Sheer reality would be the main complaint with others. "Flying Head"-hair and "fire-beast" claws sound like the chimerical kennings - girls' beards, cats' footfalls, fish-breath - that fettered Fenrir until the twilight of Asgard. As for the "exploding bird," though, we know these exist, masquerading at least sometimes as pigeons, vanishing when they choose, leaving only a cloud of feathers. In Spring 2001 one of this species was caught on film, crossing home plate right into a Randy Johnson pitch.

Iroquois Spirits

B. Miracles of Mad Bear

Medicine Men

By now the Native American medicine man (or woman) is a media icon. Though we ask New Agers to keep an even keel, it does indeed seem as if psychic healing and communication occurs far more often on the Res than in the society around it. We should all keep open the possibility of paranormal talents: we who have heard about experiments with faith healing or the mind-bending feats of Indian yogis; we who have simply seen a family dog frisking by the door moments before its owner is home. We advise others to consider the chance that preindustrial shamans had such "special" abilities, which might have been the difference in personal or cultural survival, and that the preservers of their tradition may have them, too. The Western Door may have had its own original, and it's still surprising how many people have never heard of Mad Bear.

A leader in the "pan-Indian" movement, Wallace "Mad Bear" Anderson (probably 1927-1985) had worked many years in the Merchant Marine where he'd become a spokesman for his fellows of all colors. His diplomacy was recognized among his own folk, and several times he was offered the position of tribal chief. His visions were global. In the late 1960s his "Traditional Indian Spiritual Unity Caravan" brought many far-flung native nations together to address common issues. Mad Bear also believed in involving other groups (including Whites) in the process, and this is probably how he came to prominence.

Many who knew him found Mad Bear reasonable and congenial, sensing that his sensation-making moves were crafted to highlight issues. At least outwardly, though, the burly Tuscarora lived up to his name, tending to barge first and bargain later. Many who knew him only from rallies must have thought his singular gift was getting into photographs with famous people. His ponytailed image appears in many near-backgrounds and front-rows beside luminaries like Castro, Ted Kennedy, and the Dalai Lama (whom Mad Bear met in India). The breadth of Mad Bear's friendships was imposing - Bob Dylan came to visit him on the Tuscarora Res - and some might be surprised that he'd be the subject of a chapter on "magic," and that only at this point would they hear of it. Yet it was well-known on the Reservation that Mad Bear was of the medicine people, and that many who came to him were healed. Not much was made of it on the Res, where nothing of this nature is done for show or spectacle. It took a White writer, Doug Boyd, to bring this side of Mad Bear into public consciousness, and we hope to give him fair exposure near his home.

Mad Bear remains controversial, even among his own people. It would be easy to claim that all his conflicts were political, but few human situations have sure answers that simple. Some we'd consider Mad Bear's spiritual fellows were troubled with him. We profile him as a representative of the Iroquois medicine people, a tradition deserving deepest respect. We relied upon Doug Boyd's book named for him (from which Mad Bear's conversation is almost directly lifted) and interviews with many who knew Mad Bear, one of the Western Door's true medicine men.

Spirits of the Great Hill

The Cattail Healing

In his early twenties Michael Bastine worked in a restaurant for whose young waiters it became a game to jam many tickets at once on to an old-fashioned spike-and-wood device - essentially a knitting needle in a plank - back by the kitchen. The record may have been thirteen (held by Mike, we think), but as one neared it, more and more force was needed to swat the flimsy things through the formidable spike. In an attempt to break his own record, our young Algonquin friend reared back for a fearful slam. He made it, all right, but the big needle dug into his thumb, sticking into the bone between the top joints. It was a grisly wound, likely to develop infection, and one that should have taken weeks to heal.

Mike decided to give the legendary healing powers of Mad Bear a try, and went to the home of the venerable shaman. Before he could say a word, Mad Bear proposed a bout of chess, a game he was always mad to play. They got through a diffident game or two, with Mike, in outright agony, barely moving the pieces. "Boy, you're not yourself today," said Mad Bear. "You're lucky we don't have money on this."

Mike stormed for the door, bent on finding a White doctor. "Oh, about that hand of yours..." Mad Bear said, almost as an afterthought. He gave very careful directions for getting and preparing the root of an ordinary cattail - how to find the right plant, to track its root underneath the swamp muck, to pull it up just right, to peel and cut a few small pieces... Only an inch or so was needed. He told Mike how to pound the root into a poultice and apply it to the injured digit.

Before he noticed, surely not more than a day or so, the thumb was virtually healed, supple, painless, and infection-free. Mike was sure that conventional Western medicine would have had him shot, splinted and stitched for weeks, with no surety the hand would have healed better.

Powerline

A few days after he'd moved to Williamsville in the 1970s, Mike Bastine was approached by a neighbor as he got into his car. Clearly perceiving that he was Native American, the man asked his nation.

"I'm Algonquin," said Mike.

The man sighed with relief. "Thank God. I don't need any more to do with them Tuscaroras."

Mike laughed, and asked what he meant. "There's one of them up there on the Reservation named Mad Bear that's been giving me and my whole crew the creeps. I won't go up there any more."

"Well, that's who I'm about to go see," said Mike. The man's terror was so comical that Mike calmed him, suggesting that he might be able to help and asking him the story. Mike's neighbor worked for the power company running lines across Reservation land. All was well and good for a time, but some Native Americans felt that something in the original agreement wasn't being met. Mad Bear had gotten wind of this, and showed up to work his medicine.

The project met unaccountable snags, including baffling malfunctions with equipment. Several bulldozers became utterly useless. Wires, batteries, plugs, and everything else imaginable were replaced, and none of them could be made

Iroquois Spirits

workable for long. A handful had to be junked. When the lines were finally up, power couldn't be made to flow between two simple towers, again with no perceptible flaws in the system. Furthermore, the crews were getting spooked. Apparitions, sounds, you name it. Many workers chose to quit the company rather than revisit the troubled site.

Mike had to laugh. "That was Mad Bear. He never was one to let something go by like that. He'd pull people aside privately and talk to them, but if that didn't do any good he went right to the next step in a hurry. He must have done some kind of ceremony up there. I think he had help from Peter Mitten on that one."

THE LAZARUS EFFECT

One day a boy was knocked from his bike by a car and apparently killed. He lay on the street until the ambulance arrived, and as Mad Bear came out of his house, the White paramedics were loading him into their vehicle with the blanket over his head. The mother pulled on him and cried, telling them to leave him, but there's no doubt that they thought he was dead. Then a voice rang out.

"Put him down!" called Peter Mitten the healer, coming unsteadily down from his house. He was ill, weak, and in bed most of the time, and anywhere but the Reservation they might have ignored him; but maybe not. There was something in that voice of his. They set the young cyclist back on the street.

The old man bent over the boy, almost nose to nose. Then he blew into his face, hard and quick. "Open your eyes." Nothing happened, and he said again, "Come back, I told you! You come back here and open up those eyes." The tender lids fluttered. "Now open your eyes. Open them all the way, but don't move until I tell you." The kid looked all around him, and his mother went to pick him up; but he was wild and terrified, and didn't seem to know where he was. Mad Bear kept the mother back, and Peter Mitten put something in the boy's mouth, something he must have had in his hand the whole time. In a while the boy tried to stand, but the two healers just talked to him, keeping him seated, making sure he'd come back for good and was planning on staying with the living. Then they gave him to the ambulance. All this time the White paramedics had stood aside, astonished. They told the whole story to the emergency room doctors.

"Everybody knew that those medics had found that kid dead," said Mad Bear years later to Doug Boyd. "But nobody ever put it in writing. Things like that they can't explain are never reported, they're just denied. And even when they're observed like that, they just can't be acknowledged. But I'll tell you one thing we never talked about with anybody. One of those doctors came to us confidentially with his own personal situation for help from Peter Mitten and me. I'm still in touch with that doctor, although his problem is over."

Spirits of the Great Hill

The Witching-Wall

[Mike Bastine often visited Mad Bear at his Tuscarora Reservation home. One time he observed something different, an odd contraption to the north of the house that would have resembled a snow fence had it not been augmented with tin roofing material and other assorted bits and pieces, festooned as well with rags and trinkets. Mike laughed when he saw it, but Mad Bear just laughed back. "You wait and see."]

A clan in Canada had begun working Mad Bear ill, but it had lost so many members - illness, accidents, even murders - that the rest were sure Mad Bear was fighting them back. Mike remembers several occasions when people came to Mad Bear's house from far parts, begging him to take his reverse-medicine off them. One clammy, violent night stands out.

During a visit to Mad Bear's cinder-block fortress-home, Mike reported hearing some queer sounds that at first he thought were from a radio within the house. It was a harsh male voice shouting outside. Mad Bear didn't look surprised. He rolled out the window in the back of the little space he used as a living room, and the voice came clearly: "Mad Bear, turn it off!"

"Turn what off?" Mad Bear called out, his voice turning high.

"Bear, don't go out there!" said Mike. In recent decades there had been violent disputes among the Iroquois, and Mad Bear had his enemies. There was a very real chance that they were about to get shot; but Mad Bear bolted for the door, and his guests followed.

From the porch Mike could just make out a human form twenty feet past the Dali fence, as if afraid to near it. It shouted from across the barrier. "Turn it off, Mad Bear!" Its clothes swirled; it looked unreal.

"You turn it off!" yelled Mad Bear. "It's what you tried to do to others!"

"We're dying, Mad Bear," the man pleaded, growling like an animal. "Hardly any of us are left!"

"I'm sorry for you, and I'll get working on it. Maybe I can turn this thing around," said Mad Bear. "But I warned you about getting it started."

The wretched figure stared with cavernous eyes; he looked like he'd walked a hundred miles. Then he receded backward, facing them all the while.

"Sorry about that," said Mad Bear when his friends were settled inside. "There won't be any more trouble tonight. Hey, we've had our little excitement. Anybody hungry?"

Iroquois Spirits

THE DJOGAO SKULL

[One of the great curiosities in the Americas is the well-known and well-photographed mini-mummy from Casper, Wyoming. In October, 1932 a dynamite blast opened a small natural cave in granite, and when the smoke cleared, a little human-like figure, seated and with folded arms, came into view. The leathery imp was 14 inches tall, and he's since been X-rayed to reveal adult development. What this - and his entombment in natural granite, which should have taken eons - says for sure is anyone's guess, but it's not hard to see how stories get started.]

As Charles Williams observed about witchcraft, so many parts of the world have belief in fairies that it's hard to trust a single explanation. As in old Celtic societies, "The Little People" have a role in the mythology of many Native American nations (including the Iroquois). Iroquois women who wished to see these *Djogao* left their infants in the woods and followed their gazes from concealment, believing the youngest children could see the Little People and that thus they might be aided to catch a glimpse. There are tales, even modern ones, about rare shamans possessing something concrete as a memento of an encounter with these elusive and magical folk. Mike Bastine has learned never to completely doubt any Native American belief, though he never expected to see an object like he did.

Once when he was helping Mad Bear move from his trailer to his new house, Mike noticed a small, plastic purple box. "Open it up and take a look," said the shaman, always testing his disciple.

Mike unwrapped the bundle to see a tiny human skull, perfect down to the teeth. The cranium was not significantly bigger than a ping-pong ball. Mike knew bone when he saw it, and was in no doubt that this object was made of it. "It scared the hell out of me," he said later.

As he so often did after disclosing a marvel, Mad Bear made no mention of it again. "If you want a show, get a ticket to the circus," he always said to those who asked him to show his powers. "What we're about is the message."

Was this really the skull of a supernatural being? A natural being with supernatural powers? An undiscovered human race? The conclusion is up to the reader. We believe what Mike told us.

WEAPONS OF FRIENDSHIP

Over the years Mad Bear had gotten himself a reputation as someone nobody wanted to mess with, as if a sense of fate or karma worked on those who tried to harm him, often as a result of their own attacks. It was as if his own spiritual force, his *orenda*, as some Iroquois would say, was too much to overcome.

There was the time a fellow Native American tried to shoot him one night, driving by the famous cabin. His volleys were ineffective. Mad Bear's house was pretty sturdy; people had tried without success to break into it. Those in the know have the feeling that even if Mad Bear's home was not so well physically fortified, no bullets would have gone through and hurt him, but we'll leave that without explanation. The fleeing drive-by gunman ended up in a ditch, badly hurt.

Mad Bear's techniques of physical defense seem so advanced and Zen-like that they're off the chart. Whereas the most refined Asian techniques defend

Spirits of the Great Hill

against forceful violence with, in one way or another, at least the effect of forceful violence, Mad Bear seemed able to simply defuse the aggression. "He doesn't ever put anything back on anyone. He just doesn't receive it," said someone once of his techniques. That takes real doing.

There was the time an enraged Native American came at Mad Bear with a knife, drawing and charging too fast for any to intercede. Mad Bear opened his arms wide and beamed like a mother in her kitchen surprised by a college kid returning home. His would-be assassin altered his course and walked into the delighted embrace. The blade clapped harmlessly and absently along Mad Bear's back, and the blade-artist returned to his seat, blinking and dumbfounded.

"Don't try that on your own," said Mad Bear out of the side of his mouth. "It took me years to work that one out."

Mad Bear's Magic Hat

Improper treaties - or ones improperly maintained - can lead to long-standing problems. An old deal from Revolutionary days ran the border between Canada and the Colonies right through Iroquois territory across which the Great Hill folk were to be granted free passage. In recent times, however, some were denied it during times of political demonstration, which sometimes kept them from powwows and even family gatherings. Once Mad Bear set out to make his point, crashing his Jeep through a wooden gate at a crossing. Later (sounding more like himself) he issued a statement offering to pay for or repair any damage caused by his exercise of his political rights, but the authorities were not amused. Mad Bear was told that he would be arrested if he tried to attend a rally in Toronto.

Mad Bear announced that he would attend, not to disturb the peace, but to fulfill his duties to his nation. The problem was following through. The officials at the border were on the lookout for the distinctive shaman, whose picture was in every guardhouse. Cars full of Native Americans would get the once-over for sure.

The press had become interested in the standoff, and stalked the Native American car caravans. Wearing his magic hat, Mad Bear sat in the back seat between two of his friends. In the car behind them were a reporter and photographer from, Doug Boyd presumed, Buffalo's largest paper. The customs agent looked into the car and prepared to wave them on, seeming to miss Mad Bear. "Hey! That's Mad Bear up there!" hollered the White reporter who'd been hanging out the window, evidently prepared to make a story if one did not make itself.

The customs agent looked again, this time peering into every face more closely; then he waved them on again. As they pulled away, Mad Bear was grinning faintly under his wide black brim. He was later to relate, "Every time that guard set his eyes on me it felt like trickling sand was running down over my face. What he saw when he looked at me was somebody else."

Writer Doug Boyd admits to studying, even modeling, the magic hat, a black, wide-brimmed affair a size or two too big for him. He sensed no cascading sand, but felt indeed different. As if amazed, Mad Bear looked at him so intently that Boyd turned for the mirror, but was prevented. When next he visited, the hat was not on its accustomed hanger.

Iroquois Spirits

The Medicine Case

For metaphysical protection Mad Bear wore a small leather pouch, filled with indistinct items, on a necklace. It was the height of rudeness for anyone to attempt to touch it; but the more awesome totem was his "medicine case," a leather satchel that he kept near him at all times. The case had been "doctored," and it was essential that it and people be protected from each other. On occasions such as the Fifth Spiritual Summit in New York City when he had to leave it in a strange place - say, a Big Apple hotel room - while he himself had to be away, he always deputized an ally to watch over it. This was often Anyas, a young Iroquois from Canada who had likewise been doctored to be able to handle it.

During the course of the day at the United Nations-sponsored conference, Mad Bear had received over a thousand dollars that the Native American contingent badly needed for lodging and expenses. He deputized Boyd to take it back to the hotel and put it into the safe, but insisted he take Anyas with him. Boyd had to search several floors of the building for the young Iroquois who'd been left with Mad Bear's medicine case, and found him confused and disoriented. Finally it came out. He'd lost Mad Bear's fabled satchel. "We just gotta get it back," he moaned. "Just don't tell Bear."

But Mad Bear found them, interrupting their conversation. He watched as Anyas tried to explain. "Stay here," he told Boyd. "Somebody did something to him. I think I know what's going on here." In a minute he was gone.

Back at their room Anyas was certainly not himself. He took off his clothes, got into bed, and then got up and dressed again. Boyd tried to get him to rest, reminding him of the closing banquet that night.

Mad Bear came to the door. "Give us a couple minutes," he said to Boyd. "I've got some work to do here." In a few minutes Mad Bear came out, and they went to his room. On the bed was the missing medicine case. How had he found it in New York City?

"I had to use a little medicine myself to track it down," said Mad Bear. "I found the guy who had it. He was a White guy, and he'd had his hands in it, so I had to use some medicine on him too. He's leaving. I think he's sorry for what he did in a way." Mad Bear had quite a talk with the young fellow, who'd been behind protest posters that had been put up all over the cathedral used for meetings. He didn't seem to be evil, but he was after something, Mad Bear figured, for his own ego: power, control, or recognition. He was being used by somebody, and he didn't even know it.

Mad Bear was not sure if an Indian in a Black Hat that nobody had known had something to do with it, but he conjectured that the young White guy had to have help. Anyas had been "overshadowed," as Mad Bear put it. "If he'd been on his guard like he's been taught, I don't think this could have happened. He'll learn, though. He'll be able to deal with this stuff someday. At least I hope so, because he can't escape the challenge."

Spirits of the Great Hill

The Ghost-Talker

His friends had taken him to view some petroglyphs that left Mad Bear oddly bemused. To him the rock carvings told the tale of the first Native Americans; but a strange new one began when their young guide found an ancient flint point. "You want it, Bear?" he called.

"You're the one who found it," said Mad Bear. "There has to be some reason for it." The boy beamed and put it in his pocket.

"Slow down," said Mad Bear. "You can't just walk off with it like that. If you think it's meant for you to keep, you have to make some acknowledgment, and some kind of offering. If you don't have an offering, you make a pledge."

The youth held the arrowhead up to the sun for awhile and tucked it away, grinning. "I made a pledge to quit drinkin'. I promised the Great Spirit..."

Mad Bear cut him off. "Hey, we can talk about that later. When you make a pledge, it's sacred. You've got to mean it. Otherwise, put that thing back where you found it."

A few days later Mad Bear's near-dawn knocking woke his friends. "That young Indian that took us out to the rocks," said Mad Bear. "He's dead. Killed. With a knife." They were crestfallen. How his teeth had gleamed in the sun! How he'd laughed! And they were angry. It sounded like murder, and few thought it would take Mad Bear long to name the killer. He joined the boy's family that evening.

Near dawn he called his circle together. "The ceremony went all right," he said. "I got ahold of the young man and he recognized me. I didn't feel too much from him - not too much fear or confusion." Mad Bear led the spirit of the young man around the house where he had lived, showing him his room, his things, his friends and family gathered, essentially showing him that he was dead. "This is where you used to sleep, but no more, this is who you used to live with, but no more..."

"You have to get everything closed out. That's the purpose in a ceremony like that." Confused spirits can be held, "trapped something terrible. Once every society in every part of the world had ceremonies for a thing like that. Now it's almost all lost, especially where there are no traditional medicine people left." Mad Bear got up. "It's late, and I'm tired. I did a lot of work tonight."

"How did he get stabbed?" Boyd blurted out. Mad Bear sighed as if the sadness was new and related the experience like he'd seen it through the young man's eyes.

The youth with the arrowhead in his pocket and the pledge to his gods fresh on his lips had walked a long trail to the store. When he came out with the sixpack, another young Indian's dog, a big one that had always been friendly, suddenly went after him. A fracas ensued, which the owner drew his knife to stop. The young Indian kicked out at the dog, maybe even at the knife. That was how he'd taken the wound; the blade had hit a vein in his hip, but it had seemed just a scratch at first. He was found on his walk home where he must have weakened, rested by an abandoned cabin, fallen asleep, and... The edge came in over the arrowhead in the boy's pocket, and may even have nicked it.

Iroquois Spirits

Only A Change of Worlds

[Maybe the trouble started out West where his work often took him. He'd fallen ill several times and been saved by Native American healers, but some were concerned that powerful, subtle enemies were working him ill, and finally beginning to succeed. The energy they loosed could follow Mad Bear across a continent.]

For a long time that spring people had been trying to reach Mad Bear, but nobody answered at his home. Some thought he might be off on another of his mystical rambles, sometimes (as it was rumored) in the form of a bear, but others were worried. At Niagara Falls for a series of seminars, Doug Boyd called Mad Bear's home; the great healer answered groggily, as if he'd been roused by the call. Surprised and overjoyed, Boyd arranged to meet his old tutor at a cookout that evening.

Mad Bear lacked his usual focus, talking offhandedly about a strange bite on his upper arm from a silver-and-purple ant that hardly sounded like a natural bug. "These things are bein' sent around all the time," he said. "Man, I sure got caught off guard this time." Mad Bear never took off the small medicine pouch around his neck for more than a minute or two, and that time it was for a dip in the water. In only seconds the curious insect was up his arm. It had moved like a robot-assassin.

Boyd was alarmed by his first look at the arm, swollen and discolored. The hospital doctors were as confounded by the account of the wound as by its fearful effect. Though he lived months longer, the great medicine man who always acknowledged greater never fully recovered from this attack. Toward the end his behavior alarmed some of his friends, particularly the Whites. "Mad Bear needs help," one cried to Mike Bastine. "He's got the window open at one end of the house, the air conditioning going full-blast at the other, and the heat up to a hundred."

"At least he'll be sure to find someplace he can be comfortable," said Mike.

In the winter of 1984 Doug Boyd and other friends flew Mad Bear out to Tucson and the Papago Reservation, whose traditional healers gave the same message: "Don't worry too much about the Mad Bear you see. Most of him has already crossed over, out of sight of you now." The rest of him went over for good in November 1985.

Mad Bear had been involved in a great contest, said many of his enlightened friends, in a struggle for people's hearts and minds, and ultimately over the Earth. Some felt that his prominence made him a target. Maybe he knew that all along. His allies of the spirit many had come to call "Those Who Care," and doubtless Mad Bear is with them now. In closing his own book, Doug Boyd recalled the last lines of Chief Seattle's famous speech, and Mad Bear's voice pronouncing them:

At night when the streets of your cities and villages will be silent, and you think them deserted, they will throng with the returning hosts that once filled and still love this beautiful land. The White man will never be alone. Let him be just and deal kindly with my people, for the dead are not powerless. 'Dead' did I say? There is no death, only a change of worlds.

WHITE MAGIC
A. The Path of Peace
&
B. Children of the Left Hand

Flectere se nequeo superbos, Acheronta movebo.
[If I cannot bend the gods, I will stir up Acheron (the Underworld).]
                                    Vergil, the *Aeneid*

    I shall go into a hare
    With sorrow and sighing and mickle care,
    And I shall go in the Devil's name
    Till I come home again.
                        Isabel Gowdie, English witch

White Magic

A. THE PATH OF PEACE

THE BRADFORD MIRACLE

[No aspect of paranormal research is simple, but the study of religious miracles seems especially problematic. We can reach little conclusion about some of these matters except that something far out of the ordinary may be going on. Not all reports are as they first seem.]

Up to ten thousand people may have visited Bradford, Pennsylvania's Holy Family Western Orthodox Church in a single week. This small shrine just south of Salamanca was open twenty-four hours a day after the Reverend Robert M. James noticed the ambiguous and apparently holy images on the sanctuary's corner wall.

Father James, church organist Paula Edwards, and her son Jason were working in the basement social hall on the night of Saturday, January 4, 1997 when they heard what seemed to be footsteps above them. They investigated upstairs and noticed such a strong and mysterious smell of roses that they looked around. Then they saw the images.

Soon legions of the faithful trooped to the church to peer into the weary, camel-colored wallpaper in the corner of the church sanctuary. They and others reported a variety of images. Some saw a cross; others perceived crossed swords, angels, the Virgin Mother and Child, Joseph, and Our Savior Himself.

To some observers, the images even changed. In the face of Christ, the eyes were sometimes open, at others closed. One visitor even saw the crown of thorns appear on a later viewing. One Bradford Catholic reported a single large image which seemed to her to be the face of Mary. It filled her with a vast, indescribable sense of peace. A Buffalo astrologer believed he saw three images, likely the Magi. Others - as is not unusual in such cases - saw nothing, and some were even apologetic about it when interviewed.

Official reaction from the Western Orthodox Church of America was muted to say the least - which is as it should be before investigation. "It sounds like people are seeing whatever they want to see," said Bishop Nicholas Carione from San Francisco, one of the four members of the church's Council. "There probably isn't anything there of religious significance. When God wants to speak to us, it is not with something that can be interpreted in a hundred different ways."

Oh? Bishop Carione's reserve is commendable, but we hardly agree that the signals of Whatever made us all are devoid of multiple interpretation. Slavery and the Holocaust are both creations, however indirect, of the Almighty, as is new life and parents' love. Because they, too, are ambiguous is not the reason to doubt the Bradford miracles. Sources we trust, however, in matters both religious and paranormal believe that the "Bradford Miracle" is one that never was. It may be a sign of something that the original pastor was soon transferred, and the matter made no more of after a week or two.

Spirits of the Great Hill

The Witch of the Helpers

[In *Shadows* we discussed the mystical Ebenezer Society and the energy they seem to have left behind. A legacy of hauntings and healings has sprouted in their old West Seneca domains.]

In the days of persecution many European societies linked the herbal healer - like the shaman and the Druid, other preservers of ancient traditions - unfairly with the outright Satanist, should there truly be such a thing. In this ironic sense we call the woman a "witch," but she was good. Still, there was a "powerful strangeness" (in the words of a great-granddaughter) about her past, her life in the domain of the Ebenezer Society, her years at the pilgrimage church called Fourteen Holy Helpers, and her own unexplained healings.

To begin, this is an odd church, in the community of Seneca, then Ebenezer, sacred land, taken for later settlers' Catholic faith. The German basilica on which it's modeled was inspired by a medieval boy's vision of fourteen healing saints, mostly from the Eastern Roman Empire. Behind the altar was a mural of this informal cult, and like the Greco-Roman gods who had their proclivities, each healer was assigned a body part, whose symbols once hung on the church's back wall.

She's hard to trace, the Witch of the Helpers. Her married name Mary Pfeiffer was taken from a German immigrant who bought the farmland the Ebenezers had for sale. Attempts to track her before that come up short. Her maiden name may have been Stephens or Szemanowski, but church records reveal no member of either name, and the dates on her baptismal certificate are either forged or wrong. Maybe she was never baptized, as if it was another tradition to which she belonged.

Other parts of Mary Pfeiffer's life were normal. Petite, scarcely taller than five feet in heels, she helped run a thriving farm, owned land throughout the area, and bore five children, one late in life. Her great-granddaughter Colleen Clements remembers her collecting her "botanicals" in the fields as children played by the log cabin, possibly her "medicine shed," on the lawn by the brook. The lilies-of-the-valley that grew by it were the whitest anyone had ever seen.

The top floor of her house was converted into rooms for overnight patients whom she cured of everything from acne to sepsis. A doctor wanted to amputate one man's arm, but in two days Mary's poultices shrank the reddened area and banned the creeping red veins. The Buffalo Medical Society considered prosecuting her for quackery, but to no use. She'd saved too many, and had too many prominent supporters.

She left money when she died for a statue above the family plot, of a woman in the toga of ancient Rome, with a bracelet of flowers, a classic face, and long stone curls. The right hand holds her head, the left lies on her thigh. It's a strange, wonderful, primal energy in this tale, that's at least not generally associated with the Western faiths, which at the core may be far more understanding than they are stereotyped.

White Magic

FATHER BAKER'S HEALING

[In *Shadows* we profiled Father Nelson Henry Baker (1841-1936), whom the Vatican has already titled "Servant of God." Elevation to sainthood, though, requires a final step, "an unexplainable occurrence or miracle," wrote Monsignor Robert C. Wurtz. A century of healings have made the case, and when, in 1999, Father Baker was moved to his crypt in the magnificent Our Lady of Victory Basilica, vials of blood and body fluids buried with him were still liquid and fresh. Something of a local crusade has been launched, but a miracle may be a tall order to prove in the material 21st century. Will this be the one that puts our native Father over the top?]

His body was already gray and black when sixteen-year-old Joseph Donohue III arrived at Buffalo's Children's Hospital in the first hours of August 19, 2000. His breathing had shut down, and bacterial meningitis had moved into his blood. He was bleeding from the eyes when his uncle, a Catholic priest, arrived and gave the last rites. The doctors said it might be a blessing, in a way, to get it over; that way they wouldn't have to amputate, to take the young musician apart piece by piece to the same end.

"I remember hearing people around my bed praying," Donohue recalls. "I heard my last rites. I was screaming in my head, and no one could hear me. I was saying: 'God, I'm sixteen years old. I can't die.'"

"Pray exclusively to Father Baker," Monsignor Ron Sciera advised Joseph's family. This was probably wise. Both of them could use a miracle, one to become a new saint, the other to stay alive. Joseph's family believes Somebody heard them.

They held a constant vigil. Word spread round the hospital, and people of faith came out. The community took up Joseph's cause, and links to Father Baker grew. A hospital worker whose grandmother had been his housekeeper rested a set of the famous priest's rosary beads on Joseph's chest. Someone mailed a bit of fabric from one of the Father's vestments; it napped on Joseph's chest before it joined the beads at the head of his bed. In Joseph's hair the Reverend Jerry Sheehan sprinkled dirt from Father Baker's original grave in Holy Cross Cemetery.

In three days there was a chance that Joseph would live; soon the talk turned to just how much of him. A young woman who'd survived the same complaint visited, without legs, with only half an arm. Joseph lost only a toe. Once out of his coma he recalled scenes of his family in other parts of the hospital and strips of conversation he could not have heard. He'd dreamed of his own grandmother, Estelle Donohue, interceding with Father Baker in a "really big castle" to a sense of peace and calm. She'd died days before his illness; Joseph and his father had played music at her services. It seemed the classic out-of-body experience, and a miracle.

At least publically, doctors were guarded. Every year they see patients in Joseph's condition. "Some of them die, some recover," said Dr. Alexandre Rotta. It's enough, though, for Bishop Mansell, who overheard doctors say among themselves that Joseph's recovery had "no medical, scientific or natural explanation."

Spirits of the Great Hill

The Heart of the Mountain

[Thomas Merton (1915-1968) was one of the great Christian writers of the twentieth century, maybe the most famous monastic since Crusade-launcher Bernard of Clairvaux, and his spiritual roots were in Western New York. Though he wasn't born here, didn't die here, and lived here only a few years, it was at St. Bonaventure that Merton found his direction. We address a queer natural spot.]

Thomas Merton of New York City came first to Olean in his twenties with poet Robert Lax, a steadfast friend and Olean native whose family cottage was in the hills above the St. Bonaventure campus. He graduated college with a fine record in literature, and a career as writer, teacher, and critic seemed imminent, but something in the environment here to which he could perhaps give no name called to young Merton. He came to St. Bonaventure to study and sought admission into the Franciscan Order.

Merton had fathered a child out of wedlock in England and had otherwise lived a worldly life. This the Franciscans knew only too well, and they advised Merton to wait a year or so and be sure of his decision. Though he was hired back at St. Bonaventure as an English instructor, one suspects as a sort of waiting-period, the changes in this remarkable young man were happening too fast for even the wise Friars to foresee.

Merton was a visionary, even lonely, character around St. Bonny, they say, who spent very little time with the social life of the college and a lot of it meditating in the woods and hills above the campus. "And as the months went on, I began to drink poems out of those hills," he wrote of this place and period. A special spot for him may have been a certain mountain-meadow, a gentle space several hundred feet up.

Merton's climactic moment is well known, and came while he was gazing into the grotto of St. Therese, a little shrine in plain site on the campus. Here he reached his decision to become a Trappist monk, and in 1941 left for the Abbey of Gethsemani in Kentucky.

From there Merton's story tells itself. His 1948 autobiography *The Seven Storey Mountain* was a best-seller. His inspiring verse and profound meditations are as dear to many secular readers as those of poet-questers Rumi or Rilke. One of the leading Christian writers and thinkers, Merton was a unifier the world so desperately needed. Active in social causes and the anti-war movement, Merton found middle ground between the church of the Cross and other disciplines like Zen Buddhism. As he left for a conference in Bangkok, Thailand, one of his fellows had a premonition that Gethsemani would never see its famous Brother Louis again. Merton was electrocuted by a faulty fan in December, 1968, too young at 53.

There are rumors that the trees of the mountain-space special to Merton fell in at about the time he died, creating the heartshape on the hill, a natural testament visible from campus. Though none offer proof, some locals resist the idea, claiming that the shape is a mere accident, and that the trees were mortally-felled, either for logging or oil-drilling. Tell that to the students, many of whom visit the Heart frequently, reporting spirits, mystical moments, and a sense of sanctity that keeps this space sacred still.

White Magic

B. CHILDREN OF THE LEFT HAND

BIRD OF PERDITION

[The family lived on Peckham Street in Buffalo, and their story is from around 1900.]

By eight months of age the first-born girl was the most irritable baby anyone had ever seen. She cried and carried on constantly, and no one could get any peace. Family gatherings were impossible, to say nothing of simple sleep at night. Of course the family did everything they could to understand, but no doctor was of any help. Their local priest, too, felt out of his depth, but he sensed something, and knew where to send them.

A priest from another part of the city came for a visit and examined the environment of the home, lifting and inspecting objects so curiously that they began to think he was addled. It was about then that he thought to examine the pillow usually placed beneath the baby. He felt around in it and discovered an odd-shaped lump. Many pillow-feathers were stuck together in the shape of a bird with one wing missing. It actually seemed as though the natural components of the pillow - like blood coagulating - had congealed to form an image. This was the oddest thing any of them had ever seen.

The old priest examined it carefully until he was assured that it was no natural thing, then put it in a pan, poured salt on it, and set it in the oven. "If the other wing had had a chance to form, that child would not have lived," he said. He studied it as it burned all the way.

Then he soaked cotton balls in some sort of liquid, possibly holy water, then stuffed and swabbed them into every possible avenue of the house: windowsills, thresholds, even keyholes, anything through which even air could pass. When he came again the little girl was still suffering, and the family was still in despair. "Must be something I left out," said the old priest. "Is there another door around here?"

Sure enough, behind a false wall was an old door no one had thought of at the time of the first treatment. This was seen to in the same fashion, and almost immediately the child recovered. The old priest pulled elder members of the family aside. "The person who did this has to be someone you know. I can't tell you the name, but I can tell you how to know them. Whoever it is won't be able to enter this house, ever again."

Even though we probably could have used names - the witnesses are that sure and that reliable - we chose none that might identify the house or the family, and surely not the witch, long deceased. She's almost to be pitied. It was the older sister of the child's mother, who must have envied the successful husband, thriving marriage, and new child of her younger sibling. And truly, she never again set foot in the once-troubled house. After arriving for family gatherings and balking a time or two on the steps, she never came close to the house again, making excuses thereafter. "If we were to show you a family photograph," says a witness, "she'd be the one you'd pick out." She had that look to her, that vampiric arch to the brows. May she rest.

Spirits of the Great Hill

The Hinsdale Horror

The first dramatic incident may have been a lamp flying across a girl's bedroom in the old farmhouse near Olean. Soon the rest of the family heard noises, starting with the usual poltergeist-pounding, becoming more expressive: groans, churchy chants, even a chorus of screams, as if from a pipeline to torment.

There were apparitions, as real as the living; the problem was their coming and going. One of the first and most troubling was a "black man" - not African-American, *black*, a traditional image of the Devil. From outside the house someone saw a woman on a bed within it, weeping. Several family members glimpsed a body hung from a noose on a tree and a weird female apparition near the pond. As the case developed, two young men spent the night, heard noises outside in the wee hours, and ran out into the moonlight. On a large, bare lawn and rough ground for running, they cornered a strange figure against a tree. They took its picture, then nipped in for the nab. It vanished. The ASPR - the American Society for Psychical Research - was convinced of the picture's legitimacy.

Things at least looked nasty. The family returned one night to find a letter-opener pinned to a picture of one of the children. Cars broke down strangely, and a chimney was partially dismantled from the inside. Something had been piling bricks in one spot of a crawlspace above the house from which mysterious noises had been coming. Several family members woke with unexplained burns on their bodies, one of which later affected an investigator. The family thought their old farmhouse roaringly haunted, and one of the children "targeted" - possessed. The family reached out for help. The matter hit the papers running.

The *Buffalo News*' Bob Curran addressed it in several mid-1970s articles, and Mike Vogel revisited it in 1980. A number of luminaries got on board as well, like author-psychic Alex Tanous, who gave the house a run-through. He pronounced it the scene of seven murders, even identifying spots. ("This was a hanging, here three people burned...") With TV crews and research teams, Tanous and St. Bonaventure's Father Alphonsus Trabold conducted a simple ceremony of deliverance. Prayers were said, a feeling seemed to be rising, caged birds went crazy, strange wailing sounds were heard outside, and the "spirits" seemed to split. Things calmed down for a time, but eventually they heated up again, and the spirits got what they seemed to want: the flight of a family and a house to themselves.

Father Alphonsus believed that the family were sincere and that there could have been psychic phenomena, but he was not ready to declare demonic involvement or outright possession, and he did no "solemn" - official - exorcism. To this day he is unsure this case may not have been merely that of a "simple" haunting.

These cases are often touchy, and writers need to use discretion, at least as long as the matter is fresh. What we call "the Hinsdale horror" became a hot-button issue in its day. Journalists broke the names of all parties, and the afflicted family - and the house they lived in - could be identified. A family that had owned the house for its first century felt accused by the psychics, and pointed out that no murders, dramatic or otherwise, had taken place in it. Some who'd written and said too much about the case were at least concerned about the possibility of lawsuits. The troubled family fell apart, and experienced other tragedy. They've left the area.

White Magic

DIABOLIC FROLIC

[Rumors of Satanic cults and covens have tormented the West for centuries. Most of the pros think kids are behind the vandalism and graffiti of today, often timed to the release of an Ozzie Osborne album. In the 1980s a new panic took hold.]

Along with some of his free-spirited pals, the only White dreadlocked kid in Jamestown met with some persistent harassment in the spring of 1988 that seemed much more serious than the usual teenage thing. His father, Professor Jeffrey Victor, was puzzled, and shocked to find something bigger behind it. *Satanic Panic* is his book about "the most dangerous urban legend of our time," according to Jan Harold Brunvand, who, as author of *The Vanishing Hitchhiker*, should know.

Satanic cults had been an "urban legend" since the 1960s. To some, cults like that of Charles Manson and Jim Jones promised a real war, to which the west's cattle-mutilations (often linked to UFOs) seemed just warmups. By the 1970s groups calling themselves Satanists were out, and Wicca (not related) thrived. Soon legions were imagining devilry everywhere, even in the moon-and-stars logo of Procter & Gamble. (In 1982 that stout capitalist company hired staff to deal with five hundred letters a day about its "Satanic" sign.) Even Flower Power and the New Age inspired backlashes. The mass media was not slow to see a goldmine.

In 1985 CBS' *20/20* studied Satanic ritual abuse, and its "experts" included law people, an evangelist, and a psychiatrist. Geraldo Rivera caught up with "Exposing Satan's Underground." Careers, albeit brief ones, dawned in Satan-spotting and the recovered-memory syndrome. Parents and child-care workers were accused of ritual abuse and imprisoned. Some may still be behind bars, and to many in the general public a Satanic underground seemed at least possible. Ah, Salem!

In April of 1988 a Satan-finder had spoken in Olean about the plague of ritual abuse. Soon rural parts of northeastern Ohio, northwestern Pennsylvania, and the southern tier of Western New York were swept up in rumors about violent Satanic cults, set to kidnap and sacrifice blonde, blue-eyed virgins on the eve of Friday, May 13. Girls meeting at least the first two specs would be easy to find in heavily Swedish-American Jamestown, but why did this May date settle in instead of the avowedly pagan first? Never mind. The panic had some individual peaks, mostly in or near the Western Door. The Empire State - at least some loose cannons in the Southern Tier - struck back. Like nowhere else.

"Punk"-looking youths - rare in 1980s Jamestown - were harassed, some with death-threats. People walked around town with baseball bats, and imagined robed rites and animals hung from lampposts. Four thousand bucks of vandal-damage was done to a warehouse used by rock bands (including the young "10,000 Maniacs") and rumored to be a cult convenience. On the fated night, only police barricades kept a hundred cars loaded with clubs, knives, guns, and loco locals from unleashing Walpurgisnacht in a wooded park reputed to be the hub of Beelzebub.

May 13 came and went with no savaging of virgins, at least of the Satanic kind, or evidence of anything but addled fiddle-faddle. Lord, what fools these mortals be. Sometimes, anyway, the author too frequently included.

Spirits of the Great Hill

The King of the Wood

The Celts were the first historic Europeans, linked loosely by religion, language, lifestyle, and customs. Though Celtic people once held a vast territory, the Celts were neither nation, race, nor empire, and the more technologically-advanced Roman civilization ended their European dominance and that of their culture-preservers, the Druids. The four major Celtic religious festivals were Samhain, Imbolg, Beltain, and Lughnasa, the first days of the months of, respectively, November, February, May, and August. Though all have other names whose spelling and pronunciation vary, the celebration was constant, always the night before the day, involving fires, frenzy, and occasionally human sacrifice (which, regrettably, has been practiced the world over). The first of these, the Celtic new year, is obviously our Halloween, and all were adopted in some form by the early Christian Church. Through some tortuous process, also contestable, the Celtic holy eves have become associated with Satanic witches' sabbaths, and are now sacred to Wiccans, modern "witches" (prone neither to Satanism nor sacrifice, we note).

On August 2, 1990, a fourteen-year old babysitter and her infant charge were found knifed to death behind a Palmyra school. A classmate confessed to the murders, to which a whiff of brimstone attached.

The defense did its job as best it might. There had been rumors of cults in the community; a sharp lawyer brought in a national Devil-finder to attest that Satanists were behind the local graffiti, and that brainwashing, even demonic accomplices he feared to aggrieve, had driven the boy to murder.

The DA's - and the victims' families - wanted justice, and attested back. An authority on Satanism and witchcraft, Professor Philips Stevens of the University of Buffalo came to argue *au contraire*, noting the national hysteria of Devil-scaring, such timely light with no perceivable heat. His testimony rightly disputed the link of Lughnasa to actual Satanism; it did not defy the possibility of a keen cult dull on its mythology. The jury, though, was settled. The accused was convicted of second-degree murder. Lost in the prevarication is surety.

The date of the Palmyra murders - August 1 - is suspicious. Lughnasa (Lammas was its Saxon name) is the summer festival of Lugh, the pan-Celtic solar deity. His rites may have involved sacrifice. Much was made of the Lammas Day 1100 death of an English king, William Rufus, son of the Norman Conqueror. Almost from the day of Rufus' accident in the New Forest, stories circulated that his death was ritual regicide. Margaret Murray's controversial *The God of the Witches* wondered if Rufus ("the Wiccan King") was the devotee of a witch-cult killed in a rite he'd willingly entered, a la Frazer's *Golden Bough*.

In Frazer's understanding of the basis of sacrifice, a victim was picked to represent the cycles of nature, death and rebirth, that had to be kept turning by human action. In one famous Roman rite, an individual called "the King" entered combat with a challenger in a sacred wood on Midsummer night, a solstice, a night as seminal as a Celtic holy eve. The winner reigned in splendor another year. In most times and places no combat-rite was needed, and the victim could be child, adult, or animal. Do we know the whole story in Palmyra? Some say that the infant was the goal of the ceremony, and that the girl gave up her life, not her duty.

The Sacred Roycroft

We are punished, not because of our sins, but by them.
Elbert Hubbard

Spirits of the Great Hill

The Shroud of Roycroft

[Though the famous Shroud of Turin is widely presumed to be the portrait of our Savior, the Church has never claimed it to be more than a mysterious object. That seems to fit. Controversy surrounds its dating and the production of its curious 'reverse' image on the old piece of cloth. No test, however, seems conclusive except to the side that likes what it hears. We may have something like it in Western New York.]

In 1964 Kenneth Koeppel found an unexpected treasure in the attic rafters of his family's new home in Olean, NY. He unrolled the two-foot square swatch of soft leather to see the image of Elbert Hubbard (1856-1915), the Master of Roycroft, in a coat and possibly a tie, gazing ambiguously back at him. That would be Hub, all right. The big house on North Street held other Roycroft productions - several pieces of furniture - but the first owners could give Koeppel no background on the leather two-by-two, and it's still mysterious.

We don't know when it was made. The 1994 *Buffalo News* article suggested that it was at least a century old, though the image is of an older Hubbard than the entrepreneur-publisher-writer-community-founder-country philosopher who turned 38 halfway through 1894. We don't know how it was made, and even the source of the leather is more mysterious than it should be. Those who have looked at the hide and ought to know such things can't decide on the animal once inside it.

The matter became a sort of obsession to Mr. Koeppel, who devoted the rest of his days to figuring it out. "The only sure thing is that nobody's ever seen anything like it," he said when interviewed by the *News* in 1994 (at the age of 85). Worried that he was running out of time, he contacted and visited many museums in his quest.

Roycroft historians knew of no similar images or processes, and photographic pioneers Eastman-Kodak in Rochester had few ideas. Even the Smithsonian, more or less the Supreme Court of such matters, was undecided. David Haberstich, head of the Smithsonian's photographic collections, concluded that the Hubbard hide had elements of photography, but that the image "has a very painterly quality." As was often done with 19th century studio portraits, the original photo was probably painted or retouched. Then it was rephotographed and reimprinted on the leather. Somehow. Only an expensive lab analysis could tell the whole tale.

Roycroft collector and scholar Boice Lyddell has tried to track the object and come up with only dead ends. The only certainties in the matter are that it's the image of Elbert Hubbard and that it's been compared to the shroud of Turin. Though outwardly pleasant, Hub's expression is hardly pious. There is a hollow quality to it, almost sardonic, as if challenging us to figure out how his image was made. Hub looks like a man who's just been informed that he's bankrupt and asked to smile for the photo. It's an odd testimonial, a grim portrait few of us would find flattering. Doubtless the process is purely natural, and the investment of time and money would reveal it... But we can't really say that yet, can we?

The Sacred Roycroft

MICHAEL'S MOUNT

[So much ancient sacred architecture was aimed at embodying "the world-mountain," a high point that could be declared a spiritual center. In the words of Thomas Barrie, *Spiritual Path, Sacred Place*: "The sacred place often symbolized the center of the world, the omphalos or navel of the world, the place where primordial creation took place. Frequently these sites are associated with sacred mountains, like the Greek sacred site at Delphi." Towers, pyramids and earthworks serve the purpose. Little did we guess that Roycroft might be part of it.]

In the winter of 1998 a geologist who'd read *Shadows of the Western Door* called with something he thought might be interesting. To our meeting at the Roycroft Inn that March night he brought aerial photographs of East Aurora that had a number of implications for Roycroft, a site of interest from almost every paranormal perspective.

The practiced eye of dowser-geologist George Pannella pointed out two curiosities, a pair of circular rises, perfectly spherical and symmetrical. From the sky above the winter landscape they looked like twin vanilla wafers. Only someone who has it shown to them realizes that the streets of the village rise smoothly to a gentle, flat peak just southeast of Main and Center streets, or, in other words, at the heart of the Roycroft Campus. The other dome is half a mile or so to the east.

Domes like these are neither very high nor terribly rare. Two so perfect and so close together are most uncommon, and it's possible one was incorporated into the siting of the Campus. It calls even more into play one of the possible meanings for "Roycroft" - "King's Hill."

When asked his take on it, Pannella conjectures that Hubbard must have had deeper exposure to the old ways than many of us have thought. He may have been a dowser himself, and he could have had exposure to some sort of *feng-shui*, the Asian landscape-philosophy. "It's not only a Western art," says George Pannella. Another connection comes to mind.

The fact that these two are side-by-side suggests a landscape-image of the breasts of the Earth Mother, which makes sense knowing Hub's feminist leanings. Katherine Maltwood's (1878-1961) statue "Magna Mater" ("Great Mother") was once a part of the campus.

In the lore of the modern mystics, a line of high points - major religious sites dedicated to dragon-fighting saints like George and Michael and dragon-fighters from other Western cultures - figures in a mystical landscape-message and a global alignment we discussed at the end of *Shadows*. (See "The Dragon Path.") If it exists, this feature may pass right through the Western Door.

The statue of Michelangelo, Renaissance polymath, stands out on the lawn of the Main Street school. It was once in the middle of the campus, more near dead-center of the mount. As if for guidance, the bronze of Hubbard himself looks over the left shoulder at the famous Florentine named for the dragon-killer, the archangel linked to high mystical shrines. Hub's alertness to the gestures of mysticism may be one more expression of an even deeper interest. It may also be simple coincidence; if so, it's one more of those Roycroft connections that makes such a pile by now.

Spirits of the Great Hill

"Dangerous Negations"

[Hubbard's longtime friend *St. Louis Mirror* editor William Marion Reedy (1862-1920) was widely regarded the mentor in Hub's constant quest to sift the timeless from the merely trendy. The wise and scholarly Reedy helped popularize a number of authors - like Hawthorne and Dickinson - at the time relatively unknown in America, and helped break Yeats, Thomas Hardy, G. B. Shaw, and the French Symbolists. (One of the most remarkable writers Reedy "broke" was "Patience Worth," the bestselling spook, who, in 1913, began to channel books through St. Louis housewife Pearl Curran.) It's natural for his contemporaries to wonder what Reedy thought of his protege once student had out-famed teacher.]

Even his defenders hardly vaunt Hub's poetry and fiction; even his foes respect his judgment of others' writing. In an early issue of *The Philistine*, for instance, Hubbard sides with young Irishman W. B. Yeats, then-obscure and now-legendary, against a pair of poets then-hip and now-forgotten. Wherever he could Hubbard tried to enlighten the public, publishing literary classics as if they were (or should be) popular. A piece in the June 1900 *Philistine* magazine seems to prove Hub's metaphysical interests, which were known to his contemporaries but which, until recently, needed proving in the Arts & Crafts community.

"He has a leaning towards mysticism," writes W. M. Reedy of Hubbard. "He believes in inspiration. He talks of his psychic sense as one to whom it is a great and grave verity." Reedy found Hub, as did everyone, practical, but also noted "much of the seer" about him. "He is Walt Whitman and Ruskin (two of Hub's idols)." With insight "into the things hidden from others," Hub was "filled with the essence of the Godhead," with "traces of all the dreamers, old and new, hints of all the heresies, suggestions of the great visionaries of our world." Reedy proclaimed Hub "a mystic philosopher, for all his gospel of work... a sublimated variation of one of the modern 'prophets,' 'divine healers,' 'Christs.'"

Well. We all see the tendency to complicate people we like, likening athletes to surgeons and coaches to Zen masters. Here it was a salesman-author whom the modern world no longer regards a lion of the spirit. Reedy's lingo has uneasy overtones. Hub's "gigantic dynamo of individuality," seemed now and again "fearsome" to Reedy, waking "a dread that some of its manifestations may proceed to dangerous negations."

"While we say that Mr. Hubbard is a good man," Reedy finishes, "and is doing a good work at East Aurora... We may be permitted to doubt that the many are as yet sane enough to approach the truth he teaches, without danger to what we call their souls."

In the following *Philistine* Hub praises Reedy to the skies, but finds him not yet "emancipated," not ready for some ideas Hub is with to the hilt. What sort of truth is a danger to souls? Reedy has to mean some metaphysical, even sociopolitical, attitude that could be disastrous taken without its fine points. Nietzche was like that, and even those who agree with some of the most effective rhetorical passages of all types would hardly want mobs taking them for mantras. But what was Reedy getting at? It's clear that these two men had many a private philosophical talk. This could be a philosophy well beyond anything that became public.

The Sacred Roycroft

ELECTRICKS

The spooks seem to keep up with us whatever we do. Unexplained electrical effects - lights and televisions and other appliances spontaneously self-adjusting - have been staples of paranormal rumor since the technology has existed. The reader is free to imagine those reported of the Roycroft Inn and Campus. A few examples should suffice.

First to the lights. Rumors of light bulbs going on and off of their own volition are legion over the years at the Inn. In the 1970s when the Inn was a Turgeon restaurant, the managers were repeatedly frustrated after turning everything out, locking up, and noticing one or several back on as they pulled away. Many hours were wasted going back into the empty building - the second time of an evening - to turn out lights and seek trespassers.

One of the first weeks after its 1995 reopening, the Inn's adding machine cut loose, spewing paper and figures all night long. Few employees attributed it to anything other than the froliscome spirits of the Inn.

"Electronic Voice Phenomena" (EVP) is one of the better-known modern psi effects, usually involving phones, tape recorders, or other sound-producing gadgets. Where the signal comes from and when it arrives may be of more significance than where it's received, but something of the sort may have happened in the Gift Shop in one incident we wrote up in *Shadows*. (An alarm system recorded what seemed to be footsteps, moving furniture, and even muffled voices - after hours.) The author experienced an odd case of this during his early-1980s stay at the Inn. One evening he returned to his apartment to find the answering machine flashing, signaling two messages. When they were replayed, there was a third - a woman's voice, impossibly faint, brandishing a nonsensical phrase. No matter how many times it was played it was unclear - all but her tone: stern, indignant, fixated.

Possibly the most inspiring of these effects we've recorded involve the nocturnal lights in and above the Ruskin Room, which do not seem caused by the earthly lighting. Two managers noted a veritable kaleidoscope from within it during a storm. This is reminiscent of Paul Devereaux' "Earth Lights," the mysterious luminous spheres and even shapes sometimes reported above geomantic-sacred sites, like Stonehenge, the Great Pyramid, Newark (OH)'s serpent mounds, and certain cathedrals. This is impressive in so young a building.

Colin Wilson sums conjecture with the surmise that the "spooks" - whose earthly operations may be as electrical as those within the human body - can summon up a sudden, concentrated electric charge, since many lights and radios thus operated are still switched off. Maybe... though what that says about voices and "Earth Lights" we leave to conjecture.

JOHN BARLEYCORN'S CURSE

A folkloric hex rides upon Roycroft because of Elbert Hubbard's stance as a teetotaler. Word has it that the Master of Roycroft declared that no one after him who served alcohol in the Inn could make it profitable. This one, however, seems hogwash. The current operators of the Inn surely sell drinks with their dinners, even drinks without to many who wish, and they're getting by just fine. The community, at last realizing en masse the treasure it has, seems to have rallied behind

Spirits of the Great Hill

Roycroft, and the tightrope between success and failure seems these days at least a catwalk.

One could see how some such rumor could get started. The string of proprietorships between the Great Depression and the Inn's reopening seemed so blighted that any village imagination would have been searching for some explanation. Even during that threescore string there was one glittering success.

After Hub's dip in the Irish Sea, Roycroft's fortunes ran downhill until the Inn was in receivership. In 1947 the bank that held it gave it to one of their clerks who had some money of his own. Some said this was pure fraud and an inside joke, but Lewis Fuchs became the only successful post-Hubbard owner the Inn had had, and he built the bar (which in his term was packed five deep on the traditional after-work happy hour). The Inn became a thriving restaurant, a dignified speakeasy, and the natural gathering-place for the whole town until Fuchs gave it up in 1955, launching another four uneven decades.

Lewis Fuchs gained, and he also gave back. He cared about the Inn, and installed the wondrous sprinkler system that made it fireproof and probably persuaded later desperado owners to think of torching other properties for the insurance settlement. So great was the feeling for Lewis Fuchs that, it was said, no one could be found to say a bad word about him. That has to be a record in East Aurora.

Lewis Fuchs seems also one of the few Inn owners who had some idea of its mystical significance. For instance, he commissioned a small pamphlet explaining the Roycroft seal, so far as could be explained. A later owner told an odd story to Scott Carnes:

Fuchs himself was known to laugh at the reputed teetotalist curse. "Hubbard didn't mean it," he said, on one occasion so surely that his conversation-mate pressed him for his source of information. Fuchs was said to confide that the spirit of Elbert Hubbard was his source of guidance in all matters pertaining to Roycroft. One thing is certain: Fuchs was the only owner of Roycroft (after Hubbard) who had made it prosper, and prospered by it.

The Prophecy

[This tale comes from the fall before the Inn's grand opening in 1995 when it was open only to workers and handymen.]

The renovated Inn is certainly a prettier place than its 1970s self. It's tidier, more elegant, and well-remodeled. It's also lost much of its intrigue. The dark corners and winding entranceways are mitigated. It feels more like a museum-gallery than a dungeon-become-pub. This may account for the 1990s decline in paranormal reports. Sometimes remodeling makes the spooks freak out; sometimes they just go away, wherever it is, and stay there.

During the earliest stages of the renovation of the Inn, small teams of carpenters and architects were at work within the closed building. Attempting to understand the structure, they were constantly peering under floorboards, behind walls, and into foundations. One of them found something that terrified him.

We think it was a piece of paper found in the first-floor someplace, to the east of the former bar, in the part of the Inn just beneath the Ruskin-room tower.

The Sacred Roycroft

It could have been a newspaper, or published material of some sort; its message was evidently quite personal to the man who found it. Something he read on it shocked him. Its date could have been anytime in the last hundred years, but we sense it may have been from the Roycroft's heyday.

What did he see? Was it a prophecy for the world in the coming ages, some utterance of "Frater Elbertus" (Brother Elbert), "the Fra" himself? Was it something merely paranormally curious, perhaps simply synchronistic, a headline from earlier decades that hit the nail on the head for the current day? Was it a stray piece of newspaper whose message was personal, momentous only to himself? Whatever the man read into it sent him rushing from the building. He quit the crew and left the area. No one knew how to reach him after that. A strong reaction.

NIGHTMARE ON WALNUT ST.

Known generally for his oils, sublime landscapes and pastoral settings, Alex Fournier was one of the most distinguished artists in the Roycroft fold. The impression is about that Fournier never painted people. He may have done no portraits, but people appear. Just look at the right painting.

Fournier's studio was in the back, mid-block, of the house on Walnut Street in which he once lived. Paranormal phenomena - generally of the tamer sort, sounds, voices, small moving objects - have been reported of this studio, currently a graceful teal wood building with a sense of allure. The psychic fireworks - and on only one known occasion - are reserved for the house in which he lived, owned by Kitty Turgeon.

In the mid-1970s some friends of the author had suffered a fire in their house, and needed to vacate for a few days. Kitty Turgeon, then staying elsewhere, offered them her East Aurora house for the needed period. All went well until late the first night, when some effects the pair found shocking took place. We gather that they involved rattling shades, heavy footsteps and other troubling effects. The next night they seemed to escalate, and the couple fled the house, vowing never to return. Lest we think the house is violently haunted, let it be said that this event has never been reported since. Kitty feels only a blissful presence here, a guardian angel. It would be no wonder if the spirit of Fournier had power, and intended to spread only good.

Beneath the wallpaper of this home were several murals, rediscovered and restored by Kitty Turgeon. Fournier also painted the glorious panels in the Roycroft Inn's Salon, all sites strongly featuring religious architecture. Though cities London, Venice, Rome and Paris could hardly be recognizable without their monumental churches, Fournier's shots of the Egyptian sphinx and pyramids and Classical and Asian temples seem chosen exclusively for their religious-mystical function. The fact that Roycroft and its East Aurora campus are included seems suggestive, another connection to the classically sacred.

THE HALLWAY STALKER

For much of the 1970s and early 1980s the Roycroft Inn was not as grand as it once was and is again. The condition just enhanced its psychic vigor. Most of the best tales we have come from this period.

One of the most persistent paranormal impressions of the old Inn was

Spirits of the Great Hill

that of heavy night-time footsteps in the third-floor hall, belonging to no one. Sometimes these were subtle, just below the normal range of sound. Sometimes they were thunderous, but never accompanied by other noises that would explain the sudden disappearance of living walkers - no doors opening and closing to apartments, bathrooms, or fire escapes, no steps down the stairs. They went to the fire escape at the end of the hall and never returned. One of our confidants listened for these carefully whenever they occurred. He took to chaining the fire escape closed, hoping to catch the walker. The steps ended as usual. He leaped out and caught no one. They were just footsteps, beginning and ending here, arriving nowhere.

At other times - in those days they were slick wood floors - it was the impression of someone standing just outside one's door, breaking the sheen of the hallway light where it reflected beneath the ample threshold. From just the right spot in one's room, it was an easy thing to see. There were no sounds of steps with these.

Of course, the ambitious ghostbusters of the third floor - three able-bodied, thoughtful males - did their best to leap out and catch the spook by surprise. Nothing but mystery ever waited. No mortal could have escaped so fast and soundlessly, and only elaborate special effects could have duplicated the marvel.

Never, though, did the sounds of footsteps accompany the one physical effect - the turning doorknobs. This was scary, something the writer experienced a time or two in his late-70s stay. He didn't think much about it until talking to others to whom it meant far more. The handful of budding spookhunters tried to recreate the experience; not one of them could shake the knob and escape.

They devised a scheme to catch the mystery. Late at night - they were all nightowls in those days - two of the three stayed in their rooms. The third spritzed the dark floors with cornstarch, backing into his own apartment. If any noticed the effect of the turning doorknob, he phoned the other two. They came out to check for footprints. Nothing - ever. Once, though, one was abashed to confess that when he heard his doorknob rattle and presumed it might be the famous trick, he threw the door open so fast that he conked his girlfriend, dropping by for a visit.

The Christmas Spirit

Something about the Campus atmosphere seems to put people into mood as the Yuletide nears. Volunteer docents lead tours and greet guests, and restaurant and reception business thrives. Even the Roycroft's most distinctive colors - a piny green and a citric red - are roughly those of Christmas. (These hues in combination, ivy and berry, are also associated with magic in Celtic lore.) The Campus still comes to life at this time of year, perhaps in many senses; a good deal of the modern spooklore we've recorded seems to date from the holiday fortnight.

In Hubbard's day his Campus was such a gumbo of free-thinkers that it was virtually irreligious in conventional senses; yet Hubbard timed some of his grandest gestures for this part of the year. His gathering of 'Philistines' ("The Convention of the Elect") was held just before the holiday, a grand week of feasts and speeches to which Hub invited his eclectic and brilliant friends. The fest was a week-long educational celebration for the staff and the entire town.

Some of Hub's other Christmas gestures were more personal, like ensuring

The Sacred Roycroft

jobs to imprisoned men so that they might gain early release and join their families for the holidays. It's hard to envision "The Father of Modern Advertising" keeping mum about this, but it's said he did these deeds without fanfare. There may have been a later set of Christmas miracles, according to one longtime East Auroran.

Every year that he owned the Inn, Lewis Fuchs - the one who reportedly claimed he had guidance from the spirit of Hub - had thousands of dollars worth of food, fruit, and other necessary items loaded into gift baskets and delivered to the homes of the local needy at the holiday season. "Don't you ever tell anyone where it came from," he always admonished his employees. What did he mean by that? How could word of it not get out? From where did the idea really come?

HUB IN FRANCE

[An unusual cross-fertilization exists between the families of prominent Buffalo soap manufacturer John Larkin and famous East Aurora philosopher Elbert Hubbard. Hubbard's sister Mary married Larkin Company lawyer William Heath, and sister Frances married Larkin himself. Metaphysical interests - philosophies such as Spiritualism, Masonry, Rosicrucianism, Christian Science, and Theosophy - permeated Roycroft and may run in all three families. Elbert's own father Dr. Silas Hubbard was a phrenologist, and many meetings of the society were held on the Roycroft Campus.

There are a number of theories for what truly happened to Elbert and Alice Hubbard. Of course it's most likely that they met their deaths as the *Lusitania* went down in 1915. It's not strange that neither's body was ever identified - the scene was chaos - but it is indeed curious that "the Fra" seemed to predict this event at least twice. (See *Shadows*.) Other rumors, however, have one or the other of the illustrious couple spotted alive afterward. This story became our instant favorite.]

While this author's lecture ("Elbert Hubbard's Literary Friends and Feuds") seemed to go over well, it hardly touched the subject of Roycroft supernaturalism. Nevertheless, by March 2000 the well-heeled members of Buffalo's Twentieth Century Club seemed familiar with our study of it. Afterward a woman from the audience approached the lectern with a strange and poetic tale that had been many years in her family.

Her aunt had been the nurse and companion of several prominent Buffalo families, among them that of John Larkin. She had helped bring up the Larkin progeny, who would have known their Uncle Elbert well. (Who wouldn't? He was one of the world's most famous men in his day.)

On a bright day in the early twenties - years after the *Lusitania*'s last ride - our speaker's aunt rode in a limo in the countryside of southern France with one of the Larkin grandchildren. They came upon a man walking toward them in the road. He smiled a bit as if to himself and looked intently at them as they neared, but gave no sign of anything. He just stood and surveyed the day, seeming content with the sunshine, the landscape, the moment. Something about him was familiar. Was it the long hair, the trademark hat, the walking-stick like a wizard's staff? They passed him in seconds that seemed like minutes. The women looked at each other and trembled. It was Elbert!

"We've got to turn around!" said the nurse, wondering what dimension they could have entered, wondering that earth held so many mysteries. "We've got

Spirits of the Great Hill

to talk to him... We've got to bring him back!" The driver slowed, looked in his mirror quizzically. Her companion - Hubbard's niece - leaned back in her seat, then forward.

"No," she said after a pause. "He's got things the way he wants them now. Drive on."

Some Particulars of the Memoirs of Scott Carnes

In its pre-renovation days the Roycroft Inn had a penchant for luring eccentric desperados, an unseemly number of whom came to ends untimely. One mammoth man was a former Hell's Angel, a semipro footballer whose own mass was too much for him, who fell like a tower caving. Another was a shambling, broken lad, limping from accidents until Heaven-sped by a fall in the frigid woods. A third was an affected preppie with another life, rumored wanted for questioning in Buffalo's "22-Caliber" serial murders. One of his rueful boasts was to point to a dent in the plaster along the second-floor stairs, made by his head, launched by the town cops. He took up a razor and watched his red life drip away, a despair - and a fortitude - we'd not have guessed. A fourth was another who took his own life, an uneasy lad whose many changes took him through insecure teen to Navy SEAL to karate black belt... His faith in Roycroft was almost religious, another despair we never guessed. Why didn't it strengthen him in the desperate hours? The last to go was a literate, educated fellow, a country genius living well off his inventions, spending his time in jeans and flannel as a handyman to the Inn.

While outwardly a very logical person, fond of long abstract conversations, Scott Carnes seemed to sense areas of psychic energy. We knew he had much to say about Roycroft, but he'd never consent to an interview, always planning to write his own piece. We thought it would never come. Through a mutual acquaintance it found its way to us, twenty ramshackle typed pages, after illness took him. It was touching that he would think of this in the last days of a life too short.

His notes started with his boyhood move from Wisconsin to East Aurora. The Inn at which his white-collar father had lived for months was his family's first stop. "The building was excitingly old and quiet, but felt 'alive' in that you were always aware of it." Another building with this same "present" feeling was their new house on Fillmore Avenue, home of a well-known ghost who even manifested recognizably as a former owner. For awhile the boy thought his ability to sense places with this "presence" was only the effect of newness and this part of the country. When he realized that others couldn't feel it, he wondered about it a bit more. He picked up the feeling occasionally at other buildings where no ghosts were reported, but he knew it had to mean this type of energy. By adulthood, though, the Roycroft Inn was the only place he could pick up this feeling. All other buildings felt normal, that is to say, inert.

In the 1960s our narrator worked at the Inn for several years as a maintenance man, and had a room on the third floor near one of the town's infamous ne'er-do-wells, then a Roycroft gopher and janitor. This lad was seldom free of any manner of drugs, and had fits, visions, and "you name it." He claimed to have seen a ghost in his second-floor room. As he'd played his drums, it had appeared behind

The Sacred Roycroft

him and walked through the wall. Carnes grilled the lad from all perspectives. His story never wavered.

In this period Carnes was in all spots of the building at all hours. Its "live" feeling was not uniform. It was hardly perceptible in the public areas except for the hotel front hall. It was strongest in the basement, especially the bottom of the hotel-side stairs and in the low cellar under the Salon with its famous Fournier murals. In this cellar Carnes had the strangest experience of his life.

Toward the end of his term, probably in the mid-1970s, a photographer's lights blew a fuse during a reception in the Salon. Carnes went into the cellar to replace it. He knew the Inn so well that he'd gotten into the habit of sneaking around it in the dark. He could see dimly, and used his flashlight only at the fusebox. He did his work and turned to leave.

Perhaps fifteen feet from the doorway out of the salon cellar he was suddenly aware of something behind him, of being watched. It made no sound, but grew to intensity with a forceful feeling of the greatest hostility, directed right at him. His fear was indescribable. He couldn't turn. He bit through his tongue, and later found from the experience that he had loosened a filling. He bolted for the other end, and didn't stop till he had exited through the kitchen basement door.

It was over half an hour before he could come back into the building. He entered the cellar to a feeling of "brooding but benign malevolence" and a strong musty odor new to him. The only physical evidence was his broken flashlight. Whenever he thought of this event in later years it gave him cold shivers and troubled his sleep. Oddest of all, Carnes took a camp-bed back to the scene and attempted to sleep. He took a long time to do it, still freaked, but fearfully excited. He was another whose trust in the goodness of the energy at the Inn bordered on the religious. If it wanted him, it could have him.

Carnes had some practical awareness of sacred geometry, and found it in several places about the Inn that he could easily reach. One rafter angle he remembered as just under 60°. "It may be stretching it, but the 'golden mean' or 'golden section' ratio of 1.618 is the arctangent of 58° 17 minutes," he wrote. To him this was a sign of sacred proportions.

Carnes left the Inn for a few years and came back in the 1970s to work for owner Frank Turgeon. Most parts of the Inn, he felt, were no longer "energized," and the only "hot spots" were at the bottom of the hotel-side basement stairs near the chimney and maybe in the hotel third-floor rear (probably to the east). Carnes helped keep heat in the Inn for two of the foundations that held it afterward. "I understand the government has it now so that's the death of it as a functional enterprise," he wrote. We're pleased to tell you he's wrong. He'd be pleased by the Inn today.

The Roycroft Inn was Carnes' favorite building on earth, and there have been times when its sheer survival was in question. He'd wept for it many times. Carnes had such a rapport with it that he'd have bought it if he'd ever had "the dough," as he said. It would have been his ruin, and his end was coming, as well as all those others. Dream well, shadow-lads. Live again all you enjoy. All of us who read this, all those you knew, come someday to join you. May none ever tell you the building you loved so much has gone before them.

The Invisible College
The Influence of Occult Philosophy

Whoever dares our cause reveal
Shall test the strength of Knightly steel;
And when the torture proves too dull,
We'll scrape the brains from out his skull
And place a lamp within the shell
To light his soul from here to hell.

    Dr. George W. L. Bickley, founder of the "Knights of the Golden Circle"

The Invisible College

ORENDA: THE IROQUOIS SACRED FORCE

Like the heaviest mystical words from other parts of the world, the Iroquois term *orenda* has no synonym in modern English. It might be styled "life-force," or "spirit," but it could be quite a mistake to say that the Iroquois thought what most English-speakers do when we pronounce either term, or that this word means anything as direct as "life." Something is either alive or dead; one can bear orenda in varying degrees.

In an old Iroquois tale, two mystical beings encounter each other in a wood, each seeming to know by sight the power of the other. "I see," says the great snake, confronting the Good-Minded Spirit in child-disguise, "that your orenda is greater than mine." It seems that, in concentrations such as those possessed by the greatest spirits, orenda can be a mighty, even deifying force. It's power, unaffected by the physical aspects of the possessor. Similarities mount to the Asian *ch'i*.

Yet there's another curious aspect to orenda: the sense of justice it seems to bear. It's debatable if any other world culture has concepts of "good" and "evil" like those of some dualist traditions in the West, but all folklores have their dubious critters. For the Iroquois, these evil supernaturals can definitely possess more orenda than most good humans, but since they walk out of the path of harmony, they will always have less than their good supernatural counterparts. However, this force is by all accounts connected also with landscape. It might be manifested in the way Europe is said to have its leys, lines of force about the surface of the earth.

There are sensitives who say they can feel this Iroquois force about certain sites, and that they even hear it. There may be a logical way of finding it. There are books and charts embodying the philosophy of feng-shui (*fung-shway*, "wind and water"), the Asian discipline of architecture and landscape understanding, and here in the West we have dowsing. Some say that feng-shui is not only an Asian practice, and that many Native American societies had something to the same effect. This might even have been roughly understood by the founding fathers of this nation (among them Ben Franklin), reputedly respectful of Iroquois mysteries, who encouraged their fellow citizens settling the new land to make use of the Native American paths in the planning of their own communities. Others claim that, by whatever means, the founders of many early towns of the United States incorporated Native American trackways, sacred sites, and force-lines into their layouts. It's been asserted of Buffalo.

Today Native American mysticism is a fixture of the New Age, permeating (so far as it's understood) or coinciding with almost every paranormal idea - UFOs, hauntings, mystery monsters, the lot. To the Iroquois this philosophy wasn't "occult": it was a part of their religious and natural understanding. To many of us it comes as a new idea that "supernatural" philosophy might underlay the buildings and street plans of Euroamerican, even post-industrial, cities. Get used to it, like so many other mystical ideas around the Western Door.

Spirits of the Great Hill

Iroquois Masons

[Most of the prime players in the American Revolution - Washington, Franklin, and probably Jefferson - were Masons, as were many prominent Iroquois, like Mohawk Joseph Brant and Seneca Cornplanter. Some suggest that inducting prominent Native Americans into Masonry was merely one more way (along with liquor) of controlling them. Others aren't so sure, including many Native Americans.]

Masonry is a ritualized fraternity. Though impressions of it have run the gamut throughout the centuries, opinion distills to four general possibilities:
1) It's an ancient, vast right (or left)- wing conspiracy out to run the world.
2) It's been political, but it's no older than the Renaissance.
3) It's guys who like to get out with the guys once a week. Only a fraction of them are into mysticism, and their apparent political involvement is coincidental. (Membership *has* declined suspiciously with the rise of Monday Night Football.)
4) It's a good, Godly, almost natural philosophy which all cultures in their best moments have practiced. In this sense the term *Masonry* might almost be a synonym for "theosophy."

Into the last camp fell Arthur Parker, scholar, Seneca, archaeologist, and thirty-second degree Mason. Parker's odd pamphlet "American Indian Masonry" is part anthropological treatise, part theosophy, part the disjointed tale of the night-time overland march of four Buffalo Masons into Reservation rites.

Sparked by rumors that remote Native American villages welcomed early Europeans with Masonic signs, words, and lodges (with rites underway), Parker regards Masonry as a spiritual impulse with "moral and philosophical teachings." We should be ready to accept it in different clothes and colors. Parker finds Masonry in four basic Iroquois beliefs.

In the Great Spirit, the Maker of All usually found among any Native American group, Parker saw Masonry's "Great Architect of the Universe." Iroquois stoicism, truth, charity, and consideration qualified as Masonic morality. Iroquois faith in the afterlife Parker relates to the Masonic-Christian core belief. In Iroquois pantheism Parker even descries the universal kinship of all created things, which he allies to the central virtue of Masonic "Brotherhood." How this jibes with the apparent monotheism of item one is left for Parker to explain.

Nevertheless, Parker's pamphlet sees a sort of 'natural' Masonry in the elaborate lodge rooms (like the Zuni kivas) so customary among Iroquois nations, and in any sort of initiation rite. Sacred, magical, ancient "lost words" no longer directly meaningful call to his mind the passwords and archaic lingo of Masonry. In traditions of building and craftsmanship, Parker sees the Masonic devotion to architecture. To Parker the Iroquois Genesis, the creation of Good Mind and Bad Mind, reflects more Masonic-Christian symbolism. In the old Seneca tale of "Red Hand the Brother-Friend" (a man betrayed, slain, and then reassembled by the powers of animals), Parker sees the Egyptian Osiris-myth so dear to Masonry.

To be frank, Parker's "Masonic" Iroquois traits could be found in most preindustrial groups, and we see no reason to think them distinctively Masonic. Parker, though, was in a position to know. He was the Iroquois and the Mason. *You* take it up with "The Ancient Guards of the Mystic Potence."

The Invisible College

SACRED CITY

Most preindustrial cultures recognized sacred natural places, often high points, fountains, or wells, at which they set their special buildings and often oriented them to compass points or celestial events like solsticial sunrises. Often the design of the building itself, through shapes, proportions, and ornamentation, expressed philosophy. This we call sacred architecture.

Some sacred buildings have a processional flair; paths and sightlines express a journey toward spirit. Simple forms can symbolize qualities: divine perfection shows in the Golden Rectangle, a deceptively simple, appealing shape; "the squared circle" embodies the union of opposites like soul and matter; the pyramid means (among other things) the growth of spirituality, from earth to heavens. The "vesica piscis" (of overlapped circles) expresses the union of male and female natures.

Architecture of this sort thrives still in Asia, but in the West the tradition has been underground for centuries, and now a display of sacred styles in a building is often thought to reveal the mystical interests of individual designers, and the influence of groups like Rosicrucians and Freemasons. The extent to which these "pagan" styles soak Christian churches is one of the West's little secrets. Their prevalence in American public architecture - like at Washington, DC - is one of ours. Like occultism - "hidden philosophy" - of all other types, sacred architecture undergoes occasional revivals. Two in America came at the end of the 18th and 19th centuries, as Buffalo was made and then polished.

For a young city Buffalo is remarkably rich in sacred architecture, and, as we said in *Shadows*, its potentially Masonic layout may incline it to mysticism. Buffalo was, after all, a "designed" city, set up just after Washington, DC, whose layout of streets and buildings is as mystical as any in the Nile Valley, and must reflect arcane influence. Some of Buffalo's streets (its "leys") surely point toward features of geomantic ("earth-magic") interest, and its octagon of Niagara Square is the primal *bagua*-shape of the Asian discipline *feng-shui*. Old Joe Ellicott may not have been a Mason, but brother and city-designer Andrew (who worked on Buffalo and Washington) took over the leadership of Ben Franklin's "American Philosophical Society," which many consider a trove of occultists, the Yankee cousin of Britain's "Invisible College." There was no lack of exposure to mysticism in the family team that plotted Buffalo.

We should begin with E. B. Green, the architect who virtually built Buffalo. Green is less studied than some other sacred stylists, and without a lot of measuring it would be hard to know how closely traditional ratios lie within his work. Yet it seems safe to say that most of Green's Buffalo designs display at least the gestures of classic sacred patterns, and it's interesting to note how many of the buildings he designed or remodeled - Delaware Avenue mansions and brownstones, the Old Genesee Hotel - come with ghostlore.

The founder of the "Chicago School" of architecture, Louis Sullivan (1856-1924) designed only two churches, one a cathedral, but that was enough to proclaim him an inspiration to sacred designers (among whom was pupil Frank Lloyd Wright). Sullivan built only one Buffalo structure, the terra-cotta Guaranty

Spirits of the Great Hill

Building on Church Street, but it's his monument, in Claude Bragdon's words, "the finest concrete embodiment" of his ideas.

A style of Romanesque even bears the name of sacred architect H. H. Richardson (1838-1886). New Orleans-born Richardson worked well in Gothic flavors and did a number of fine churches, including one with giant trumpeting angels (nicked "Church of the Holy Bean Blowers") too splendid for its Boston congregation to afford. Buffalo architect John Conlin finds the Buffalo Psychiatric Center Richardson's greatest work. He's enthralled by the 1870 Administration building's "complex, organic qualities," envisioning a "negative tower" between the real two. No wonder the sublime building has its tales.

No American architect is more admired or more original than Frank Lloyd Wright (1867-1959), and Buffalo is stocked with his work. Wright's abstruse "organic architecture" uses the natural features of a site, and grows the building into it like a plant. Where people dwell is its heart, its germ. He may have invented his own type of sacred architecture, one that goes to the root of it all, the Creator. We shouldn't undersell Wright's technical mysticism, and his attachment to concepts like the "first architecture," in line with Masonic visions of God as the prime architect. John Conlin notes Wright's devotion to the Golden Ratio, the sacred proportion so central to Classical aesthetics. "Such an interesting, basic rule," muses Conlin. "So hard to apply."

Wright built a series of houses in Buffalo's Parkside area, including the Darwin Martin house. The Graycliff mansion on the Erie shores, commissioned by Isabelle Martin, holds many traditional features, even an almost megalithic earthwork (whose incorporation came "at the cost of many mirrors," Martin told his Christian Scientist wife). Evidently approving its religious tones, the Piarist Fathers were its last owners before the Graycliff Conservancy. Pat Mahoney, Vice President of the Graycliff Project, freely describes both Wright and Roycroft's Elbert Hubbard as creators of "sacred space." Wright's Buffalo buildings seem notably unhaunted, but we have the ghost of one: the Larkin Administration Building at Seneca and Swan, considered the greatest building ever built in Buffalo and (as of 1950) the United States' "most infamous parking lot."

We can't forget other prominent buildings about Buffalo, obviously conceived along sacred outlines. The Buffalo and Erie County Historical Society (the last building left of the Pan-Am Expo) had the benefit of young Rochesterian artist, architect, and mystic Claude Bragdon, though not likely as a designer. George Dietel and John Wade's City Hall defies labels, but "Eclectic Classicism" may do. Though too elaborate to be truly megalithic, City Hall's profile has a subtle, primal quality, and its ornamentation holds mystical symbols. Daniel Burnham's 1895 Ellicott Square was once the largest office building in the world. Toss in Richard Upjohn's St. John's Cathedral, East Aurora's Roycroft, Father Baker's Basilica, and the overtly Classical Albright-Knox Art Gallery, and we have the appearance of a regional pattern.

It's stunning to note how many buildings that could be considered "sacred" because of the architecture are also allegedly haunted. Even if they don't have ghosts, they draw the folklore. They must have juice of some sort.

The Invisible College

WHITE SHAMAN OF THE LANDSCAPE
[It's no surprise that some message we'd consider "mystical" could be hidden in any design of Olmsted's day; the idea that it's something non-Western is new.]

At the April 1998 conference of the New England Antiquities Research Association (NEARA), New York filmmaker Ted Timreck presented a paper on Frederick Law Olmsted and his landscape-designs. "The Devil's Footstep" noted in Olmsted's use of natural features a balance of the "pastoral" in the Classical sense and the "sublime" in the Romantic. This is bizarrely coincident with a way of regarding natural features based upon Iroquois and Algonquin creation myths.

A giant water bird dove for prey into the original sea. The mud it brought up became the land. The primal female, the Earth-Mother, delivered twin sons ("Good-minded Spirit" and "Evil-minded One") who fell into conflict. European minds could see of these only God and Devil, but the matter may be subtler, and hold no value-judgement. One of these grand earth-born spirits was the embodiment of earthly features - gentle, nurturing, pastoral places ideal for habitation - with related qualities and substances. The other stood for the sublimities, the landscape-challenges: sharp vertical forms, crags, declivities, and a range of its own associations. This is like Asian ideas of yin and yang, and their enactment into landscape *feng-shui*. This way of regarding natural features is totally non-Western, and Omsted did indeed visit China at 21. Those who need it explicated should turn to Timreck, whose work this is.

Timreck merely observes, however, the aesthetic coincidence. He asserts no Olmstedian steeping in Amerindian mysticism that affected the famous landscape-work. It's not impossible, though. Young apprentice Olmsted (1822-1903) spent years in the Hudson Valley and New England's fields and woods. There's no accounting for what he might have learned from the Native Americans.

Mystical artist Franklin LaVoie finds classic Western patterns in Olmsted's Buffalo circles and streets, of which Soldiers' Place (at the intersections of Lincoln, Bidwell, and Chapin parkways) may be the hub. The shape of the primal boat, symbolic of the sail into spirit, appears in his design of streets and circles, pointing into the due north point on the horizon. Mathematical symbolism seems associated with far-off Agassiz Circle to the east, the line of which back to Soldiers' Place bisects the sacred angle (144°) of the other points. An apparent lunar alignment (northeast from Colonial Circle to Soldiers' Place) points to the moon's northern major standstill. Even the image of a landscape-giant, possibly the famous and symbolic statue of David, may be suggested within this design. (One of the rare copies of the original statue does indeed exist near the Buffalo Historical Society inside Olmsted's layout.) Delaware Park lake may be a key feature of the image, whatever its message. What this said to Olmsted is up in the air, but like alignments were part of the landscape-mysticism of many monument-building world cultures. It all suggests that within our urban landscape may be an avenue of sacred ways, incorporating ancient mystical features. To walk or simply regard them could be an opportunity for meditative growth, for peace within urban pressure. Quite a mystical gift to have left a city; may the motorists on the speedy, smoggy Scajaqueda cut-through enjoy it. No one else can.

Spirits of the Great Hill

The Cohocton Head-Readers

[In the early twenty-first century the discipline of phrenology - "understanding mankind through the scientific study of the shape of the head" - is less than, let us say, politically correct, but it once caused a world sensation, and its American pioneers were a pair of brothers from the Western Door, Cohocton's irrepressible Fowlers. Not since Hamlet went off on Yorick has anyone made so much out of a skull.]

As undergraduates at Amherst College the brothers Fowler, Orson Squire (1809-1887?) and Lorenzo Niles (1811-1896), heard a lecture that changed their lives. German doctor Johann Gaspar Spurzheim must have delivered a barnburner about phrenologists Franz Josef Gall and George Combe. The calls of medicine and ministry came suddenly fainter.

Phrenology had been around for awhile. By the end of the eighteenth century the idea was started that the human brain is organized into areas, which is roughly right. The notion that these brain-regions were well-developed according to moral, personal, and physical qualities, and would leave skull-bumps detectable to the touch - well, we think that's wrong. Crazy. It didn't matter. A star was born.

After graduation the brothers Fowler set out talking about reading heads and doing it. Opening offices at various times in Baltimore, Philadelphia, and the Big Apple, the skull-scoping siblings visited many cities and read famous heads: politicians, publishers, painters, physicians, poets. Doors opened. Bro Lorenzo opened a New York office that published two magazines and employed poet Walt Whitman as editor (briefly).

It's a kick to regard: the Fowlers' master diagram, the pleased-looking human head with his egg-bald pate apportioned into irregular territories like a map of counties, with images suggestive of their Latin-rooted functions. (A fattie tucking into a roast embodies "alimentiveness." A sly cupid drawing his bow stands for "amativeness." A father doting on a family scene shows "philoprogenitiveness.")

The Fowlers were entertainers as much as educators, a tag-team "What's My Line" constantly tested by people from one walk of life attempting to give all the signs of another. Hemming, hawing, fretting, feeling their subjects' heads, calculating bumps, and then pronouncing on likely talents and proclivities, never were the brothers fooled. Politically correct or not, it makes you wonder.

The Fowlers' entourage (their "cabinet") came to include sister Charlotte, her husband (publisher Samuel Wells), and Nelson Sizer, a medical student. This freed Orson Fowler to write articles with a phrenological take on every trendy subject of the day - human rights, marriage, sex, parenthood, health, clothing, tobacco and alcohol. War he blamed on people using the wrong organs in their heads. The elder Fowler even sensed his own cranium changing with his efforts to improve himself, and tried to teach others how to help themselves and gauge the effect by reading their own skulls.

With notoriety the Fowler museum grew. It must have been a ghastly Gandalf's-den of busts, casts, and human and animals skulls. Tours of this still menagerie/cranial zoo usually ended with a study of the visitors' skulls. The largest mail order house in New York was devoted to selling Fowler books, journals, and even model skulls to be used in the home-study course. The Fowlers devised an

The Invisible College

Inquisition-like contraption - seemingly a lampshade branching from a commode - in which a trusting participant might sit to be officially head-read.

The Fowlers heard of few metaphysical subjects that did not interest them, and it does not surprise us that elder brother Orson was a student of Spiritualism, even observing the Fox sisters in person (see *Shadows*). He also heard the faked rappings of Charles Chauncey Burr and found them no more like the Fox sisters' percussion "than a church bell is like a Scotch fiddle." Curiously, the Fowlers had little to say about the subject of abolition; not metaphysical enough, we guess.

Always concerned with healthy living, Fowler soon studied the American home, for which he decided that the octagon - a basic *feng-shui* shape - was the ideal. Octagonal homes became the rage. The great Mark Twain retired to such a study near Elmira, and number of others about Western New York are (or were) in Akron, Red Hook, Hammondsport, Stockport, Millbrook, Friendship, Madison, Geneva, Lily Dale, Randolph, and other towns. It may be the Fowlers' most lasting legacy.

Fowler had a host of practical reasons for favoring the octagon (given at length in *A Home for All*, 1853). An eight-sided frame of the same outer area provides about a fifth more inner space than a traditional one, and the increased light and open air helps human moods. It's also hard to believe that Fowler was ignorant of traditional folk wisdom, which maintained that spirits, particularly negative ones, prefer small spaces and tight corners. The octagonal frame eliminates right-angles, chronic gatherers of "bad vibes." Fowler even designed an eight-sided church, but he may have overstepped himself with his multi-leveled mansion in Fishkill, NY. Too big to be stable, it was declared unsafe and dynamited in 1897.

Like an old soldier, phrenology just seemed to fade away. The world tires of any trend sooner or later, if from no other cause than the parody of waves of imitators; but this demise may have been brought on by the rise of more dramatic forms of short-cut wisdom. Helen Blavatsky and her new style of mystical spiritualism ("Theosophy") came along, and the impact of Freud's subtler methods of reading what was inside the head may have doomed the Fowlers' study of its outside.

We have a question mark next to Orson Fowler's death-date since even the Cohocton historians aren't sure when or how he passed. Many historians presume 1887 was his last year, but that was just when he set out in a new direction and (in his early 80s) started a new community in Colorado. We imagine he's passed on by now, but we don't know when, and the Colorado people aren't sure of it, either.

Spirits of the Great Hill

Cthulhu Country

[In *A Ghosthunter's Journal* ("My Vengeance Lurks") we profiled a fictional Buffalo occultist. There was a real one... we think.]

Someone calling himself William Lumley came to public notice when letters began to arrive with famous writer H. P. Lovecraft (1890 - 1937), founder of an ominous, horrific literary cycle, totally fictional, we hope. Lovecraft's "Cthulhu (*Ka-THOO-loo*) mythos" has enduring popularity and a formidable cult of imitators.

This William Lumley (probably 1880-1960) may have been eager then to cry his word, but he's suspiciously hard to trace now, and good scholars and trackers have been on the job. ("I can find people the FBI can't find," says bill collector and ex-Marine Mike Lesner, and author and Lovecraft authority Daniel Harms has also been on the trail.) The possibility has occurred to more than one of them that the Lumley who wrote to Lovecraft lifted a name from the one who lived in Buffalo. The fact that no relatives have ever claimed royalties on his one published and oft-anthologized story may be a sign of something.

At some point Lumley may have toured the world as a sailor, but his long-time residence was on Buffalo's east side. Records suggest that his local occupation was "watchman." Night watchman? A likely-enough job for a solitary occultist. We see why Lumley made no splash as a writer. His poems are ghastly, like heavy metal lyrics without quite such a high degree of symbolic development. His single story ("The Diary of Alonzo Typer," *Weird Tales* magazine, February 1938) is derivative of Lovecraft, to whom it was even handed for editing. Lovecraft never met in the flesh other writers linked to him, like "Conan" creator Robert E. Howard and Clark Ashton Smith, so it's less strange that he never knew Lumley, about whom, nevertheless, Lovecraft's chatty notes give us most of what we have to go on.

In Lovecraft's account, Lumley was a mixed bag. He seemed a real occultist of "unusually wide" reading, yet he claimed familiarity with nonexistent books like the *Necronomicon* and horrific scholars whose very names Lovecraft knew he'd invented, like the "mad Arab," Abdul Alhazred. ("All-has-read," get it?) His blubbering gratitude seemed pathetic to Lovecraft, and his "best friends" were other writers he knew only through letters. His point in contacting Lovecraft seemed to be none other than to tell him that he was right in his horrific visions, because Lumley had seen with his own eyes two of the Elder gods. Lumley was dying to tell someone who would listen that his own region - Western New York - gave the goods.

In 1932 Lumley hosted a man he calls "the Oriental Ancient" for a long Buffalo pow-wow. Lumley frequented a "haunted" valley nearby, of strange elemental spirits and a misty "white presence." He slept in pre-human ruins, witnessed monstrous rites, and claimed "strange and marvellous results" of cryptic chants and spells involving clay images. His 'Typer' tale features a ruined mansion, a lost settlement, and an ancient monument. (The now-vanished Abell mansion was in the lost community of Williamsburg, a region of many ancient earthworks.)

Today Lumley sleeps in an Erie County grave, and we bid him untroubled dreams. Knowing the desecration visiting another cemetery (possibly due its mention in *Shadows*), may Cthulhu keep the name of this one.

The Invisible College

NICOLA TESLA'S FALLS EXPERIMENT

["I am become death, the destroyer of worlds," said Oppenheimer, lifting a line from ancient Indian texts upon realizing the power of his atom bomb. Another inventor may have been even more in tune with the wisdom of the ages, and his goal was only life.]

    Rambo inventor Nicola Tesla (1856-1943) was distinguished as much for his eccentricity as for his science. Today known mostly as the inventor of alternating current, Tesla's means were more those of a psychic than a scientist. He seems to have come to most of his inventions alone in a dark room, simply visualizing. Some of the greatest pioneers in many fields have been astonishingly intuitive, but Tesla has become a cult figure, a New Age darling. Tesla believed there was a natural, inexhaustible energy source - "The Luminiferous Ether" - out there in the universe, free for the taking, and his aim was harnessing this power and giving it to all the nations of the world. Tesla's advanced concepts included:

- Super-batteries, storing years of electricity from environmentally clean solar engines. There'd be no need of nuclear power if these were built, and if they worked.
- Bladeless, pollution-free power turbines for planes, cars, and industries.
- A "thought-transference" machine, putting images from the mind onto a screen.
- Free electricity and communications - TV, radio, and telephone - for all the world.

    Obviously, Tesla had detractors, and outright enemies in the industries his inventions would make obsolete. Some of his ideas had problems of their own. Take his "natural night-light," an artificial aurora borealis made by charging the upper atmosphere. (When do we sleep?) His impermeable electric force field might shield cities and make war obsolete, but could we turn it off? His "artificial earthquakes" sound more like weapons than presents. Who wants an earthquake?

    Tesla's most spectacular experiment was effective, though, and at our own Niagara Falls. In 1895 on behalf of Westinghouse, Tesla harnessed the force of the Falls and sent electricity to Buffalo, introducing the world to alternating current, the death-knell of Edison's politically-correct direct current which failed across distance. Whether Tesla saw this as a result of natural electricity is another question.

    Tesla's grandest vision involved the delivery of electric power, pollution-free vehicles, and communications, free to all parts of the world. The first step depended on a strategic setup of widely-spaced towers and transmitters. The main "Tesla Coil" was to be in Colorado Springs (probably because of its elevation), and a tower at our Falls was only one of four. The others were in Bermuda, Wardenclyffe, NY, and the Azores (Atlantic islands often thought to be survivors of Atlantis). To many, the Falls are unique in the world, and it might seem that Tesla's grand design downplayed them. It's significant that a figure like Tesla sensed a mighty power source at the Falls. He will always be linked with them, and the goal of all his inventions: to benefit humanity.

Spirits of the Great Hill

Human Dimensions

[One of the most adventurous modern explorations into the human spirit had its day in a Buffalo burb.]

Human Dimensions Institute (HDI) was "in response to growing public hunger for solutions to the mystery of the human being, our most critical frontier." The brainchild of Professor Jeanne Rindge, HDI started in 1967 as a lecture series at Rosary Hill (now Daemen) College, then run by Franciscan nuns. Rapid success resulted in the establishment of HDI as a separate entity, a freeform "college within a college," separately incorporated and financed.

As much a venture for its faculty as its students, HDI addressed almost any subject of body or mind that might lend insight into the "piece of work" that is humankind. HDI also conducted its own research program and library service, and sent speakers and workshop leaders throughout the country and abroad. Before it was through, HDI gained international recognition for its research in fields of healing and nutrition. Over 72,000 people participated in its lectures, seminars, classes and conferences, and spinoffs included a publishing house, a magazine with global circulation, and a summer center at Canandaigua Lake that opened in 1973.

HDI did actual lab research in areas of health, nutrition, hypnosis, ESP, and the dream-experience. It studied spiritual philosophies of many types, including Zen and Western meditation, Tibetan mysticism, reincarnation, and Christology. The Institute also worked with a variety of what we might call "holistic" disciplines: creativity, yoga, the environment, and leadership. Even "softer" types of study focused on adult-play, Gestalt, sensitivity, and family therapies.

HDI's members around the world reported creative breakthroughs, self-realization, better health and human relationships, and growth in civic, spiritual, and environmental senses. They felt deeper meaning in their lives and the world around them, and reported that other people noticed the improvements.

For over a decade HDI was "a tax exempt, not for profit, educational, scientific, and charitable corporation" whose program included seminars, workshops, experiments, experience groups, and an irregular series of lectures by some pretty heavy hitters. Among its star speakers: Edgar Mitchell, sixth man on the moon, founder of Noetic Sciences Institute; bio-feedback pioneers Elmer and Alice Green; Eva Reich, daughter of "orgone energy" inventor Wilhelm Reich; parapsychologists Jule Eisenbud and Stanley Krippner; Andrija Puharich, author, mystic, and researcher; Hugh Lynn Cayce, son of "Sleeping Prophet" Edgar; psychic Joan Grant; philosopher Alan Watts; spiritual healers Olga Worrell and Moshe Feldenkrais; and Western Door Seneca historian and teacher Twylah Nitsch.

The glitz shouldn't blind us to the hits, however, and HDI had several in the 1970s. HDI's research director Dr. Justa Smith suspected that the success of faith (or "magnetic") healers might be due to their effect on enzymes in the patient's body. She ran controlled experiments, putting renowned healers to work on test tubes of trypsin, obtaining remarkable results that could demonstrate the effectiveness of faith healing.

Another of HDI's apparent successes was in its study of the discipline known as "psychic photography." Famous proponent Ted Serios was famous in the

The Invisible College

1960s, seeming to project images onto blank film by staring into a camera, focusing his energies, and firing the flash. Sometimes like a pool player the "thoughtographer" called his shots, declaring the images he intended to produce. Most of the time the effort revealed only self-portraits of an agitated Serios, but some occasional triumphs occurred, sometimes images of the things he'd declared he was imagining. Even one should be a miracle. Fred and Jeanne Rindge brought less-famous thoughtographic colleague Joseph Veilleux to HDI, and their study of him under very controlled conditions may validate the practice of such psychic imagery.

In the mid-1970s HDI commenced a relocation to Canandaigua. Upon its rebirth and relocation to North Carolina 50 miles west of Asheville, HDI under its new name VERITAS (Latin, "Truth") set forth these emerging needs to which it answered: *A planetary imperative for humanity to become co-creators (rather than exploiters) of the environment; a growing yearning in people for an environment which is physically, mentally, and spiritually fulfilling; the need to discover meaning in the world and understand expanding human possibilities; a desire to share with others, and gain insight from people of different backgrounds.*

The WNYX-Files

Pan, the goat-footed god, is not so funny when you encounter him.

F. W. Holiday

The WNYX-Files

The Top 10 UFO's

In some circles, UFOs (whether lights or objects) are thought to be the actual air-and-space craft of higher-tech extraterrestrials, our own secret military, entities from alternate spaces or times, or some other possibility we've missed. In other quarters, of course, the subject is considered nonsense. There may be a middle ground, and the answer at least more complex than a yea or nay to the question of objective validity. Some researchers regard UFOs as hallucinations induced by earthly energy of some sort, linked to ghost reports, fairy sightings, and apparitions. Some devotees suspect that one must be in an altered state even to see a UFO, in which case it's a mystical privilege like a religious vision. We think UFOs - at least the en masse reports of them in specific regions - mean something more than mass fantasy; we're not sure what.

We'd heard that Western New York was a UFO hotbed, but the picture never came clear till we put together this list of cases, based on some combination of validity, prominence, and dramatic impact. There are, of course, hundreds of reports, and surely others might have qualified for our list. At all times we've relied upon the conjecture of experts.

Much of the way the world looks to each of us depends on the attitudes through which we behold it. Skeptics are justified in their frustration with all matters paranormal. You can't disprove a negative, i.e., ghosts. (All you can say is that you haven't seen one, and that many reports were illusory.) Some debunkers, however, eager to presume prevarication, seem to ignore good evidence in certain paranormal cases. Whatever; do not expect a resolution to the UFO question soon. If UFO designers are slick enough to cross galaxies, they should be able to keep guessing forever the species that actually debated the standing of "Piss Christ" as a work of high artistic craft.

The Top Ten:

10) Mars Attacks! (1954): A disk-shaped UFO to the west of Griffiss Air Force Base set the jet jockeys scrambling. The chase shot out along the southern shores of Lake Ontario. An F-94 was closing in when the inside of the jet suddenly overheated and seemed likely to catch fire. Pilot and radarman parachuted to earth, but the plane tore off on its own, finally slamming into a tiny town (Walesville, NY, according to Hugh Cochrane) and setting fires. The Air Force sent out a statement to the effect that engine failure caused the accident. This one could be scary, if it's what it looks like.

9) The Ellicottville Flap (1994): The first sighting was reported the morning of February 6, 1994, by two people in a car on Rt. 219, about five miles north of Ellicottville. (Let's see, that would put them... leaving Gypsy's bar.) More would follow into the early spring, a smorgasbord of shape, size, and habits, and with a dozen people checking in. One described a wobbly object, "incredibly bright lights," and "a really beautiful noise, like a distant waterfall." He took a photo of a beam of light which Buffalo News reporter Donn Esmonde acknowledged *could* have come from a UFO. Few other witnesses were willing to go public. "Some of them are professional people," said Hank Dubey, editor of the town paper *Special E-*

SPIRITS OF THE GREAT HILL

Fects. "They're afraid people will think they're a little crazy." UFO people think they were afraid of something else, like "MIBs" (Men in Black). In the same year, Syracuse and Rome, NY experienced flaps of their own.

8) The Seneca Line (1966): In August and again in October, New Yorkers from Sodus to Port Gibson (25 miles south) were shocked to see a fierce light move above the region before heading northeast over Lake Ontario, apparently toward what Hugh Cochrane calls "the Marysburgh Vortex," a patch of understandable turbulence where the water of the Great Lakes funnels into the St. Lawrence River. Starting at about 8 PM, state police received reports of a brilliant light that hovered 30 minutes at one spot, flashing red, green, and white before it moved off. This is also an area of many lake-serpent sightings.

7) Light in Lyons (1891): On December 9, 1891, people in Lyons, NY saw a bright light in the sky, described as "a blue-white aurora-like glow" that stayed over the town and rose and fell in intensity, lighting the whole area like a flare. For the next four months of 1892 the same blue glow appeared each night, then finally faded. No official explanation was ever offered.

6) The Case of the Missing Bellybutton (1980s): One of the most persistent rumors about the entities aboard UFOs concerns their fascination with human reproduction, constantly tinkering with people's navels and privates. Among the recovered-memory images is that of a needle being painfully inserted in either area, taking samples of who-knows-what, or depositing who-knows-what worse. The bellybutton of one alleged local abductee became so badly infected by some mysterious pinprick that it had to be removed by surgery. Yes, the bellybutton. This is an interesting case because the Southern Tier woman was a multiple UFO-experiencer whose recovered-memories were especially convincing. She may even have developed psychic abilities, like perhaps Uri Geller, as a result of the experience.

5) The Jamestown Flap (1968): In June 1968, Thomas Wedemeyer of Jamestown, member of an amateur UFO group (CAP, Commission on Aerial Phenomena), claimed to have been approached by a man posing as "Major Smedley," USAF officer, who interrogated him about his group's knowledge of a reported UFO landing near Buffalo. The encounter left him with a severe headache, and checks of the Air Force found no such officer anywhere. It would develop that this Major Smedley had been seen in other areas, like Erie, PA, where another interview gave another sighter a two-week-long illness.

This episode may be related to a "flap" (the term for an outbreak of sightings) in Salamanca and Jamestown, maybe in the early 1970s, in which a cult of local UFOlogists got scared silly by something - Men in Black, a string of escalating psi events, whatever. They don't return phone calls from inquiring writers. We hear of another impressive late-1990s series from this region, part of a nationally-prominent zone, at least to judge from the reports.

4) Southwestern Lake Ontario (1975): Spring 1975 was a big period for sightings in this part of the lakes. Dramatic, multiple events were reported in and about the eastern end of Lake Ontario, on both Canadian and American shores. While reports of landings and sightings (one of them even lasting six hours) come from other parts of Canada in the general region, the focus seemed to be the southwest corner of Lake Ontario. A young photographer even set up his cameras and caught them at Niagara-on-the-Lake, where sightings were prevalent for weeks. Bright,

The WNYX-Files

deep-orange lights were seen often from 1975 to 1980. They zipped fast, erratic courses and made 90-degree turns.

There may be a pattern to the reported UFO activity and related phenomena about this part of our region and its siting at the juncture of Lakes Erie and Ontario. Some in the Northeastern UFO Organization suspect that Ivan Sanderson's theory of underwater UFO "bases" could be right on track in two deep depressions in Lake Ontario's western end, joined by a long narrow trough.

3) The Circus Animals' Desertion (1975): The *Edmund Fitzgerald* went down on Lake Superior, but the mighty storm called "the Witch of November" had a long reach, and a series of other incidents at the time could point to some super-natural disturbance. There were many UFO sightings from that region of the lakes on the day of the disappearance, and the switchboards of the NORAD center had been flooded with calls. UFOs, including several over southwestern Lake Ontario, were reported 200 miles east of the site of the fabled disappearance. Animals flipped at a Niagara Falls zoo. Several buffalo battered their cages and blew the big house. Amok on a highway, one had to be shot.

2) The East Coast Power Blackout (1965): This was a major event that started at the immense power plants at Niagara Falls. UFOs were spotted at the Falls, Rochester, Syracuse, New York City, and other spots along the power line at the time of the blackout. Whether they were extra-terrestrial craft or natural effects involving lights, shapes, and forces, the might and strangeness of the event satisfies everyone with a taste for mystery. It's been part of the UFO mythology ever since.

1) The Cherry Creek Incident (1965): The feature event - in which a giant silvery football hovered at the treetops and may even have made a touchdown - seemed to be just the keynote of a summer of them in the same small region of Chautauqua County. As *Shadows* noted, the imposing August 19 incident involved electrical oddities, spooked animals, and purple goo on the ground. Testimony had its glitches, but few researchers ever doubted that somebody had seen something. The fact that several witnesses recalled so little of the event implies a whole "missing time" scenario to some UFOlogists. Since becoming the most nationally-prominent UFO event on the Western Door, the Cherry Creek incident has gotten proportionally little attention, especially in light of the fact that it was one of the few acknowledged as "unexplained" by Project Blue Book, the US Air Force UFO-investigation group.

Spirits of the Great Hill

War in Heaven

[Immaterial "battles in the sky" loom large in the annals of the paranormal. One of the most famous from the British Civil War replayed itself several times in the skies near Warwickshire. A member of the detachment Charles I sent to view it recognized an uncle among the cloudy combatants. Rather than psychic events, these spectacles are often thought to be historic ones caught in some natural VCR and shot across the sky for all observers; maybe such are ghosts, however, merely house-or-land-bound. The only phantom battle we've heard of stateside happened above our own Chautauqua County.]

In 1904 Ross Mills' staunch citizen Emery Armstrong Ross compiled the memoirs of his Scottish-American clan. He stuck mostly to family recollections and events from the pioneer history of the region. Other than stratospheric assessments of Scottish poets Burns and Scott, there's little fantasy in his book. At the end comes his one brush with it, recalled from his teens.

The *Aurora borealis* - the "Northern Lights" - had been vivid in the fall of 1843, and the Ross family and friends often ended their evenings watching the display. One cool, clear twilight something drew their attention to the northern sky.

Ross describes a change, like a wide-screen coming into focus. Bright belts of colored flame streamed up from the horizon into the pale milky way. Shifting bands of opaque airy fluid gradually resolved into marching armies, approaching the witnesses, growing in size and clarity as they neared. They were observing a film in the indigo dusk.

These aren't the Miltonic "Wars in Heaven" of an armchair army-man. Ross describes legions, weapons, warriors, and tactics in realistic detail. His rendition can't place the encounter in history, though from the armament we judge that it had to be within decades of his day. From its size and splendor, it seems a European battle, possibly a Napoleonic clash before him, maybe from the American Civil war to come.

Strange for ghostly effects are the dramatic sounds Ross describes, as if "all the combined bolts of the god of war had shot out in one preconceived burst of fury." Even stranger are the light, color, and movement before and after the battle-visions. Ross devotes pages to these impressions, which it's hard to think of anyone envisioning before seeing them in twentieth-century film.

Others besides those on the Ross family's porch witnessed the event, but it was not widely reported. Ross didn't wonder. Like a movie-screen, the spectacle might not have been visible from all points, and it came well past the bedtime of this thin farming community. Ross does well enough on his own to recreate them, the stunned hours his family, guests, and neighbors watched. Finally, after a renewed surge, the armies withdrew as if each gave the field and vanished into the million-starred dark. Then "the dark borders of the belt faded away and blended with the color of the sky, unveiling the hidden stars that again twinkled in all their brilliancy; and nature asserted its prerogative and calmed the troubled skies, and God reigned over all the universe."

The WNYX-Files

THE RANDOLPH FRANKENSTEIN

[The prospect of man-created life still touches nerves. Something curious, even terrifying, may have gone on at Randolph.]

John Murray Spear's aforementioned Kiantone community ("Spiritual Springs") had a predilection for spirit-guidance. In one of these trances came directions "through the organism of Brother Spear" for a perpetual-motion machine powered by "the magnetic life of Nature." Sometime in 1853 a group of devotees in Lynn, MA, set about making the "Physical Savior," only one of its many names.

As of the summer of 1854 the "Universal Infant" - to some a virtual Second Christ, to others an "Electrical Walking Frankenstein" - was still incapable of motion, and its designers were roundly mocked in the Bay State. Though their magazine columns professed "the deep satisfaction which Truth alone gives," they packed the parts off to Randolph, NY, where, "the spirits" maintained, electromagnetic properties in the earth and conditions peculiar to Randolph were friendlier to a machine expected to come to life. Critics, though, believed that the move had two points, both material: to duck the mockery of the intellectual east, and to tap the resources of wealthy Randolph supporter Thaddeus Sheldon (1818-1868).

The scene had to be seen. The new Mrs. Spear climbed a high rock and lay beside the metal contraption, writhing two hours in labor pains "of the spirit," in theory, giving the metal critter some of her generative life. "At precisely the time designated," Spear wrote, "and at the point expected, motion appeared, corresponding with embryotic life." Pulses were detected, continuing for weeks. The critter was cared for like a newborn. But Randolph would prove a prickly nursery. Word spread that man might make himself God, and his consort the Virgin Mary. A mob, maybe led by the local Baptists, beat the zinc out of the fiendish machine, burning Sheldon's barn that stored it (probably on the site of today's Sammy's Diner by the longtime Randolph Inn).

Cynics noted that the machine's disaster freed Spear of the need to show that it worked. Even the great Spiritualist Andrew Jackson Davis conjectured to the effect that Spear's guides this time were the ethereal correspondents of Ace Ventura, Pet Detective, having some fun. They consoled Spear when next they spoke: "Earth's inhabitants cannot be harmonized until there exists a universal method of conveying thought." To that end they proposed "a central telegraphic station" on a Randolph hill christened "Highrock Tower." The trick of building it they never revealed.

We should not forget that in its early days electricity seemed almost a psychic force, as "new age" or counterculture as any idea of Tesla or Reich today. "Magnetism" was linked to all the fads - rappings, octagonal houses - of 1850s spiritualism. Some conjecture that were Spear to come back today, he'd see all his predictions about "psychic" power in our use of electricity; yet others think he may have had something even more metaphysical on his mind, and that we're the ones who'd be amazed could we go back to his and regard this "New Messiah." It would be interesting to see what the excitement was about.

Spirits of the Great Hill

The Lake Erie Serpent and Friends
[Maybe we gave her short shrift in *Shadows*, the famous "South Bay Bessie."]

    The idea of a huge unknown animal living in one of the Great Lakes looks, on the surface, absurd. It would seem impossible for the critter to escape official notice, and Erie, as the only Great Lake to freeze over, seems the least likely home; yet "South Bay Bessie" has gone big-time. We list a few sightings from Erie and, where specified, its eastern neighbor.

- 1793: A giant snake, described as over a rod (sixteen and a half feet) in length, allegedly chased a daffy duck hunter on Middle Bass Island for 100 yards. Suffrin' succotash, that's a fast one.
- 1817: A ship's crew spotted a Lake Ontario critter thirty to forty feet long, with nearly black skin. A naturalist among them thought it might be some type of eel.
- 1880: The crew of the *General Scott* observed a serpent 35 to 40 feet long, with a foot-thick neck and dark mahogany skin, nearly black.
- 1892: The schooner Madeleine left Buffalo for Toledo and drew up on a foaming mass in the water, as if two marine titans grappled. Soon quiet reigned, and a serpent, 50 feet in length and up to four feet around, lay weakly. Its fearsome head projected four feet from the water; its eyes sparkled. Its body was dark brown and had apparently vestigial fins, small in proportion to the rest of it.
- 1896: At Crystal Beach near Fort Erie, four people reported observing a 35-foot serpent with a doglike head. It disappeared just before dark.
- 1900: Three sightings in July of a fast fifty-footer: off the Buffalo breakwall, near Elmwood Beach, and off Stony Point. The latter observers, being sportsmen, loosed a volley of rifle fire; the critter dove.

    Yet reports continue. In August 1992 Bessie, its head as big as a car, was blamed for attacking a sailboat and killing three folks. Three times in the summer of 1993 a snake-like critter (30-feet and then some) was seen in Lake Erie. Its body moved up and down through the water, not side-to-side like a water-snake. In western Lake Ontario in 1829 several children reported a giant snake, twenty to thirty feet long, with a head 10-15" in diameter. The papers noted that this was not the first area sighting.

    Of course pranksters have gotten into the act. In 1993 Larry Tocha and friends made a snake of their own at a boat-building and repairing business. "A Monster Party" was arranged off the mouth of Cattaraugus Creek, and a fiberglass reptile did its best "Muppet" moves.

    Lakes Ontario and Onondaga have their serpents, according to Native American lore. Onondaga's reptilian monster "Mosqueto" was said to have killed several people. Ontario's Great Horned Snake, ever at war with the Thunder-God Heno, was even a creature of actual report, surfacing in Oneida legend (probably around 700 BC, according to Loren Coleman) with a stench so mighty that it killed several people. Other critter-spotters think these beasties are giant worms or eels, gill-breathers moving between the lakes through tunnels, never needing to surface. The reader is going to have to make up his or her own mind on this one. We find ourselves strangely devoid of conviction, despite two centuries of reports.

The WNY X-Files

Creepy Critters

"Sasquatch," "Snookum," "Bigfoot," or whatever else you call the big hairy, has been spotted in most wooded states of the Republic. In *Shadows* we discussed a number of Western Door sightings, and here have a few more to add.

Former residents of the "Lost Nation" area of Allegany County reported overnight pranks with farm equipment during a late 1960s bout of sightings. Something had been playing with the switches on a tractor overnight, and one well-laden trailer was picked up and moved by its hitch, a feat requiring prodigious strength. A neighbor herding cattle saw her large, aggressive German shepherd suddenly cowed by something in the trees. She led the entourage back to the barn, looking over her shoulder all the way. In the same region, it may have been the the utterly indescribable "Black Creek Whodat" years before the 1970s folklore cycle started.

The 1990s saw numerous Western Door Bigfoot reports. An internet tracking site mentions some mighty spooked hunters along the Allegany River near Salamanca in Fall 1996, and a running Bigfoot reported in a Monroe County wood in September 1997. Veteran woodsmen have gotten impressions of tall, moving, black "things" in the Alleganies and some of the tracts of Erie County. It's hard to tell what to make of any of these. One of the most interesting reports we have is of plaster casts of giant footprints from Cattaraugus County in the late 1990s. We heard about this within a week of its alleged instance, but have been unable to view the items, should they truly exist.

A fifteen-year-old witnessed a huge, white, hairy monster - a "double for a prehistoric sloth" - walking about near Sherman, NY in 1965-66, claims John Keel. It was said to be twelve to eighteen feet high, with a tail six to eight feet long. Lest we think it merely "The Case of the Imaginative Teen," the kid's whole family and two other men reported the critters (sometimes in pairs) on several occasions. Sometimes we wonder if ancient events and even animate beings can sometimes resurface as apparitions like ghosts.

Big cats aren't native to the clammy British Isles, thus reports of them since the 1970s are true mysteries. That we catch them on film and nowhere else lends an aura of the paranormal to the subject. Phantom panthers (reported in Eden in 1947 and Elmira in 1977) are less out of place in the states, but mysterious nonetheless. In late fall 2000 a very big black cat was seen and photographed several times near Fort Erie and Point Abino, Canada, once by a humane society official. In March 2001 Hamburg had many reports. As prints were found after a sighting that same month in West Seneca, this one is evidently a natural beast. Witnesses, though, called its eyes "yellow, demonic," and "spooky."

"We get a lot of reports of bears and mountain lions and black panthers and so forth," biologist Jim Snider told the *Buffalo News*. "Then after a few days we never hear from them again. If there's one out there, it's from someplace in captivity. There isn't a habitat within thousands of miles." Maybe there is a spirit in the woods. Walk softly, and carry a big stick. Yeah, maybe one of those that has a trigger on it.

Spirits of the Great Hill

The Medina Croppies

[Crop circles have been found in fields of grass or grain in most parts of the world. They've come to wide attention only in recent decades, but some evidence suggests that they've long been with us. Some circles are hoaxed, of course, but theorists (called "cereologists") regard the rest as possibly psychic effects, misunderstood natural ones, or UFO touchdowns. In England, where they're often elaborate, there's even a nickname ("croppies") for the human devotees. In the US where these things are simple and scarce, a 1998 study knew of only 50 reports. We've had four upstate, one nearby.]

As Todd Roberts harvested his field on July 5, 1991, a dark space in the wheat caught his eye. Its stalks were flattened and whirled into a circle over twenty feet in diameter, as if the hand of providence had stamped it with a gigantic beer-bottle. In the week that followed there were many writeups and thousands of sightseers at the corner of Salt Works and Maple Ridge roads.

"It was a finely-woven fan-like pattern," reports Daryl Hardes, chairman of the Ultimate Frontiers Organization (UFO), who studied the circle before the mobs got to it. "Layers of grain laid down in different directions, several deep, without breaking the stalks. They looked like they'd grown with a 90-degree bend to lie on the ground. Soil taken here tested 100% sterile, while it was normal outside the circle. That couldn't have been done with ropes and boards." Some massive radiating force may have been at work. The original circle was a visible discoloration until the snow fell.

"Crop circles are much more common than people realize," continued Hardes, who found a second in a cornfield nearby. Researcher Shane Sia noted four more found the same week near Culvert Road.

So often the Old World crop circles form near ancient monuments. Near the Medina circle is the three and a half acre "Neuter Fort," named for the Western Door's pre-Iroquoian nation. It may once have been five feet high and topped with wooden palisades. Time and agriculture have left only two low circular dirt walls, one inside the other, twelve feet apart, and 430 feet in diameter. Queerly, entrances - gaps in the walls - are differently aligned. Some think these works go way back, before the known Native American groups in the area. Only half a mile off is a large pit in which several hundred ancient skeletons were found.

About a third of the world's crop circles come with UFO reports. The night before the Medina circle was found one neighbor spotted strange lights in the air, and across the road from it lived someone who'd seen a UFO at another time. UFOs are also commonly reported near or above ancient monuments like those in Medina, which are "places of ancient sanctity" as described by John Michell.

A few years after the circle on her property, Joan Roberts witnessed a queer, dust-and-wind effect like an earthy water-spout cross her yard. This might back the theory that some crop circles are caused by quirky weather conditions like tornado touchdowns, but it doesn't explain all the world's circles, sometimes in intricate patterns and glyphs. The Roberts family seem to have heard the theories, and felt sure that no UFO made their circle. "The wheat wouldn't have grown back like it did." Maybe.

The WNY X-Files

ANCHOR OF DOOM

[Many have studied this case, and only those who love mystery are satisfied. Some suspect "vortexes" about the lakes, and we think of this story as a natural-supernatural phenomenon. One wonders, though, whether it might not be all supernatural. The *Admiral* (having been built in 1922 as the *W. G. Meyer*) had just undergone a name change, always considered a bad omen.]

    In early December 1942, the *Admiral*, a ninety-foot tug, towed the million-gallon tanker barge *Clevco* through western Lake Erie. Visibility weakened as night drew, but each vessel could navigate and communicate. The crew of the *Clevco* were alarmed, though, when they looked at the towline to the tug which, instead of going straight across the water, dropped into the ominous depths. The *Admiral* had become an anchor. This should have been impossible, at least without warning.
    The *Clevco* gave the Coast Guard her exact position, and everyone expected her to be waiting when help arrived, but the cutters *Ossipee* and *Crocus* met only wonder, an empty stretch of lake. After circling the area, the officer in charge called for aircraft. Soon a plane from the Civil Air Patrol arrived and widened the search area. The *Clevco* was sighted, but sixteen miles to the east, *Admiral*-anchor and all. This also should have been impossible. The plane was instructed to circle the *Clevco* until the cutters arrived. Nature had another surprise.
    It started to snow - heavily. The pilot was not only losing sight of the tanker *Clevco*, he could hardly see the coastline. He had to return to base.
    The *Clevco* was still there when the two cutters neared its new position and prepared to fire a line to it. The snow swirled anew, and again the tanker was lost.
    At that point the commanding officer aboard the *Ossipee* requested the tanker to dump some oil, an eco-unfriendly tactic which would aid in the search. The oil would float and point a way to the ship that had discharged it. No one knows if the dump was attempted or the order ever received. The two cutters had developed mysterious problems of their own that would take them out of the action.
    A strange fire aboard the *Crocus* was controlled, but the cutter was forced to return to base. The *Ossipee* was soon rendered *hors de combat* herself, since, in the sudden turbulence, her gyro compass stopped working. In a curtain of white, her crew could neither plot their position nor be sure they were not crashing into the ship they were there to save. In a sudden toss the steel vault in the *Ossipee*'s main cabin tore loose from its bolts and slammed into the facing wall. The crew - veteran seadogs - started getting sick from some undescribed complaint and couldn't carry out their duties. Sensing no trail of oil and in trouble of its own, the *Ossipee*, too, had to give up the fight. Whatever had done for the steel tug *Admiral* called, too, to the tanker *Clevco*, and seemed to see that its ministrations would be private. No one knows why disaster struck either.

Spirits of the Great Hill

The Black Creek Whodat

[Something was surely afoot about the Allegany County town of Black Creek for a stretch of the mid-1970s. What, though?]

It started in 1973 when some Cuba high schoolers built a cabin on open land. Overnighters were routine, and almost from the first there were unsettling noises - like feet running around the cabin, eventually heading off into the nearby swamp. Dogs often chased them, but never caught up. Maybe it's lucky. So far it sounds like an Iroquois bogie called "the Legs," though this pair had something on them.

One very late night in 1975 a camper took a walk. By a fence he looked up and saw it: humanoid, big, and white. Kid and critter made eye contact, then split, one into the brush ("at astonishing speed") and the other back to the cabin, little slower.

Years after his three friends would recall his streaming tears, but at the time they were unimpressed, sure he was just trying to scare them. The panicked camper headed home in his truck. The others slept, and laughed when something banged and shook the cabin an hour later, presuming it their missing mate, whom they'd never noticed was so tall or strong. At daylight the joke was over. Their cabin had visible dents. They went to their pal's house. He'd gone home and stayed.

In the year that followed, there were strange reports about the region of Spring Valley Road. Big white "things" were spotted in the woods and in car headlights, and few dogs would chase them. People felt watched when outside. A strange horrible smell surrounded a barn full of terrified livestock. ("Their eyes were just fire," said a witness.) A mutilated calf was found outside. Hunters scoured the region, but the swamp - in which beeping noises and strange lights were rumored - was nearly impenetrable.

As with any paranormal report, there's the chance that Black Creek's white Bigfoot is all make-believe. No direct physical evidence of it was ever found, and people were clearly fishing for things to add to the story, the folkloric "piling on" effect. For those who'll listen further, the beastie has paranormal possibilities:

An extraterrestrial: The sounds and lights are fixtures of UFO tales.
A ghost: It was pale, fitful, and supernaturally elusive.
A white-ass Bigfoot: It was big, white - and stinky. Also linked with killed livestock and rattled cabins, the fiendishly fulsome Bigfoot is in some quarters called "The Skunk Ape."

The last reported sighting of the Black Creek Whodat was in the spring of 1976. At three in the morning two young men camping in a pickup truck woke to hear themselves circled by footsteps, which ominously stopped. Someone opened the back door of a nearby house and a dog tore out howling. The young men came out of the truck and saw the apparition - way too fast to be human - outracing the dog to the woods. After that, the sightings and all other reports simply stopped, and Black Creek's beige Bigfoot retreated into its own legend. It's been two decades since the contentious cabin burned and its site was cultivated and cleared.

The WNYX-Files

THE MAN WHO LIVED TWICE

A New Englander by birth, the man, born around 1910, suffered a serious illness in his boyhood. He was near death, and his family gathered. At some point during the long, delirious days, he had an electrifying imaginary experience. It could have been anything: dream, reverie, vision, clairvoyance... He saw himself as an old man, looking back on his life, this illness, and every event in between. It was an odd hall of mirrors, that quick flash, his life in reflections from within it, right up until that point of age in the dream. It was at that point that he knew he would recover, and then go on to live all he had seen in fact.

He came to Western New York with his family. Even in his boyhood, he could tell many of his neighbors about events to come in their lives. So many of them came true that grumblings about "witchcraft" started, and he learned when to shut up. The man married and lived an unassuming life in the Southern Tier as a middle-class father and provider. It's a good bet that his occupation was blue-collar, and, though he was not the possessor of graduate degrees, he was intelligent, and a rational thinker. He had no mystical pretensions or paranormal interests, and no other wonder to relate than this one event... that he always remembered.

None of us can be sure of all he knew or even the nature of it. Did he see the world to come? Was he surprised by Pearl Harbor, by the assassinations of the Kennedy brothers, by the mission to the moon, by the fall of the Berlin Wall? Or did he see only his own life ahead of him? Did he also know what was to come after? All we know is that from time to time, almost as an offhand gift, he'd dispense a little treat of prophecy to one of his neighbors, dropping broad hints with a wink of something about to come to them, almost as a little test to see if, when it happened in fact, they remembered who told them. And it gave some of them the creeps, including the man's wife.

Either from religious or simply social perspectives, she despised all mention of her husband's single, evidently psychic vision and the insights that seemed to come from it. A smart, competent, and well-liked woman who inspired much loyalty in her community, she remarried after her husband's death and since has moved across the country. As long as she lives, mortally opposed to the subject, others' loyalty to her keeps us from revealing some of the details we have and learning many more. Had we not sworn to reveal no more than this we'd have learned nothing.

In some psychic circles, particularly those well-connected with the East, this sort of experience seems familiar as a "walk-in." The thinking goes that in such a case, another being steps into the body of the sufferer at the near-death moment, the time of deepest weakness and trauma. Usually this "walk-in," possibly another human soul wishing to live on earth again, carrying vast knowledge from the afterlife, becomes the stronger personality; every one of the rest of their days together they walk in a single body. There are cultures that recognize this and know how to cure it or forestall it, probably our own Seneca; but ours, of course, has trouble acknowledging the likelihood of ESP. Who knows what this experience truly was?

Spirits of the Great Hill

The Quest for the Holy Shale

[Henry Kissinger once said that academic turf wars were so bitter because the stakes were so small. We might presume a deep alliance among people linked by interests so abstruse that they are taken out of the mainstream by them, but Dion Fortune (*Psychic Self-Defense*) notes that jealousy and conflict are especially rampant among occultists, maybe for the reasons Dr. Kissinger observed.]

God give you better health and more sense.
(William III, refuting the premise that the king's touch could heal, to a scrofula sufferer, the only person he was ever persuaded to attempt so to cure.)

If this book has had any single point, it would be to demonstrate the enormous psychic-spiritual energy of Western New York, extending from its long and obscure prehistory to the present through its short history. To do so, we needed to detail its many manifestations. Some think the root of it all might be a natural energy source, maybe the Falls ("a cosmic vortex generator," says one mystic), maybe the quartz-crystal ("Black Rock") underneath. Some of these manifestations are on the daffy side.

A pair of lady psychics convened a regular group across the mid-1990s. There may have been twenty regulars, a handful from Rochester, many from Erie County, all from the Western Door. They began as friends who met for group meditation and discussions. Many of them were members of the informal network of New Age sympathizers, people whose interests would have been on the edge: psychic phenomena, Native American spirituality, Wicca, UFOs, mystery monsters, occult philosophy - the interests of this book.

Inspired by the idea of "simulacra" - landscape that, from high above, looks like something symbolic of what it's named - the women took their group into trance and emerged with knowledge of a vast, perfect emerald crystal pyramid buried beneath a Western Door hill. It was a beacon, a vortex, and a rendezvous-site for UFOs. The Native Americans knew about it, claimed their sources, but never revealed it to Whites. Its mighty radiation explains the spiritual activity in our region. To find it became a quest.

"New Age joyrides," comments a disaffected member of these wagon trains through Western New York and Northwestern Pennsylvania, psychic tours in which one of the leaders would stop the cars, feel the "vibes," and launch a hike up a hill, or a in new direction. Sometimes these caravans lasted days.

There were problems maintaining the group. Not just everyone was admitted, a reason for both its slow replenishing and the difficulty of tracking its details. No one outside the nucleus could join before an interview with one of the founders. They were brought to the psychic's home, given herb tea, and "studied." Though metaphysical discussions doubtless ensued, one senses that the expression of suitable hipness-cum-obeisance was the key to the ditty. (Most of us know this test we disdain on the path to something we think we covet. It reminds me of my 20-year-old self's exclusion from the course of a midwestern poet-prof: "If you *care* about writing, you are welcome." A saint to his circle, he had a lot to teach. I learned only that I must not have cared enough.)

The WNYX~Files

There were other difficulties involving time and money. Many of these folk worked for modest livings, and others' ends didn't meet as it was. When the shrine-seeking advantages of private fortune became clear to the group, a psychic solution was sought. Someone emerged from deep trance mumbling the phrase, "Stun-guns." We hear that the group actually pursued the idea. Time, energy, and money may have gone into a franchise, even a small factory.

The failure of the mystic hill ever to turn up was another issue. How they'd have known it for sure, even were they standing on the top of it, is a side question, this perfect, green, lucent pyramid hundreds of feet high, beneath hundreds more of mountain. It may lack the virtue of existence.

The leaders fell out. "Two big goddamn egos," noted one offended former member. It may have been more complicated than that. The spirit-personae who rap, channel, or automatically-write their dictates through such mediums are usually presumed majestic, so often Native American, presences. (Victorian psychic Emma Harding enjoyed the protection of spirit-chief "Arrowhead," who, in times of danger, stood above her "with drawn hatchet.") We may imagine that each of these women's spirit-guides likewise stooped to conquer and was death to disobey. Apparently one psychic received steady guidance from an even tenderer source, the spirit of her dead child. Any who quibbled with her visions dared imply that this source would lead her wrong. Soon the group was on two quests, and questers were forced to take sides. Others wearied simply of conflict. The group lost critical mass. One envisions them still, the two falling-out former friends, still stalking the region's roads and hills, squalling at storms like Lear, waiting Godot to the end.

Make no mistake, though, we are told: these women had power. "It was alarming to feel yourself so... probed," said a man they "interviewed." And psychics of integrity claim that there is something analogous to what they were seeking in one of the ancient hills of our region, and that several times they were very close, and they may have known it. The idea that there could be some vast treasure for the world in this small region is one we share with them. It may not be an emerald pyramid, but it may be something as abstract and mystical as the Grail.

In Western Door UFO-and-Bigfoot circles they still joke about this: A whopper-telling critter-sighter, a ringer for Stooge Moe, had climbed a tree. In full sight of a picnic of fellow fanciers, he slipped, struggled, and fell, and then started flapping his arms wildly as if they were wings. The group rushed, but, seeing him unhurt, convulsed with laughter at the sight of the bandy chap waving the air of the bright sky like the desperate Icarus. *Why*, they asked, *did you flap your arms like that? Did you really think you might be able to fly?* "It couldn't hurt," he replied.

Maybe we laugh, too; but the quest for the chimerical pyramid parallels this book about the spirit-life of the region that never trusts in the good it has, that lusts a certain type of flight and reminds everyone it lacks it, flapping bare wings. Maybe some sorts of flight are overrated, and more subtle ones go unnoticed. Maybe that's human nature, and this area one that embodies the trait on masse; but by setting down some of its folklore I hope (to horribly paraphrase James Joyce) to forge the uncreated conscience of my place. It couldn't hurt, this delve into its indirect legacy of spirit. There is something here. We just don't understand it yet. It may not be what people expect it to be.

Spirits of the Great Hill

Sources:

Other Council Fires:
Kingdoms of the Cattaraugus: *Mound Builders of Ancient America*, Robert Silverberg; *The Adena People*, Webb & Snow. **Giants in the Ground:** *The History of Livingston County*, Lockwood Doty; Silverberg; Webb & Snow; internet paper, Ross Hamilton, "A Tradition of Giants." **The Sodus Bay Spearhead:** Paper, "Let History Be Written," Ralph C. Brendes. **The Buried Causeway:** *Ancient Man in America*, Frederick Larkin; H. C. Taylor, *History of the Town of Portland*; Obed Edson, *History of Chautauqua County*; A. W. Young, *History of Chautauqua County, New York*. **King Solomon's Mines:** *Ancient Mines of Kitchi-Gummi*, by Roger Jewell; *Bronze Age America*, Barry Fell; *Atlantis America*, Zapp & Erikson. **Fort Hill:** 1880 report of Dr. Berlin Hart Wright; papers "Mysterious Ruin at Bluff Point on Keuka Lake in New York State," by David D. Robinson, and David B. Kelley's "Pre-Colonial Earthen and Stone Ruins in Yates County, NY." **The Great Circle-Henge:** David D. Robinson's article "Saint George, the Serpent, and the Seneca Indians," NEARA Journal XXIII, Winter/Spring 1989. **The Mastodon Rider:** *American Antiquarian* magazine, Vol. 9, NO. 4, 1887; *American Antiquarian* 25, 1903; notes from Carl Johannessen; Robert Silverberg *Mound Builders of Ancient America*; "A Tradition of Giants," paper by Ross Hamilton; *The Genesee Country*, Vol. I, Ed. by Lockwood Doty; *The History of Livingston County*, Lockwood Doty.

The Power Points:
The Peace Queen: Arthur Parker's *Analytical History of the Seneca Indians*; Rosemary Ellen Guiley's *Atlas of the Mysterious in North America*; J. Sheldon Fisher's *Genesee Country Magazine* article of April/May 1993. **Ontario Atlantis:** *Lake Chautauqua*, Emma C. Dewhurst; *Gateway to Oblivion*, Hugh Cochrane; the papers of Norman Carlson. **The Angel's Mountain:** *Field Guide to Mysterious Places of Eastern North America*, Salvator M. Trento. **The Spiritual Springs:** "The Elixir Spring of Kiantone," NY Folklore Quarterly, Vol. 2, 1946; "Utopian Theme with Variations," Russell Duino, Pennsylvania History, April 1962; "The Kiantone Movement," Oliver Chase, *Centennial History of Chautauqua County*, Vol. II. **Garden of the Gods:** Interviews; articles of Earl Plato. **The Devil's Hole:** W. Haden Blackman, *Field Guide to North American Hauntings*; Dennis William Hauck, *The National Directory of Haunted Places*; Orsamus Turner, *History of the Holland Purchase*. **The Valley of Madness:** Alfred Hilbert, "The Forbidden Trail," *Crooked Lake Review*, July 1991; interviews. **The Great Hill:** Lecture by Arthur Parker, "Legend of the Serpent of Nundawaono"; paper by David Robinson, "Saint George, the Serpent, and the Seneca Indians"

On the Spirit Way:
Byzantium by the Lake: *Chautauqua: A Center for Education, Religion, and the Arts in America*, by Theodore Morrison; *Chautauqua: An American Utopia*, by Jeffrey Simpson; Obed Edson, *History of Chautauqua County*; **City of Light:** Larkin, *Ancient Man in America*; pamphlet: "Cassadaga Lily Dale Sesquicentennial." **The Millennial Millerites, "That Place is Burnt!":** *Genesee Valley People 1743-1962*, Irene A. Beale; Michael Barkun, *Crucible of the Millennium*; Whitney Cross, *The Burned-over District*. **"Whosoever Will May Come":** *Jamestown Post-Journal* article of 10/6/1962, by

Sources

Dennis Pritchard; Paper, "Field Trip to Shiloh" by Jack Ericson, April 1968. **Calvin of Oak Knoll:** *Dunkirk Evening Observer* article by Jim Fox, 7/29/87; interviews. **Father X of the Western Door:** Many interviews.

Spooks, Spirits, Specters:
The Niagara Frontier
Psychic Symphony at the Circle: *The Metronome* article by Terri Hettrick, Dec. 1994. **Niagara Square:** Pamphlet: "The Life, Trial, Condemnation, and Dying Address of the Three Thayers." **The McKinley Curse:** Arch Merrill, *Down the Lore Lanes*; interviews. **Mark Twain's Buffalo Ghost:** *Mark Twain at the Buffalo Express*, McCullough and McIntire-Strasburg; JASPR 1918; *Buffalo Express*, 4/24/1910; *Hartford Courant* article, 6/25/1995, by Garret Condon. **The Lockwood Mansion:** Info supplied by Child & Family Services; interviews. **Lady in Lavender:** *Buffalo News* article of 4/5/92 by Burt Erickson Nelson. **Team Spirit, The Imaginary Friend:** Interviews. **The Lemon Angel:** Turner's *History of the Holland Purchase*; interviews. **Clet Hall:** *Buffalo News* article of 1/30/1998 by Paul Chimera. **Tale of the Tailor:** *Union-Sun and Journal*, Clarence O. Lewis, 10/9/1968; *Lockport Daily Journal*, 12/10/1867; *Lockport Daily Union*, 12/9/1867. **The Cold Springs Whatever:** *Niagara Gazette*, Eric Stutz, Oct. 29, 1978; *Union-Sun Journal*, 10/30/1982, by Chris Salamone. **Spirit-Sisters:** Interviews.

The Left Side of the River
The Dollhouse: Articles in *Fort Erie Extra*, 5/1 & 5/8, 1990, by Charles Davies and *The Review* (Niagara Falls, Ont.) by Kevin Harding, 10/27/2000. **The Lighthouse:** *The Review*, Kevin Harding, 10/27/2000; interviews. **Houdini's Halloween:** *Buffalo Courier Express*, 11/24/74, by Mike Healy. **The Niagara Poltergeist:** *Ghost Stories of Ontario*, John Robert Colombo; *PK: A Report on Psychokinesis*, Mike Brown. **The Buttery, The Angel Inn, The Kiely:** Rosemary Ellen Guiley, *Atlas of the Mysterious in North America*; info supplied by the proprietors; interviews.

Rochester & Region
Poor Tessie Keating, Hill of 1,000 Ghosts: Shirley Cox Husted, *Valley of the Ghosts*. **Mother of Sorrows:** *Rochester Democrat & Chronicle*, 10/31/1993, by Ad Hudler; Husted, *Valley of the Ghosts*; *Rochester Times-Union*, 10/30/1986, by Amy Wilson. **Of Widows and Windows:** Interviews.

Lake and Lakeside Wights
Flying Dutchmen, The Phoebe Catherine: *Haunted Lakes*, Frederick Stonehouse. **The Point Charles Marker:** *Rochester Democrat & Chronicle*, 5/13/1921. **"Wherever You Can Place Your Eyes...":** "Pultneyville, A Harbor of Shadows & Spirits," Chuck and Sue Glisch, *Great Lakes Cruiser Magazine*, October 1995; "Haunted Houses in Wayne County," paper by Rebekah M. Porray. **The Black Dog of the Erie:** *Haunted Lakes*, Stonehouse. **The Box of Red Jacket's Bones:** "The World's Wonder Corner," by Everett R. Burmaster; papers of Everett Burmaster. **The Fyfe and Drum, Fredonia's White Inn, Flittin' at the Dock of the Bay:** Info supplied by the proprietors.

Chautauqua-Allegany Spirits
Boos & Brews: Interviews. **New Ireland:** *Buffalo News* articles of 6/4/98 by Harold McNeil and 6/8/98 by Donna Snyder. **The Ashford Hollow Witch:** Interviews. **Little Lucy's Theater:** "Allen's Opera House," B. Delores Thompson; Pamphlet of

Spirits of the Great Hill

"The Reg" opening, October 1990.
Western Finger Lakes
Portrait of the Grey Lady: Interviews. **Seth Roberts:** *PK*, Mike Brown; Guiley, *Encyclopedia of Mystical and Paranormal Experience.* **Message from Mehitabel:** *Genesee Country* article by Nancy Lyon, Fall 1999; interviews. **Eliza of the Trackways:** *The Fish Horn Alarm,* by J. Sheldon Fisher
Genesee Country Ghosts
The Legend of Buttermilk Falls: *Batavia Daily News* article of 5/27/ 1950. **The Abell House:** *The Livingston Republican,* 7/6/1933; *Rochester Democrat and Chronicle,* 11/29/1925; *Picket Line Post,* 7/25/1937; *Mt. Morris Union,* June, 1965; *History of Livingston County,* Lockwood Doty. **Flower of Avon:** Pamphlet, "A Tour of the Genesee Valley," Big Spring Historical Society.

Iroquois Spirits:
A. The Charmholder's Bundle
Seneca Witch Belief, A Charmholder's Bundle, The Stealer of Childrens' Hearts, Catching a Blood-Bone, The Hair-Bone Token, A Witch's Bag: Arthur Parker, *Seneca Myths and Legends.* **The Wailing Spirit of the Genesee Flats:** *Genesee Valley Herald* article, 5/27/1868. **Maker of the False-Face:** *Masked Medicine Societies of the Iroquois,* by W. N. Fenton; Journal, American Society for Psychical Resesarch, V. 46, article by Edmond P. Gibson; *Smithsonian Report,* 1940, by Willliam N. Fenton; interview.
B. Miracles of Mad Bear
General: *Mad Bear* and *Rolling Thunder* by Doug Boyd; interviews. **The Djogao Skull:** *Lost Cities of North and Central America,* David Hatcher Childress. **The Lazarus Effect, Weapons of Friendship, Mad Bear's Magic Hat, The Medicine Case, The Ghost Talker, Only a Change of Worlds:** Boyd, *Mad Bear.*

White Magic:
A. The Path of Peace
The Bradford Miracles: *Buffalo News* article of 1/9/1997; **The Witch of the Helpers:** "Scientific Standards vs. My Great-Grandmother" (the *Medical Post,* 3/21/1995), Colleen Clements; "Postmodern Malpractice: A Medical Case Study in the Culture War," Colleen Clements. **Father Baker's Healing:** *Buffalo News* article of 11/5/2000, by Lou Michel. **Heart of the Mountain:** "Thomas Merton at St. Bonaventure," by Paul Spaeth; article by Art Jester, Dec. 1998, *Knight Ridder Newspapers.*
B. Children of the Left Hand
Bird of Perdition: Interviews. **The Hinsdale Horror:** Bob Curran's *Buffalo Evening News* columns 2/22/1974, 5/3/1974, 5/27/1976; Mike Vogel's *Buffalo News* "The Magazine," 10/26/80; *Echoes of a Haunting,* by Clara Miller. **Diabolic Frolic:** *Buffalo News* article of 2/5/95 by Dale Anderson; *Satanic Panic* by Jeffrey Victor. **King of the Wood:** *Satanic Panic,* Victor; Sir J. G. Frazer, *The Golden Bough.*

The Sacred Roycroft:
The Shroud of Roycroft: *Buffalo News* article by Tom Buckham, 6/12/94. **Michael's Mount:** *Twelve-Tribe Nations,* John Michell; interview. **"Dangerous Negations":** *The Philistine,* June 1900. **Electricks, John Barleycorn's Curse, The**

Sources

Christmas Spirit, "Some Particulars...": The papers of Scott Carnes; interviews. **The Prophecy, The House on Walnut, The Hallway Stalker, The Christmas Spirit, Hub in France:** Interviews.

The Invisible College:
Iroquois Masons: *American Indian Freemasonry*, Arthur Parker; *Buffalo Saturday Night* magazine, Feb. 3, 1923 (article by "CLM"). **Sacred City:** Interviews, John Conlin and Paul Redding of *Western New York Heritage* Magazine; *Spiritual Path, Sacred Place*, Thomas Barrie; Peter W. Williams, *Houses of God*; *Sacred Architecture*, A. T. Mann; Marilyn J. Chiat, *America's Religious Architecture*; Anthony Lawlor, *The Temple in the House*. **White Shaman of the Landscape:** Interviews. **The Cohocton Head-Readers:** Report of Vivian Shafer Wheaton, 1985; Irene Beale, *Genesee Valley People 1743-1962*; "Orson Squire Fowler and the Octagon," *Heritage* Magazine, Winter 1996. **Cthulhu Country:** Letters of H. P. Lovecraft; papers of Daniel Harms. **Nicola Tesla's Falls Experiment:** Paper, "Nicola Tesla," by Robert Sheridan; *Tesla, Man Out of Time*, Margaret Cheney. **Human Dimensions:** "Paranormal Effects on Enzyme Activity" by M. Justa Smith, Human Dimensions Professional Paper No. 2, Vol. I, No. 2; *Psychic Mysteries of the North*, A R. G. Owen.

The WNYX-Files:
The Top Ten UFOs: Buffalo News articles by Bob Galganski (8/13/2000) & Donn Esmonde (4/24/1994); *Gateway to Oblivion*, Hugh Cochrane; Rosemary Ellen Guiley's *Atlas of the Mysterious in North America*; *Mysteries of Time and Space*, Brad Steiger; article by Carol Fisher, 8/19, 1994, *Special E-Fects* (Ellicottville). **The Randolph Frankenstein:** *The Lynn News*, Oct. 27, 1854; *An Eccentric's Guide to the US*, Robert Damon Schneck. **The Lake Erie Serpent and Friends:** *Haunted Lakes*, Stonehouse; Rosemary Ellen Guiley's *Atlas of the Mysterious in North America*; *Buffalo News* articles (7/30/1978) by Mike Vogel, and Michael Levy (12/29/93); John Robert Columbo, *Mysterious Canada*; Loren Coleman *Crypto-zoology A to Z*. **Creepy Critters:** John Keel, *Strange Creatures from Time and Space*; Buffalo News article of 3/23/2001 by Janice Habuda. **The Medina Croppies:** *Buffalo News* article of 8/2/1991 by Jeff Burdick; (Syracuse) *Herald-Journal* article 8/24/1994 by Mark Weiner; (Medina) *Journal-Register* articles by Brian Kozody, 7/23 and 7/30/1991; *Landmarks of Orleans County*, Isaac Signor; interviews. **Anchor of Doom:** *Gateway to Oblivion*, Hugh Cochrane; *Haunted Lakes*, Stonehouse. **The Man Who Lived Twice:** Interviews. **The Black Creek Whodat:** John Arden-Hopkins' *Cuba Patriot* article. **The Quest for the Holy Shale:** Slayter Brown, *The Heyday of Spiritualism*; interviews.

CREDITS:
Without Tim Bailey, Rob Laux, and Katy Fronczak of S&G Press the art in this book would not have been possible. To these true professionals we give deep thanks. Special thanks to these people who went far out of their way to help in compiling information:

Michael Bastine, Cassandra Joan, Norman Carlson, Daryl Hardes, Daniel Harms, Katherine Johnson, Franklin LaVoie, Elizabeth Marshall, Shane Sia, Sharon Stanley, Rodger Sweetland, Father Alphonsus Trabold.

Some of the people who helped us find the information in this book have been credited within the text. So many have helped us that we must have missed someone. To them regrets; to the rest, thanks:

J. P. Allan	Adie & Mary Jewett	Andrew and Elizabeth
Jamie Baran	Becky Jones	Sachs
Marion Barden	Nancy Kieran	Pat Schaap
Carol Bailey	Julia Kittsley	Ernie and Caroline Scheer
George Besch	Al Kleinschmidt	Ron & John Schenne
Helen Besch	John Koerner	Sandy Schneider
Ken Boring	Chris Krtanik	Sue Scott
Doug Boyd	Dan Larkin	Veronica Scott
Barbara Brant	Carole Larsen	Bill Severin
Debbie Brooks	Martin Leal	Dave Shaffer
Diane Brosius	William Leslie	Richard Shulte
Lisa Bunce	John Licota	Steve Simon
Kevin Burke	Hal Limebeer	Diane Sinton
June Burkett	Mark Lozo	Alan Sipprell
Paul Cain	Sharon Lubitow	Sr. Justa Smith
Mike Campanella	Denny Lynch	June Spear
Philip Chang	Armand Mabee	Phil Stevens
Barbara Chernogorec	Dick Mabee	Larry Sticht
Sue Conklin	Jason Marr	Rich Taczkowski
Connie Constantine	Vince Martonis	Frances Teculver
Martin Costello	Carl Mazzu	Claudette Thomas-Heller
Wilson & Karen Curry	John McKendry	Dr. Carolyn Vacca
Marshall Dahlin	Gerry Mead	Officer Jimmy Valentine
John Danieluk	Rev. John Mears	Quain Weber
Don Dayer	Randy Melanthine	Vivian Shafer Wheaton
Cheryl Delano	Mike & Travis Melnik	Chanel White
Ernie Dellas	Becky Mercuri	Jeff Wiedrick
Chris Densmore	John Morgan	Rob Wilkinson
Frances Dumas	Philip Morris	Jim Williams
Don Eckler	"The Navagh Clan"	Elaine Winter
Su Ewing	Sam Nasca	Patrica Wisniewski
Tom Ferri	Danielle Nati	Ric Wyman
Lydia Fish	Rick Naylon	Moury Zeplowitz
Michael Gesel	Joe Nickell	Rick Zuegel
Ramond Gianfrancesco	Natalie O'Doherty	
Virginia Gibbs	Marlynn Olson	
Tom Gleed	David Parrish	
E. J. Gonser	Marjorie Allen Perez	
Dwight Halstead	Jason Phoenix	
Jean K. Hanson	Ronda Pollock	
Dan Harris	Paul Redding	
The Hayes family	Jeanne Pontius Rindge	
Beth Hoag	Orren, Joan, Todd, & Lee	
Bill Huddle	Roberts	
Joe & David Ippolito	Laird Robinson	
Melissa Jacobs	Lyn Rogers	
Peter Jemison	Robert Rust	

THE ART:

FRONT COVER:
    BACKGROUND IMAGE: *MOONDANCER*, BY FRANKLIN LAVOIE; FANTASY LANDSCAPE AND FOREGROUND IMAGES, FRANKLIN LAVOIE; COLONEL ABELL, BY MASON WINFIELD; CITY HALL BY KEN SHERIDAN; *THE PEACE QUEEN*, BY FRANKLIN LAVOIE.

TITLE PAGE: BACKGROUND PHOTO BY WILLIAM MALONEY; COVER, *SHADOWS OF THE WESTERN DOOR*, VARIOUS ARTISTS

PAGE 8: BACKGROUND IMAGES BY JILL RUSSELL; SKULL BY FRANKLIN LAVOIE; ELEPHANT PLATE BY MASON WINFIELD

PAGE 16: FORT BY P. K. DUGAN; OTHER IMAGES BY FRANKLIN LAVOIE

PAGE 20: *HENO THE THUNDERER*, BY FRANKLIN LAVOIE

PAGE 30: PHOTOGRAPH, "GATE AT THE HALL OF PHILOSOPHY" BY RICK ZUEGEL

PAGE 43: PHOTOGRAPH BY WILLIAM MALONEY; RED JACKET BY FRANKLIN LAVOIE

PAGE 45: BACKGROUND, *CROOKED HOUSE* (CROPPED) BY JILL RUSSELL; RED JACKET BY FRANKLIN LAVOIE; COLONEL ABELL, BY MASON WINFIELD

PAGE 90: *THE PEACE QUEEN*, BY FRANKLIN LAVOIE.

PAGE 106: PHOTOGRAPHY AND COMPUTER WORK BY ROB LAUX AND KATY FRONCZAK

PAGE 115: DARD HUNTER ILLUSTRATION AND ELBERT HUBBARD PHOTOGRAPH SCANNED BY ROB LAUX

PAGE 126: *THE INVISIBLE COLLEGE*, BY FRANKLIN LAVOIE.

PAGE 137: *ILLUMINOIDS*, BY FRANKLIN LAVOIE.

PAGE 138: *MOONDANCER*, BY FRANKLIN LAVOIE

BACK COVER: *HENO THE THUNDERER*, BY FRANKLIN LAVOIE

    ALL ARTISTS MAY BE CONTACTED THROUGH THE PUBLISHER

MASON WINFIELD

TEACHER AND WRITER MASON WINFIELD STUDIED ENGLISH AND CLASSICS AT DENISON UNIVERSITY AND RECEIVED A MASTER'S DEGREE IN BRITISH LITERATURE FROM BOSTON COLLEGE. FOR THIRTEEN YEARS HE TAUGHT, COACHED, AND SERVED AS ENGLISH DEPARTMENT CHAIRMAN AT THE GOW SCHOOL IN SOUTH WALES, NY. DURING THIS PERIOD HE WAS NAMED AMONG THE TOP TEN TENNIS PLAYERS IN BUFFALO SEVERAL TIMES AND WON A CROSS-COUNTRY SKI MARATHON. MASON IS A REGULAR CONTRIBUTOR TO SEVERAL MAGAZINES AND WON A FICTION CONTEST WITH HIS VAMPIRE TALE "THE HUNTERS." HE IS THE AUTHOR OF TWO OTHER BOOKS PUBLISHED BY WESTERN NEW YORK WARES, *SHADOWS OF THE WESTERN DOOR* AND *A GHOSTHUNTER'S JOURNAL*.

THE BIRTH OF A PUBLISHING FIRM

The Buffalo area's most innovative publishing company will celebrate its 18th anniversary in 2002 by hitting a benchmark that few regional publishing houses manage to achieve.

Since its inception, Western New York Wares Inc. has moved more than 140,000 books and games into homes, schools and libraries around the world. Not bad for a company that sprouted its roots in trivial turf!

The year was 1984 and the trivia craze was taking the nation by storm. As Buffalo journalist Brian Meyer played "that other trivia game" with friends in his North Buffalo living room, he came up with the notion of creating a local game that tested players' knowledge about the people, places and events in their hometown. Western New York Trivia Quotient hit store shelves several months later, selling out its first edition in only six weeks. The game's success established Meyer as an up-and-coming young entrepreneur.

A year later, he compiled a book of quotations that chronicled the feisty reign of Mayor Jimmy Griffin. Meyer refuses to disclose how many six-packs were consumed while sifting through hundreds of biting "Griffinisms." An updated volume was published eight years later, during Griffin's last year in office.

Meyer, a City Hall reporter for the Buffalo News, spent nearly 16 years at WBEN Radio where he served a managing editor. Over his two-decade journalism career, Meyer has won more than 20 state and regional awards.

As founder and president of Western New York Wares Inc., Meyer has collaborated with dozens of local authors, artists and photographers on many book projects. By 2001, the region's premier publisher of local books had been involved in more than 50 literary ventures.

The Buffalo native is a graduate of the Marquette University College of Journalism, St. Joseph's Collegiate Institute and Buffalo Public School #56. He teaches communications courses at Buffalo State College and Medaille College. Meyer also serves as treasurer of the Greater Buffalo Society of Professional Journalists' Scholarship Fund and is active in the Buffalo Newspaper Guild.

He enjoys spending weekends canoeing, hiking and hanging out with friends at his cottage at Rushford Lake in Allegany County.

**Visit our Internet Site at:
www.buffalobooks.com**

Other Regional History and Architecture Books
Visit our Web site at www.buffalobooks.com for a complete list of all titles distributed by Western New York Wares Inc.

Shadows of the Western Door: Haunted Sites and Ancient Mysteries of Upstate New York – A supernatural safari across Western New York. Guided by the insights of modern research, author Mason Winfield pens a colorful, provocative and electrifying study of the paranormal.
ISBN: 1-829201-22-4 $12.95

Shadows: The CD – Haunted sites and ancient mysteries never sounded so intriguing. Listen as author Mason Winfield reads more than a dozen of his most popular supernatual vignettes, including "The Grave of Jack the Ripper" and "Fort Niagara." The 70 minute compact disc comes with a full-color insert.
ISBN: 1-879201-26-7 $9.95

A Ghosthunter's Journal: Tales of the Supernatural and the Strange in Upstate New York – A delightfully diverse smorgasbord of strange encounters, all of them set in Western New York. The 13 fictional stories are inspired by the files of Mason Winfield.
ISBN: 1-879201-29-1 $12.95

Symbol & Show: The Pan-American Exposition of 1901 – A riveting look at perhaps the greatest event in Buffalo's history. Written by the late Austin M. Fox and illustrated by Lawrence McIntyre, this book offers a lively assessment of the Exposition, bringing to light many half-forgotten facts.
ISBN: 1-879201-33-X $15.95

The Erie Canal: The Ditch That Opened a Nation – Despite its shallow depths, the waters of the Erie carry an amazing historical legacy. It was in canal towns like Lockport and Tonawanda where the doors to the American frontier were unlocked. Written by Dan Murphy, the book includes dozens of photos.
ISBN: 1-879201-34-8 $8.95

Erie Canal Legacy: Architectural Treasures of the Empire State – Photographer Andy Olenick and author Richard O. Reisem take readers on a 363-mile journey along the canal route. This hardcover book is comprised of full-color photos and an enlightening text.
ISBN: 0-9641706-6-3 $39.95

Frank Lloyd Wright's Darwin D. Martin House: Rescue of a Landmark – The untold story of the abandonment and rescue of the region's most architecturally-significant home is recounted in vivid detail by Marjorie L. Quinlan. The book includes color photos and detailed architectural plans.
ISBN: 1-879201-32-1 $13.95

Nature's Niagara: A Walk on the Wild Side – Learn more about the wild animals, plants and geological formations at Niagara Falls. Written by Paul Gromosiak, the book includes many full-color photographs and maps.
ISBN: 1-879201-31-3 $8.95

Niagara Falls Q&A: Answers to the 100 Most Common Questions About Niagara Falls – Author Paul Gromosiak spent four summers chatting with 40,000 Falls tourists. This invaluable guide answers 100 commonly-asked questions. The book also includes photos, many of them in color.
ISBN: 0-9620314-8-8 $4.50

Daring Niagara: 50 Death-Defying Stunts at the Falls – Paul Gromosiak pens a heart-stopping adventure about those who barreled, boated, even bicycled to fame. The book includes vintage photos.
ISBN: 1-879201-23-2 $6.95

Water Over the Falls: 101 of the Most Memorable Events at Niagara Falls – Daredevils who defied the Mighty Niagara. Tragic rock slides and heroic rescues. More than 100 true-to-life tales are chronicled by local historian Paul Gromosiak.
ISBN: 1-879201-16-X $6.95

Zany Niagara: The Funny Things People Say About Niagara Falls – A lighthearted tour of humorous happenings and historical oddities. Penned by Paul Gromosiak and illustrated by John Hardiman.
ISBN: 1-879201-06-2 $4.95

Exploring Niagara: The Complete Guide to Niagara Falls and Vicinity – Filled with 77 spectacular full-color photos, the guide includes dozens of wineries, canals, waterfalls and mansions. Authors Hans and Allyson Tammemagi also chronicle the history that shaped the region.
ISBN: 0-9681815-0-3 $14.25

Victorian Buffalo: Images From the Buffalo and Erie County Public Library – Visit Buffalo as it looked in the 19th century through steel engravings, woodcuts, lithography and other forms of nonphotographic art. Author Cynthia VanNess has selected scenes that showcase everyday life and views of historic structures created by luminaries like Frank Lloyd Wright, Louis Sullivan and E.B. Green.
ISBN: 1-879201-30-5 $12.95

Classic Buffalo: A Heritage of Distinguished Architecture – this full-color hardcover book showcases dozens of local architectural gems. The 176-page book includes stunning photographs by Andy Olenick and an enlightening text by Richard O. Reisem.
ISBN: 0-9671480-0-6 $39.95

John D. Larkin: A Business Pioneer – The riveting story of a Buffalo man who built a small soap manufacturing outfit into one of the largest mail order houses in the nation. Daniel I. Larkin, a grandson of John D. Larkin, has penned a book that reflects on the American dream at its best.
ISBN: 0-9619697-1-7 $14.95

Church Tales of the Niagara Frontier: Legends, History & Architecture – This first-of-a-kind book traces the rich history and folklore of the region through accounts of 60 area churches and places of worship. Written by the late Austin M. Fox and illustrated by Lawrence McIntyre.
ISBN : 1-879201-13-5 $14.95

Buffalo City Hall: Americanesque Masterpiece – local historian John Conlin has penned an authoritive guide that chronicles the history and architectural significance of a regional icon.
ISBN: 1-879201-14-3 $5.95

Buffalo Treasures: A Downtown Walking Guide – Readers are led on a fascinating tour of 25 major buildings. A user-friendly map and dozens of illustrations by Kenneth Sheridan supplement an enlightening text by Jan Sheridan.
ISBN: 1-879201-15-1 $4.95

Buffalo's Waterfront: A Guidebook – Edited by Tim Tielman, this user-friendly guide showcases more than 100 shoreline sites. It includes a handy fold-out map. Published by the Preservation Coalition of Erie County.
ISBN: 1-879201-00-3 $5.95

Buffalo's Brush With the Arts: From Huck Finn to Murphy Brown – A fascinating adventure behind the manuscripts and million-dollar book deals, highlighting the Niagara Frontier's connection to many creative geniuses. Authored by Joe Marren, the book contains more than 20 photographs from the Courier-Express Collection.
ISBN: 1-879201-24-0 $7.95

Beyond Buffalo: A Photographic Journey and Guide to the Secret Natural Wonders of our Region – Full color photographs and informative vignettes showcase 30 remarkable sites. Author David Reade also includes directions and tips for enjoying each site.
ISBN: 1-879201-19-4 $19.95

Western New York Weather Guide – Readers won't want any "winteruptions" as they breeze through this lively book written by former Channel 7 weather guru Tom Jolls. Co-authored by Brian Meyer and Joseph VanMeer, the book focuses on historic and humorous weather events over the past century.
ISBN: 1-879201-18-1 $7.95

White Death: Blizzard of '77 – This 356-page softcover book chronicles one of the region's most dramatic historical events. Written by Erno Rossi, the book includes more than 60 photographs.
ISBN: 0-920926-03-7 $16.95

Great Lake Effects: Buffalo Beyond Winter and Wings – a unique cookbook that is filled with intriguing historical facts about the region. The hardcover book has been compiled by the Junior League of Buffalo.
ISBN: 1-879201-18-1 $18.95

Please include 8% sales tax for all orders in New York state and $3 for shipping per order (regardless of the number of books in the order.) Visit our Web site at: www.buffalobooks.com or write for a catalog:

Western New York Wares Inc.
P.O. Box 733
Ellicott Station
Buffalo, New York 14205